JERRY BAKER'S

OLD-TIME
GARDENING WISDOM

✽

by Jerry Baker,
America's Master Gardener®

Text, Design, and Layout by Kim Adam Gasior

Mechanicals by Graphic Arts & Production, Inc.

Illustrations by Graphic Arts & Production, Inc.

OTHER TITLES BY JERRY BAKER, AMERICA'S MASTER GARDENER®

To: Who else? The best grandma
a boy could ever have — Ethel Grace Puttnam,
a/k/a Grandma Putt —
my friend, teacher, confidant, and much, much more.

I have no doubt she is still
helping folks laugh while they learn in that
Great Garden in the Sky!

Publisher's Cataloging-in-Publication Data
(Provided by Quality Books, Inc.)

Baker, Jerry.
    Jerry Baker's old-time gardening wisdom / by Jerry Baker ; text, design, and layout by Kim Adam Gasior ; mechanicals by Graphic Arts & Production, Inc. ; illustrations by Graphic Arts & Production, Inc.. – 1st ed.
    p. cm.
    Includes index.
    "Lessons learned from Grandma Putt's kitchen cupboard, medice cabinet, and garden shed!"–Cover.
    ISBN 0-922433-35-6

1. Gardening. I. Gasior, Kim Adam. II. Title. III. Title: Old-time gardening wisdom.

SB455.B35 1999   635
                                     QBI01-200808

Distributed in the book trade by LPC Group.

4   6   8   10   9   7   5   3   hardcover

Jerry Baker
P.O. Box 1001
Wixom, MI 48393

http://www.jerrybaker.com

Printed in the United States of America

Contents

3
YOU WANT ME TO EAT...<u>WEEDS?</u>

4

AH, THE SPICE OF LIFE — HERBS!

5

A BERRY, BERRY GRAPEFUL GARDEN

6
AN APPLE A DAY...

7
NUTS TO YOU!

8

PUTTIN' BY AND STORIN' AWAY

9

SHARE YOUR LOVE...
WITH FLOWERS

10
GRANDMA'S ALL-AMERICAN LAWN

EPILOGUE: PLANT A TREE!
339

OLD-FASHIONED GARDEN RECIPES INDEX
341

INDEX
347

INTRODUCTION

My Grandma Putt always had a way with youngsters, and when I first went to live with her, she took me for a walk in her fantastic garden, introducing me to all of her friends. Quite simply, the plants in her garden were her friends—she looked out for them, and they looked out for her.

It never seemed even a little odd to me that Grandma treated her plants just like people, or that she would spend long hours conversing with them. And she never seemed to feel the slightest bit awkward about including her grandson—me—in those conversations.

It wasn't long before I was also wandering around the place, jabbering away to "Grandpa Putt," the big horse chestnut tree out front by the road, and to "Great Grandpa Coolidge," the old maple tree near the back porch. My favorite tree was a huge white oak way back at the edge of her property which Grandma and I named "Chief Black Feathers." I would lie on my back, look up at the branches, and start talking out loud. Before long, I could see the Old Chief take form in the thousands of leaves shimmering black against the sunlight.

Grandma Putt was a remarkable woman—a real honest-to-goodness pioneer. As a small girl, she had helped Great-

Grandpa Coolidge carve their farm out of the Indian Territory. She was part Indian herself, and she treated each plant, tree, and flower as an individual, with a spirit and personality all its own. She taught me how to recognize these plant peculiarities, and how to use them to make a successful garden.

There was a time in my life when I was convinced that Grandma Putt knew just about everything. Most of her knowledge came from hard work, experience, and the school of hard knocks. Some of it was handed down from her Indian and pioneer ancestors. I don't remember ever seeing her read any books except her time-worn Bible and her dog-eared almanacs. But, somehow, somewhere, she accumulated an amazing amount of information on the art, history, lore, and science of gardening. To tell you the truth, I learned a lot more about gardening from her in a few short years than I have learned in all the years since.

And I wasn't the only one! People would come from miles around to see Grandma Putt, bringing their sick house plants, diseased patches of lawn, weeds they wanted identified, and a multitude of questions about their toughest gardening problems. Grandma never charged for her good advice or home remedies, and as often as not, she sent the person away with new hope, and a basketful of berries or fresh vegetables.

THE REST IS HISTORY...

For a ten-year-old, city-born and city-bred boy, coming to live with Grandma Putt in the country was like a leap to another universe. I was looking forward to fun-filled days and

INTRODUCTION

restful nights, when one day, Grandma came up with a bright idea that dashed my hopes, and changed my life forever!

As I recall, we had gone to town that day to do some shopping. We were walking along Main Street, and I was thinking about how good an ice cream cone would taste. All of a sudden, Grandma Putt jolted me out of my reverie!

"Junior, I think it's about time we laid out some chores for you to do. A little work never hurt a boy your age."

Work! That word had a nasty ring to it—work was taking out the garbage, cleaning up my room, or shoveling snow off of the driveway. Work was no fun; as a matter of fact, it was the *dirtiest four letter word* I knew at the time!

"Yes, it's about time you got acquainted with my friend, good ol' Mother Earth," she said.

And, as they say, the rest is history. Those seemingly innocent words started me off on a life-long journey spreading the gardening wisdom that I first learned working beside Grandma Putt. Over the years, I have added to that storehouse of gardening know-how, picking up thousands of tips, tricks, and tonics along the way. In my travels, I've discovered that Grandma's old-fashioned methods really aren't all that old-fashioned after all; some of the "newest" discoveries are techniques that she effectively used more than fifty years ago!

Of course, there have been some revolutionary break-throughs in the past five or six decades that have made certain aspects of home gardening safer, easier, and less time-consuming. But over the years, I've found that Grandma Putt's common-sense methods still work best. They have withstood the test of time, and proven themselves over and over and over again in my garden.

In this book, I'm going to share the gardening gospel according to Grandma Putt with you. Some of the anecdotes, techniques, and remedies you'll find in the chapters ahead are very old-fashioned, while others are relatively new.

Even back in Grandma Putt's day, it was a mixture of old and new ideas that made our country, our families, and our gardens great. The same is true today. I hope that in these pages, you'll discover the knowledge, joy, and pleasure I first gained from gardening with Grandma Putt, and that you use some of her old-time gardening wisdom to create the garden of your dreams!

Grandma Putt and me

The future America's
Master Gardener

Grandma Putt

GRANDMA PUTT'S HOMESTEAD

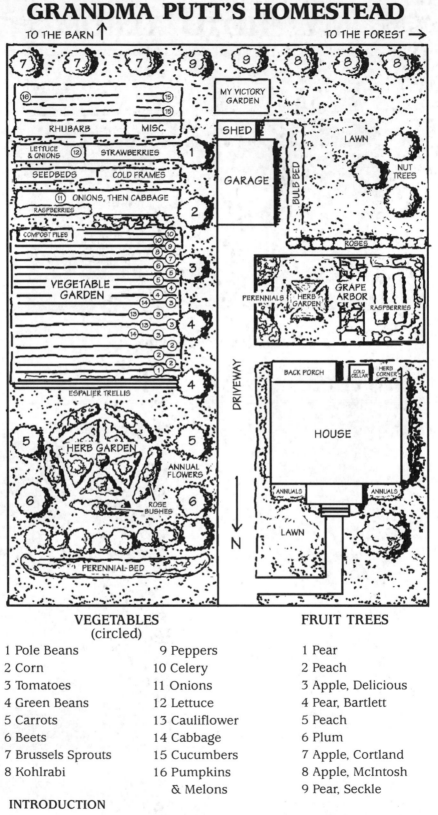

TO THE BARN ↑   TO THE FOREST →

MY VICTORY GARDEN

SHED

GARAGE

RHUBARB | MISC.

LETTUCE & ONIONS · 12 · STRAWBERRIES

SEEDBEDS | COLD FRAMES

11 ONIONS, THEN CABBAGE

RASPBERRIES

COMPOST PILES

VEGETABLE GARDEN

ESPALIER TRELLIS

HERB GARDEN

ANNUAL FLOWERS

ROSE BUSHES

PERENNIAL-BED

BULB BED

LAWN

NUT TREES

ROSES

PERENNIALS | HERB GARDEN | GRAPE ARBOR | RASPBERRIES

DRIVEWAY

BACK PORCH | COLD CELLAR | HERB CORNER

HOUSE

ANNUALS | ANNUALS

LAWN

N ↓

VEGETABLES
(circled)

1 Pole Beans	9 Peppers	
2 Corn	10 Celery	
3 Tomatoes	11 Onions	
4 Green Beans	12 Lettuce	
5 Carrots	13 Cauliflower	
6 Beets	14 Cabbage	
7 Brussels Sprouts	15 Cucumbers	
8 Kohlrabi	16 Pumpkins	
	& Melons	

FRUIT TREES

1 Pear
2 Peach
3 Apple, Delicious
4 Pear, Bartlett
5 Peach
6 Plum
7 Apple, Cortland
8 Apple, McIntosh
9 Pear, Seckle

INTRODUCTION

HERE'S THE SCOOP— KNOW YOUR DIRT!

PLAN BEFORE YOU PLANT

Nowadays, when I read most vegetable gardening books, I can't help but remember how foolish I was in planning my first Victory Garden with Grandma Putt. The books usually recommend starting with hundred-foot rows! After a lifetime of learning the hard way, believe you me, my recommendations for you are a bit more modest!

Grandma Putt always said that planning a garden is like ordering food at a restaurant—*don't let your eyes get bigger than your stomach!* She knew that many short rows of vegetables would receive the proper care and attention through the long growing season, and would produce as much, if not more, than a few long rows that you can't handle.

"Planning a garden is like everything else you'll do in life," she used to say, "so be sure it's of a size you can do well. If you show Mother Earth that you're earnest and willing to work, she'll reward you with a bountiful harvest." This came from one of her favorite sayings from Henry Ward Beecher: "A half well-done is better than a whole half-done." Confused? So was I! Nevertheless, we plodded on.

Those were the days...

Grandma Putt was never one to mince words, and she saw no sense in me wasting a good summer just rambling around. So as I've already told you, one spring day, she decided to put me to work—in my very first Victory Garden!

The Big War was underway at that time, and everyone was doing their patriotic duty. I had been doing my part by smashing tin cans, saving tinfoil, and collecting bubble gum cards commemorating the Battle of Midway.

But now, I was being given the opportunity to take on more responsibility by planting a Victory Garden! The idea seemed very commendable to me; not quite as exciting as bombing the enemy, but better than a stupid old paper drive! It was easy to picture whole regiments of "our boys" enjoying my corn, beans, and cucumbers. I couldn't wait to begin!

Grandma Putt's vegetable garden was a thing of beauty. Already, there were rows of radishes, lettuce, beets, and carrots standing crisp, green, and leafy against the dark brown, loamy soil. Tomato seedlings were in flats, ready for transplanting; peas, beans, and potatoes had been put in the ground, and were marked by seed packet envelopes tacked to sticks at the end of each row.

I remember thinking that if an old lady like my Grandma could grow a

(cont.)

STICK TO YOUR PLAN!

Grandma said that before you start to plan a garden, you need to decide what kind of a gardener you want to be. As far as she was concerned, there were three kinds of gardeners:

1. Those who gardened for the fun of it;

2. Those who gardened for work (cash crops); and...

3. Those who gardened for the fun of work!

If you've never had a garden before, and you don't need to sell what you raise, my advice to you is to start out small, with ten-foot rows. That way, gardening doesn't become too much of a burden, which will only turn you off altogether. If you have the time, energy, and patience (plus a little experience), and you want to store, give away, or sell some of your harvest, plan a medium-sized garden with up to twenty-five foot rows.

Finally, if you are looking to hit the mother lode (a.k.a. "pay dirt"), then plan a garden that is limited only by the space available, the amount of resources, and your imagination!

LOCATION, LOCATION, LOCATION!

Those are the three key words in real estate, and what is a garden if not a piece of real estate? Well, I now know that it's a whole lot more, although most folks act like they're ashamed of their garden, tucking it away in some hidden corner of their yard. Not Grandma Putt! Her vegetable garden was in plain view of her back porch, for all to see. Besides saving on the walk, she liked to sit out on the porch on nice summer evenings, and watch her friends grow.

Those were the days...

(cont.)

garden that looked this good—just wait and see what a big, strong boy like me could do! It would be great! I could just imagine my garden, stretching out for acres, until it blurred into the distant horizon.

When it came time to lay out my garden, was I ever in for a rude awakening! Grandma Putt told me to put it "over there," pointing to a small, weedy patch of ground just beyond her garden. "It's best to start small, with something you can handle," she said.

"Who is she kidding?" I thought to myself! I knew I could handle a garden ten times that size. "I'll probably have to cut down a couple of those trees, and clear some of those brambleberries over there, so I can extend this little plot," I bragged to myself.

"All right, Junior, let's get at it—take your string and some of these sticks, and stake out this plot. Figure on twenty rows, 10 feet long, with a foot in between each row."

I was horrified—such a tiny garden! It took me a few moments to swallow my pride, and fight back the tears. But then, I thought I'd start small, and do such a good job that she'd want me to double it in no time at all. Already, those regiments I was going to feed had grown. By the end of my first day of gardening, my Victory Garden was going to take care of the entire African invasion force!

Since those days, I've always been in favor of using landscaping space to grow plants that will also pay their way. So why not have food and flowers, as well as foliage? Grandma Putt taught me that strawberries and squash make attractive ground covers; they also provide the fixins for some very tasty meals!

As you'll soon find out, all of Grandma's yard was a garden; there was no wasted space. Her asparagus and stocks grew, mixed together, along the stone fence down by the road. Rhubarb, or "pie plant" as she sometimes called it, came up every year in a small patch by the well, mixed in with some calla lilies. Behind the lilies were four rows of grape arbors. Pantry herbs were thrown in the flower beds below the kitchen window, while garlic and onion grew with the roses. What I am trying to say is— *DON'T HIDE YOUR GARDEN*! Besides working in it, looking at it, and talking to it, the best part is having your friends and neighbors share in your success!

With that said, it's time to get down to some serious business, and find out exactly what you need to consider when you are looking for that ideal spot to raise your vegetables.

Green Thumb Tip

Grandma Putt knew that some vegetables were handsome enough to grow in any flower bed. The tall feathery fronds of asparagus made a beautiful background for her flowers. She used frilly, fresh-looking lettuce and parsley, and colorful heads of red cabbage in borders. Both artichokes and eggplant grow into handsome, bushy plants that can produce strikingly attractive fruits in a flower garden. She also grew climbing plants like beans and tomatoes on the downspouts next to her house.

FULL SUN IS BEST

Sunlight was the first thing we considered when deciding on where to place my vegetable garden. Most vegetables need a good six to eight hours of full sunlight each day if they are going to do a good job producing for you.

The best time to look for an area in your yard is in the summer or early fall (when the trees are fully out) early in the morning, when you'll be able to determine if the location will get the warmth of the early morning sun. If your garden is one of the first places to warm up during the day, it will also be one of the first places to warm up in the spring, which will give you a jump on the growing season. If you have to choose between morning or afternoon sun, choose the morning sun because plants make better use of morning sun for photosynthesis.

If you don't have perfect sunlight, then you're going to need a helping hand. The trick is to carefully choose the vegetables you are going to grow. Some leafy vegetables can take more shade than most, so cabbage, lettuce, broccoli, beans, spinach, and chard are good choices for an area that gets a little respite from Ol' Sol during the hottest parts of the day!

Grandma Putt's Words of Wisdom:

"Plants, like people, need lots of sunlight to survive."

Made in the Shade!

Veggies that do well in part sun include:

Chard
Chicory
Collards
Kale
Lettuce
Parsley
Peas
Spinach

How-to Hint

For those of you who have back problems, can't handle a tiller, or are simply too lazy to remove the sod, I've since learned that sod can be smothered out of existence. Keep in mind, however, that this method takes some time.

What you need to do is cover the ground with cardboard or several sheets of newspaper, wet it down, add several inches of grass clippings, and then thoroughly hose the whole thing down. Allow it to sit for several weeks, and then plant your vegetables through the cardboard/newspaper.

Add plenty of mulch during the growing season, and hand-pull any grass or weeds that appear. By the end of the second year, the grass should be gone!

newspaper

grass clippings

sod

Also, keep your vegetable garden as far away as possible from tall trees, particularly those with shallow root systems. In addition to the shade, the trees will also rob your garden of valuable food and water.

No Sod Allowed!

If you're going to plant your garden in an area where sod is now growing, you need to get rid of it, *pronto!* So either take it off in pieces, and use the pieces to fill in the bare spots in your lawn, or put them on your compost pile (sod makes *excellent* composting material).

Over the years, I've seen too many folks try to turn the sod under, which often results in big trouble later on! The grass, weed seeds, and runners continually pop their ugly little heads up to the surface of the soil, where they germinate, and become a troublesome bother when all you really want to do is grow vegetables. Spending a little time in the planning and preparation stage will save you a lot of time and effort later on!

YOU NEED...WEEDS?

The area Grandma Putt pointed out to me as a good location for my first Victory Garden was, believe it or not, *full of weeds!* That's right—nasty old weeds! And just when I thought things were going to be easy!

When I asked her about this, she said that weeds are a good indication that the soil is fertile. If there's nothing much growing in a given area, then you should think twice before trying to plant *anything* there. On the other hand, if the area was overgrown, then you know the soil is good for growing *something*. Her general rule of thumb was the thicker the weed cover, the better the soil fertility. This old adage remains true to this day.

Weeds Worth Noting

The type of weeds growing in an area can tell you an awful lot about the soil below. Here's what to look for:

Good Drainage—humusy, well-drained soil is often indicated by the presence of burdock, chicory, pigweed, purslane, dandelion, and lamb's quarters.

Bad Drainage—if mosses, sedges, curly dock, horsetail, may apple, or joe-pye weed are thriving on your property, then you have poor drainage.

Heavy Soil—soil that is heavy, but not necessarily poorly drained may have buttercups, broad-leaved dock, dandelion, and plantain growing in it.

Light Soil—sandy, light soil is often home to sheep sorrel, wild cornflower, white campion, and yellow toadflax.

So watch out!

SOIL IS MORE THAN JUST DIRT!

Grandma Putt always said…"A person doesn't know anything about life unless she puts her own two hands in the soil, and makes something grow." Why? Because a spadeful of good garden soil is an amazingly complex world, full of an infinite number of living things. Grandma Putt called it **"Mother Earth's Boardinghouse."**

Unfortunately, not all soil is good for growing. As I learned, "good" soil has good drainage, good structure, the availability of nutrients, a proper balance between acidity and alkalinity, good aeration, the ability to hold up to 40% of its own total content in moisture, and is the right temperature.

Back in the good old days when folks were close to the land, farmers played their soil conditions pretty much by ear. They would spread a layer of manure every year or so, and toss a few shovelfuls of lime on whenever they thought the soil was getting "sour."

Nowadays, most of us have been separated from the good earth for so long that we don't have any "feel" for what we are or should be doing. So, if your soil instincts are dull, here's how Grandma Putt taught me to sharpen them.

The Quick Test

Here's a quick and easy test to determine how the drainage is in your garden area. First, dig a hole in the lowest part of your garden, about one foot wide by one foot deep. Then fill it full of water. If the hole drains quickly, then the soil is too light. If the water is still there the next day, then your soil is too heavy. The perfect soil should drain in about 30 minutes or so.

THINK PERPENDICULAR!

After sunlight, the next most important thing that Grandma said we needed for my garden was good soil drainage.

"People who want to garden," she said, "have got to learn to think perpendicular. Begin to think about what's going on under the ground, instead of merely concentrating on the part of your garden that sticks up out of the ground."

Grandma Putt had gardened in my Victory Garden spot for many years before I had, so she knew that the drainage was excellent. But if you're the least bit unsure about the drainage in an area you intend to use, check it out before you begin.

Determining Soil Structure

When master gardeners talk about soil structure, they are referring to the size and proportion of the particles in the soil. With soil, you can either have sand, silt, or clay, with sand being the coarsest, and clay being the finest particles.

Sand—drains well, but loses nutrients quickly.

Silt—tends to compact, which hinders nutrient penetration.

Clay—drains poorly, which prevents nutrient penetration.

DOES YOUR SOIL STRUCTURE STACK UP?

It has to, literally, in order for your garden to grow. Here's a quick and easy way to check your soil structure that I saw Grandma Putt use many times, particularly when she was getting ready to break ground on a new bed.

She took a large glass jar and added two cups of water and a cup of soil to it. She shook it thoroughly, and let it settle for an hour or so. Then she shook it up again, and let it settle for a week to ten days, or until the water in the jar became clear again. Then she examined the way the soil had settled in the jar to determine what she needed to do to the soil.

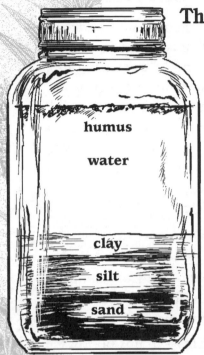

The Perfect Mix—Good Sandy Loam

If the soil is what it should be…fine sandy loam…then it will have layered itself out into the following proportions: the bottom layer will be sand, with coarser sand at the bottom, and fine sand just above it. This sand layer should make up about two-fifths of the soil in the jar. The next layer will be silt. This layer should make up the second two-fifths of the soil in the jar. The top layer of soil will be clay. This layer should be only one-fifth of the total soil content. If your soil stacks up this way, then you've got a good sandy loam, which is perfect for growing fruits and vegetables!

Light Soils

Soils that contain too much sand are called light soils. They are very easy to work, and they usually warm up first in the spring. The problem with these soils is that they are often unable to hold enough moisture for growing plants: water runs through them as fast as it does off a duck's back! As a result, you're fighting a never-ending (and quite often, losing) battle to keep enough moisture in the soil.

Heavy Soils

Soils that contain too much silt or clay are called heavy or clay soils. Once you try spading up a plot of clay soil, you'll understand why it's called *heavy soil!* These soils either retain too much moisture, or will not accept any moisture because of the limited space between the soil particles. This soil has a tendency to stay cold and soggy late into the spring planting season, which spells trouble for your seeds and seedlings. If this is a problem in your area, then you may have to dig down into it and lay drain tile. The other solutions? Move your garden, or build raised beds!

Humusy Soils

What's left in the jar? Well, when you test your soil, you will probably see some material floating on the top of the water after the soil has settled, and the water has cleared. This floating debris is called humus. The perfect mix, good sandy loam that I mentioned before, contains a proper balance of sand, silt, and clay. It also contains plenty of humus.

Humus is a dark brown or black substance that is the remains of decayed or decaying organic matter. It's made up of either plant or animal matter, including bacteria and fungi, that has been returned to the soil. Humus is essential for supplying the soil with nutrients, texture, and the ability to hold moisture.

In nature, rain and snow are Mother Nature's way of working humus into the soil. But in your garden, you can act like Mother Nature by giving your soil the life-sustaining organic substances it needs.

CORRECTING SOIL PROBLEMS

Good drainage and good soil structure are closely related. If you have a drainage problem because your soil is too light or too heavy, here's how Grandma Putt taught me to correct it.

BULKING UP LIGHT, SANDY SOIL

Grandma Putt's Words of Wisdom:

"Cover up your garden in fall, and it'll be rarin' to grow in spring."

To improve light, sandy soil, you need to mix in plenty of compost, peat moss, leaf mold, wood by-products (shredded bark, chips, and/or sawdust), or green manure. These materials are listed in their order of effectiveness.

Another soil-building technique to use when you're *not* in a hurry is an age-old technique known as **cover cropping.** Farmers and back-to-the-landers like Grandma Putt have planted cover crops for many, many years. By planting a fast-growing crop early in the fall, then plowing it back under as soon as it "covers" the ground, your soil has a chance to decompose (and extract the nutrients from) the green plant material and the roots.

HERE'S THE SCOOP—KNOW YOUR DIRT!

There are probably two dozen cover crops you can use, although the following crops are suitable for planting in most parts of the country:

Annual Ryegrass	Hairy Vetch
Buckwheat	Oats
Clover	Winter Rye

If you are going to try this technique, sow somewhere between 2 and 4 oz. of seed per 100 sq. ft. of garden area, making sure that you soak the seed first in **Grandma Putt's Super Seed Starter Tonic.**

Super Seed Starter Tonic

Grandma Putt used to soak *all* of her seeds in this tonic before sowing them:
1 tbsp. of Fels-Naptha Soap Solution,*
1 tbsp. of Epsom salts, and
1 tbsp. of tea water
in 1 gallon of warm water.

LIGHTENING UP HEAVY, CLAY SOIL

To improve heavy silt or clay soils, you need to work in gypsum, wood chips, green manure, compost, peat moss, or leaf mold. If it's <u>real</u> heavy clay, you may even need to add perlite, vermiculite, or sand. But don't add sand to the mix unless it is absolutely necessary.

To add humus to your soil, try working one or more of the organic wood materials to it. Clay soil already has all of the water it needs, and wood materials are perfect because they don't add to the problem. Wood materials also force soil particles apart when they are mixed together, which will help speed up the drainage process.

*See page 341 for instructions on how to make this solution.

Other Humus Building Additives

In addition to green manure, there are several other organic soil additives that work just as well in improving the structure and texture of your soil. Here's a list of what's most commonly available:

Bark
Compost
Oak-leaf mold
Peat moss
Redwood products
Sawdust

GREEN MANURE

Green manure is best applied to your garden in the fall. It can take one of two forms: either cover crops or plant debris.

If you don't want to try cover cropping, then do what we used to do: take any plant debris you can get your hands on—grass clippings, old pea plants, leaves, sawdust, wood chips, etc.— and work them into the top 6 inches of your garden soil in the fall. By the following spring, the bacteria and microorganisms in the soil will have broken down this debris into a rich, dark brown humus.

Keep in mind that wood chips and bark are better for clay soils, while shredded leaves are best for sandy soils. Grass, pea, and bean plants will also return a great deal of nitrogen to the soil, which is great for your plants.

BLACK GOLD—COMPOST!

Any organic gardener will tell you at the drop of a blade of grass (on his compost pile, that is) that compost is the best darn humus-building material you can give to your soil! The difference between compost and green manure is that with compost, you lay your grass clippings and other organic debris in a pile, and let the decomposition take place *above ground* before you work it into your garden soil.

HERE'S THE SCOOP—KNOW YOUR DIRT!

There are at least a hundred different ways to compost, and it seems that everyone's got an opinion on which method works best. Many old-timers, including Grandma Putt, had two or more piles going at once: one that was ready for spreading, and others that were in various stages of "working."

You can use just about any material in your compost pile as long as you keep turning it often enough to let the airborne bacteria get at it. Before long, your pile will heat up, which will not only help with the decomposition, but will also eliminate a lot of the odors.

Where you put your compost pile has a lot to do with where your garden is, and how close your neighbors are. Try to keep it as close to your garden as possible; at the same time, if the prevailing winds threaten to blow your neighbors away, either locate it somewhere else, or feed it plenty of brown material that doesn't tend to putrefy. You can do much to ward off putrefaction by turning the pile every ten days or so. In the worst cases, you should liberally sprinkle baking soda on top of the pile, and work it into the layers; it works to remove odors in your compost pile just like it does in your refrigerator!

To Compost...

Things you can (and should) compost include: **leaves, grass clippings, young weeds, plant prunings, vegetable peelings, eggshells, coffee grounds, used tea leaves, soil, manure** (from cows, horses, sheep, pigs, or chickens), **rock powders** (rock phosphate and granite dust), **bone meal, seaweed, fish scraps, and hay.**

or Not To Compost...

Definitely <u>do not</u> try to compost the following: **oils, fats, or meat products; pet manures** (which contain pathogens that will not be destroyed, even in a hot pile); **diseased or pest-infested plants** (which will only spread the problem); **weeds that have gone to seed** (the compost will distribute the weed seed throughout the garden); and **poisonous plants** (like poison ivy, caster bean, datura, and oleander).

Grandma Putt's Surefire Compost Recipe

For those of you who have never made compost before, this simple recipe will help. It's the same one Grandma Putt used and passed on to me many, many years ago.

STEP 1. Locate the spot where you want to build your compost pile in an out-of-the-way area.

STEP 2. Dig up the sod, turn it over, and then wet the area slightly.

STEP 3. Build a wire perimeter out of chicken wire or hardware cloth to keep the pile in shape.

STEP 4. Raise the pile up off of the ground on a screen for better air circulation.

STEP 5. Build the bottom layer of the pile out of sod or grass clippings, making it about 10 inches high.

STEP 6. On top of the sod/clippings, place a layer of old newspapers, and wet them down thoroughly.

STEP 7. Add a 2" thick layer of well-rotted manure or other organic animal waste on top of the newspaper.

STEP 8. Then add a healthy dose (4" or more) of grass clippings or any plant waste.

STEP 9. Add more wet newspaper.

STEP 10. Then sprinkle on a layer of topsoil.

Keep alternating the layers of **newspaper/manure/grass clippings/ newspaper/topsoil** until you've built your compost pile approximately 4 feet high. Each layer should be no more than a few inches thick. Keep the pile moist, but not soggy, and cover it with a sheet of black plastic

topsoil
newspaper
plant waste
animal waste
newspaper
sod

HERE'S THE SCOOP—KNOW YOUR DIRT!

so the nutrients don't leach out. Use a bottle of beer per 5 bushels of material to jump-start the process, or sprinkle it occasionally with **Grandma's Compost Starter Tonic.**

Turn your compost pile every ten days to two weeks; at a minimum, at least three times during a season. When the mix is nice and dark, and rich and crumbly, it's ready to use in your garden.

Compost Starter Tonic

After adding grass clippings to her compost pile, Grandma Putt sprayed it with her Compost Starter Tonic, which she made by mixing up:

1/4 bottle of beer, and
1/4 cup of ammonia
in 1 gallon of warm water.

This really got her pile cookin'!

FEED THE SOIL!

As we all know, plants need plenty of food to survive. Unfortunately, most folks are confused about the simple process of how plants get their food. They think that soil nutrients are taken in as food by their plants. That's not exactly true. Nutrients are the chemicals and minerals in the soil the plants need to manufacture their own food.

The first thing Grandma Putt told me as we were working the soil in my garden was that a happy, healthy patch of vegetables requires a certain amount of minerals to be present and available in the soil. The most important of these minerals are **nitrogen, phosphorus, and potash or potassium.** By adding organic matter and those nutrients to the soil, you are building a reservoir of nutrients for your plant roots to absorb. Then they can come and get it!

From the Garden Shed

Back in Grandma Putt's day, there weren't a lot of "miracle" fertilizers available; about all they had in the way of fertilizers were homemade, organic ones. The best sources were:

Nitrogen—animal manures (but <u>not</u> pet droppings), fish emulsion, cottonseed meal, and dried blood or blood meal.

Phosphorus—bone meal, rock phosphate, and colloidal phosphate.

Potassium—wood ashes, greensand, or granite dust.

Trace elements—seaweed and algae products.

Nitrogen (N) encourages leafy growth and succulence. It's supplied by rain and snow, but your garden also needs additional applications. Your soil has the ability to hold some nitrogen in the form of humus.

Phosphorus (P_2O_5) promotes the development of a good, strong root system. It also helps plants mature quickly. Most vegetables require large amounts of phosphorus. Soil doesn't hold phosphorus very well, which is why you'll need to fertilize with a material that has a high phosphorus content.

Potash (K_2O) helps build plant tissues, root development, and disease resistance. It is necessary for manufacturing starches and sugars. In sandy soils, a particularly high amount of potash is needed in your fertilizer.

All-Purpose Organic Fertilizer

Grandma Putt made her fabulous All-Purpose Organic Fertilizer by mixing up:
**1 part dehydrated manure,
1 part bone meal,
3 parts granite dust, and
5 parts seaweed meal**
in a large, old wheelbarrow. Come chow time, she'd wheel it out into her garden, and put it into action!

Trace elements are also vitally necessary to promote healthy plant reproduction and growth. Among the most common are boron, calcium, chlorine, copper, iron, magnesium, sodium, sulfur, and zinc.

THE ACID/ALKALINE TEETER-TOTTER

For a healthy garden, it isn't enough that all of these minerals are present in the soil. For plants to thrive, the nutrients must also be available on demand to the plant roots. Sometimes, too much acidity or alkalinity in the soil inhibits mineral availability.

Grandma Putt used to pay close attention to her plants, and what they were telling her. If she spotted a yellowing of new young leaves, she knew the soil was turning alkaline, and was not making enough iron available to her plants. So Grandma would mix a little lime into the soil to "sweeten" it up.

You can test the balance between the acids and alkalines in your soil by a very simple test which will check what is known as the pH content of the soil. You must remember, however, that the soil on one part of your property may be completely different from that on another part.

From the Kitchen Cupboard

Here's a quick and easy way Grandma Putt used to test her soil. She'd put **a couple of spoonfuls of dry soil** into a jar, and add **an equal amount of white vinegar.** She screwed the lid on, shook the mix up, removed the lid, and held the jar close to her ear. If she heard a loud, fizzing sound, she knew her soil was quite alkaline. A faint, fizzing sound meant that the soil is only a little alkaline. Then she'd go to work.

pH Content

Since my days in Grandma Putt's garden, I've learned that the acidity of soil is measured by its pH, which means "potential of hydrogen." It's calculated on a scale from 0 to 14, with 7 being the midpoint. A soil pH of 7.0 is neutral, neither acid or alkaline. A pH above 7 is called a "sweet" or alkaline soil, while a pH below 7 is known as a "sour" or acid soil.

Most garden plants grow best in soil with a pH range from 6.0 to 6.8. In this range, the breakdown of organic matter, nutrient release by microorganisms, and availability of most nutrients is greatest.

So the general rule to remember is the closer you can keep your soil to neutral pH, the better it will be for your plants!

"Ah So"—
"Sweet" and "Sour" Soil!

It is difficult—and foolish—to drastically try to change the pH of your garden soil. You'll spend a lot of time and money with mixed results. But you can raise or lower it a bit to create a more comfortable home for your plants. Sulfur or limestone is needed to make the change; sulfur is used to make alkaline soils more acid, while ground lime-

Plant pH Indicators

Plants growing wild in an area can tell you a lot about the type and quality of the soil. Here's Grandma Putt's rules of thumb:

Acid Soil

These weeds grow well in acid soil: sorrel, dock, knotweed, wild strawberries, cinquefoil, and plantain.

Alkaline Soil

These weeds grow well in alkaline soil: wild peppergrass, bladder campion, and goosefoot.

Adjusting Soil pH

The following amounts are approximations, and soil type and conditions may alter the results. As Grandma Putt always said, **"PROCEED WITH CAUTION!"** Ideally, do not apply more than 1 pound of sulfur or 5 pounds of limestone per 100 square feet in any one application. If larger amounts are needed, apply half of the material in spring, and the other half in fall to create a gradual increase or decrease.

pH change		Material used	Sandy loam	Loam soil	Clay soil
from	to			lbs. to apply per 100 sq. ft.	
7.5	6.5	Sulfur	1-1/2	2	2-1/2
7.0	6.5	Sulfur	1/4	1/2	3/4
6.5	6.5	——	0	0	0
6.0	6.5	Limestone	3	4	6
5.5	6.5	Limestone	5	8	11
5.0	6.5	Limestone	7	11	15
4.5	6.5	Limestone	10	13	20
4.0	6.5	Limestone	12	16	23

stone is normally used to make acid soils less acidic.

If your soil is sour (acidic), add lime to sweeten it. The amount of lime needed will depend upon a lot of things. A general application consists of 50 pounds of lime to each 1,000 square feet of garden area. You can use agricultural lime, and apply it with a spreader, or you can take a tip from the old-timers, and apply hydrated lime, which is lime suspended in water. Other soil "sweeteners" Grandma Putt used from time to time included plain old **wood ashes from her fireplace, bone meal, and crushed eggshells.** If you live near the seacoast, ground oyster, clam, and seashells contain lime, and are available generally at local garden centers.

If your soil is too sweet (alkaline), you will want to help lower the pH, making it more acidic. Good old gypsum will help do the trick. Apply it in a fairly thin layer at a rate of about 35 pounds per 1,000 square feet of garden area. Other acid-adding ingredients that are handy include beech or oak sawdust, sulfur, peat moss, cottonseed meal, and old-fashioned pine needles.

Those were the days...

"Plough deep in the fall, and shallow in the spring"—was the rule that successful farmers of the nineteenth century lived by.

Grandma Putt said that when she was a young girl, farmers who worked just the top 6 inches of their soil were mocked and derided, often being called "fools" or "lazybones" behind their backs.

She said when she checked later in the season, sure enough, the fellows who plowed shallow had the worst-looking farms, and the poorest harvests. By the same token, the farmers who plowed deep had the best-looking and most productive farms, with the biggest harvests!

AERATION IS HALF THE BATTLE!

Aeration is another key to a great garden. How do you do it? By working your soil to a depth of 18 inches in the fall or winter (if you live out West). This creates lots of little passageways for air to filter down to the subsoil level. This air will supply the plant roots with oxygen and nitrogen in amounts that are critical to your plants' well-being.

When winter is over and spring arrives, soil plowed in the fall will be easier to work. It will get more air, and thus, warm up and dry out more quickly.

Don't think that you can cheat Ol' Mother Nature by doing

HERE'S THE SCOOP—KNOW YOUR DIRT!

this deep plowing in the spring, and everything will be okay. If you do, you'll get good aeration, but you'll also bring inferior and infertile subsoil up at the wrong time, and put it in contact with your tender plant babies!

CATCH AND HOLD... *MOISTURE* THAT IS!

Grandma Putt was fond of saying nothing happens in nature without water, and that includes gardening, of course; I don't know how many times I heard that one! Water is the only medium that allows all of the chemical processes which are so essential to plant life and growth to take place.

Grandma Putt explained to me that plants use water like our bodies use blood. The difference, however, is that plants continually lose water (in the form of vapor) from their leaf surfaces, so they need to replenish what is lost. They do this by obtaining a new supply from the soil through the root system. The root hairs on most plants are able to absorb incredibly tiny amounts of moisture from the thin film of water that surrounds each particle of soil.

Plant scientists now know that the conditions in which plants grow best allow the soil to catch and hold up to 40% of its own content in moisture. By creating the proper soil structure and texture with the additives that Grandma Putt taught me, and by aerating your soil, you will be able to prepare a garden seedbed with the moisture-holding capacity so necessary to your soon-to-be "plant people."

KEEP A WEATHER EYE OUT...

As a final measure, all too often, first-time gardeners fail to take temperature into account when they begin to plant. I know I thought that just because it was warm outside, I could plant anything I wanted, even though it was only early May. Grandma said that in order to grow healthy vegetables, you must pay attention to the soil temperature as well as the air temperature. Remember, light, sandy soils warm up quickly, while heavy clay soils remain cold and soggy, sometimes well into May or even June.

None of us can control the weather. Try as they might, even today, no weatherman can accurately predict exactly when planting should begin. Many farmers rush to get everything in the ground as soon as the last frost of the spring has passed. A good gardener, however, knows that there is a lag period between the last spring frost, and the day when the sun has warmed the soil to "growing temperature."

Those were the days...

Grandma said that the nighttime temperatures are more important to us gardeners than daytime temperatures. Her many years of experience and experimenting had proved to her that many vegetables, like corn, tomatoes, potatoes, beets, turnips, and sweet potatoes "set" their crops at night. When I asked her why that happens, she just smiled and said that it was one of many mysteries that take place in a garden. (I didn't want to ask her about **the birds and the bees** because there was no tellin' where that one would end up!)

Another mystery was why each plant "sets" best within a certain specific temperature range. A summer with cool nights will be better for potatoes than for tomatoes, which is why Maine and Idaho have always been such good potato-growing states.

Why worry about the soil temperature? Because many helpful microorganisms, soil bacteria, and even earthworms are immobile if the soil is too cold. And if they're immobile, they're _not_ doing their stuff! They become much more active as the soil temperature warms up.

This is one important factor that you have no control over, so you need to be particularly observant and adaptable to Mother Earth's timetable. If the spring is cold and wet, delay your planting until the warm, sunny days are here to stay. Plantings put out in too cold of soil will only wait for the warmer days before they start to grow. Time, experience, patience, and accurate record keeping will teach you a great deal about the temperatures needed for proper plant growth.

Getting "a feel for" the soil in my garden, learning not to rush the natural way of

Old-Fashioned Forecasting

Phenology is the modern term for the way old-timers used certain plant forecasters to determine what the weather was going to be like. It's a little more sophisticated than finding out if Aunt Minnie's gout is acting up, but not much. For example, according to Grandma Putt, you should plant:

- Cabbage and broccoli after dogwoods have dropped their flowers because there was less of a chance of the crops being damaged by root maggots.

- Swiss chard, spinach, beets, and onions when the daffodils are in bloom.

- Peas when maple trees flower.

- Potatoes when white oak leaves are the size of a cat's ear.

- Bush beans, pole beans, and cucumbers when the apple blossoms are dropping.

- Warm weather crops like tomatoes, melons, and eggplant when black locust and peonies flower.

things, and becoming aware of Mother Nature's comings and goings were among the most important lessons I learned that first year at Grandma Putt's place. And you know what? Those lessons have stuck with me to this day!

2

THE VICTORIOUS VEGETABLE GARDENER!

Grandma Putt taught me many valuable lessons, and as the seasons I spend in my garden turn into years, and the years pass all too swiftly, I have come to understand that it is crucial for all of us—especially our children—to reestablish and reaffirm our fragile interdependence with all living and growing things on God's green earth.

For a young boy or girl, growing a vegetable garden can be quite an education. In my case, it was the most fun and most satisfying experience I've ever had!

With Grandma guiding me, I learned how to plan; how to make my plan work; and that work can be a joy and a pastime, rather than a duty. I learned that extravagant rewards can result from practicing simple economics, the usefulness of keeping good and accurate records, and the importance of self-reliance. I also learned how to observe and converse with nature and plants, how to benefit from the good and bad experiences of people far older and wiser than me, what it is to be bone tired and satisfied at the same time, and how to be humble and grateful for a harvest that exceeded my fondest hopes and greatest expectations. Quite an education, wouldn't you say?

SET YOUR SIGHTS HIGH!

Grandma said you should always have a reason to dig into Mother Earth, or she wouldn't help you grow anything but weeds. You may never need to raise vegetables to feed yourself or your family like so many folks in other parts of the world, but before you begin, you'd still be wise to set a goal for yourself or your children. Otherwise, you'll let your mind and muscles wander from the job in the months ahead. Then, the weeds will take over, and get the best of your garden. Your vegetables end up with the short end of the stick, and that, my friends, doesn't do anyone any good!

Grandma Putt's Words of Wisdom:

"Think big, but grow small."

THAT GOOD OLD GARDEN PLAN

Grandma Putt loaned me the money to get my first garden started, and knowing that I had to pay it back made me plan more carefully, and plant more wisely. My first garden was roughly 200 square feet (compared to the acreage most garden books tell you to plant); my grubstake at the time was just $5.00.

At first, I was tempted to spend it all at once, trying to jam as much as I could into that small patch of ground. I was quickly shown the error of my ways when I reviewed my first garden plan with Grandma Putt.

After hearing me out, Grandma said that a good garden plan can only be drawn up after you get to know the

THE VICTORIOUS VEGETABLE GARDENER!

different types and varieties of your vegetable people. Before spending a dime of her hard-earned money, she said I'd have to learn about their soil requirements, the area they liked to grow in, their temperature requirements, and the time it takes them to grow ripe for harvesting.

In addition, she said I'd have to learn a little about "brotherhood gardening," interplanting, succession planting, seeds, seedlings, and the lay of my land. Only then, she said, would I be ready for planting.

I remember shaking my head at the time and walking away thinking how that was a whole lot to digest for someone who was ready to dig a hole in the ground, throw in a handful of seeds, cover them, and then walk away! But even today, Grandma Putt's simple advice is sound, and practiced by some of the most experienced gardeners around the world.

Those were the days…

Grandma Putt had her own reasons for getting me out into the garden, but she knew they wouldn't carry much weight with me. So, she used the Victory Garden "hook" to get me to look at the project as though it was going to be a great adventure. And that's exactly what it turned out to be!

Grandma lent me the money to get started, and said that I could either pay her back from what I raised and sold, or work it off by weeding and taking care of her garden. She even helped me set up some potential customers for my vegetables.

Grandma said that if I paid her back, I could use the leftover money for war savings stamps. Plus, if I earned enough to buy a war bond, she promised to match it.

War bonds cost about $19 at the time, and were worth $25. Having that much money in those days was like being rich! The whole idea of doing something for the war effort, *and* filling my wallet at the same time was a goal guaranteed to spark my imagination, and kindle my enthusiasm!

WHO'S WHO?

If you want to be a successful vegetable gardener, you need to know some basic facts about vegetables before you run right out and buy seed or seedlings.

Vegetables can be divided into two basic types—**annuals and perennials.** Most are annuals which grow, flower, and set seed all in one short growing season. The perennials, however, if carefully tended, will give you tasty crops year after year. Some, like asparagus can live for five years or more.

We raise different types of vegetables for their different edible parts—some for their roots, some for their foliage, and some for their fruit or flowers. Grandma Putt always taught me it's not always necessary to wait until these plants are mature in order to harvest them. In fact, most vegetables are firmest, crispiest, and tastiest if they are dug up or picked before they are fully grown. And with a little forethought and effort, you can reap the rewards of your efforts all season long!

For the beginning vegetable gardener (like I was at the time), Grandma Putt said that a good, general way to tell your vegetable friends apart is by the temperature they grow best in. She divided them into two basic groups—cool-season crops, and warm-season crops.

ROOTS
beet

FOLIAGE
lettuce

FLOWER
broccoli

COOL-SEASON VEGETABLES

With these vegetables, we're interested in the roots, leaves, and stems. Short, cool days are key—rising temperatures and lengthening days cause these vegetables to flower and produce seed. If your area has a short growing season, then these vegetables are your best chance for garden success. The perennial vegetables that grow best in cool weather include artichokes, asparagus, and rhubarb—or "pie plant" as Grandma Putt used to call it. In the very early spring, just as soon as the frost is out of the ground, you can plant beets, carrots, Chinese mustard, lettuce (several kinds), and onions (either seed or seedlings).

As soon as <u>all danger</u> of frost has passed, you can plant cabbage, broccoli, Brussels sprouts, cauliflower, celery, collards, early corn, garlic, kale, kohlrabi, leeks, more lettuce, New Zealand spinach, spinach, early peas, more radishes and turnips. This second planting usually can be put in a week or ten days after the first. Because of their hardiness, these plants generally have the ability to weather some slight late frosts.

Guide to Planting Dates

Early Spring Plantings

4 to 6 weeks before last frost:
Broccoli, Cabbage, Onions, Peas, Spinach, Turnips

2 to 4 weeks before last frost:
Beets, Carrots, Chard, Lettuce, Mustard, Parsnips, Potatoes, Radishes

Late Spring or Summer Plantings

After danger of frost is past:
Beans, Beets, Cukes, Melons, Sweet Corn, Squash, Tomatoes

2 to 4 weeks after last frost:
Beans, Beets, Lima Beans, Sweet Corn

Late Summer or Fall Plantings

6 to 8 weeks before first frost:
Beets, Collards, Kale, Lettuce, Mustard, Spinach, Turnips

My First Victory Garden

Here's how you can grow 13 great vegetable varieties in a garden measuring only 12 x 15 feet. Use this as a starting point for your own garden plan. Be sure to include your favorites I may have left out.

Back Fence: Cucumbers and beans are natural climbers, so it's a good idea to plant them near a fence or some sort of support.

Row 1: Includes a clump of flavorsome chives plus a few parsley plants for tasty garnishes. Fill out the row with peppers.

Row 2: Plant your favorite kind of lettuce: head, leaf, or romaine.

Row 3: Is for carrots. Remember to dig this row a little deeper than the rest; carrots like plenty of depth to grow in.

Row 4: Is devoted to beets. Both greens and roots are tasty.

Row 5: Is for onions—the pungent bunching type or the flavorsome bulbing variety.

Row 6: Will supply your salad bowl with radishes and endive.

Row 7: Has tomatoes and your favorite type of squash (summer or winter).

WARM-SEASON VEGETABLES

These vegetables require warm soil to germinate, and long days and high temperatures (day and night) if they are to develop and ripen fruit. With most warm-season vegetables, the fruit is the object of the harvest, instead of the leaves, roots, or stems. Heat is the key—warm soil and no frost, and adequate growing temperatures.

After all danger of frost is past, go ahead and plant your warm-season crops including green and yellow string (snap) beans, lima beans, borage, chard, Chinese cabbage, cucumbers (early hybrid), endive, muskmelon, more peas (spread them out over several plantings throughout the spring and early summer), peppers, potatoes (white), tomatoes, watermelons, and a week or so later, sweet potatoes. Some of these vegetables won't begin to grow until after the ground warms up, but it's all right to put them in a little early.

In late June/early July, you should plant more cucumbers, okra, gourds, eggplant, squash, late cabbage, more beets, more radishes, late corn, late beans, and pumpkins. These should be ready for a late-season autumn harvest.

> ## Green Thumb Tips
>
> *Tip #1*—Plant tall and trellis-grown vegetables on the north and west sides of your garden.
>
> *Tip #2*—Plant early crops which will be succeeded by late crops near each other.
>
> *Tip #3*—Plant early season peas, lettuce, and spinach where you'll be planting hot-weather crops like tomatoes, peppers, and eggplant.
>
> *Tip #4*—Follow early leafy crops with fall root crops, and early root crops with fall leafy crops.
>
> *Tip #5*—Don't plant peas and beans successively in the same spot.
>
> *Tip #6*—Don't plant cabbage family members in the same place year after year.
>
> *Tip #7*—Don't plant tomatoes, peppers, and eggplant side by side, or where they have previously grown.

Foolproof Vegetables

These vegetables are easy-to-grow confidence builders for the beginning gardener:

Beets	Lettuce
Bush beans	Onion
Cherry tomatoes	Pole beans
Garlic	Radish
Green pepper	Summer squash

HOW SOON DO YOU WANT IT?

With the exception of radishes which germinate in a couple of days, few, if any, vegetables are quick growers. This doesn't stop seedmen from calling anything that takes less than three months to grow a fast-growing variety.

You'll just have to get used to the speed with which Mother Nature and Mother Earth get things done. Once you get into the slow but sure natural swing of things, you'll feel more at ease in your garden. For a list of approximate growing times, consult your seed packets, or follow the guidelines listed in the "Vegetable Gardening At-A-Glance" chart on page 43.

Do Yourself A Favor

Just a few words about selecting your vegetables before you complete your plan and begin planting your garden. First and foremost, plant some or all of the "foolproof vegetables" I've listed above. This will get your confidence up and growing.

Then, as silly as this may sound, be sure to include your favorite vegetables in your garden. After all, you're the one who's going to be doing all of the work! Then poll everyone else in the family for their favorites, and add as many of these as you can.

If you don't have a lot of time to work in your garden everyday, grow crops that won't need frequent harvesting. These include cabbage, peppers, squash, and tomatoes.

Grandma Putt's Forgotten Vegetables

From what I can remember, at one time or another, these vegetables appeared in Grandma Putt's garden. Some of them are old standbys that have dropped out of common use, others may not be very easy to find. So, study your seed catalog carefully, and scout about your local nursery if you're interested in tasting some of that old-time flavor.

Leafy Vegetables
borage
burnet
Chinese cabbage
Chinese mustard
collard
corn salad
cress
good King Henry
kale
kohlrabi
lovage
mustard greens
orache
rampion
roquette
sea kale
watercress
wood sorrel

Root Crops
black salsify
caraway
celeriac
chicory
golden thistle
groundnut
hamburg-
    rooted parsley
Indian breadroot
Jerusalem
    artichokes
rocambole
salsify
skirret
solanum
    commersoni
tuckahoe
turnip-rooted
    chervil
wapato

Seed Pods
black-eyed peas
Chinese okra
lentil
Martynia
okra
peanuts
pea pods

Stalks and Shoots
alexander
angelica
bean sprouts
cardoon
samphire
sweet Cicely
udo

Then once you get a little experience and gain a little confidence, try experimenting a bit. Every year, try to include at least one vegetable that is new to you and your family. Don't let a neighbor's or your own bad experience with canned or frozen samples of a vegetable keep you away. Somehow, each one improves when it's fresh-picked out of *your* garden, and cooked immediately. Remember, it never hurt anyone (except Dr. Frankenstein) to experiment!

GRANDMA'S GARDEN DIARY

As I've already mentioned, drawing up a planting plan for your garden is one of the most, if not *the* most, important step in vegetable gardening. Once you've made your final selections for your first planting, go ahead and put them in the ground. Then record the date, location, and expected growing time for each vegetable you plant. You can get these expected growing times from seed catalogs, the backs of your seed packets, or the "Vegetable Gardening At-A-Glance" Chart on page 43.

Of course, after many years of experience, I can honestly tell you that it will be a miracle if any plant comes up exactly on the day these reference guides say they will! Your plantings will germinate and grow according to local soil conditions, temperature, climate, and moisture. The growing time references relate to ideal situations set up by the seedmen to study their new offerings and old standbys. So the lesson is—give yourself ample leeway on either side of the expected growing time!

Every year, Grandma Putt kept a garden notebook that was jam-packed with detailed information and her own keen observations. Boy, I wish I had my hands on one of her notebooks now; there's no telling what I could still learn from her!

Grandma believed that having a record of each planting according to the variety, expected growing time, location, and success or failure of the crop was as important as having a garden plan. She kept her records current through the season, and from year to year. They helped her remember how each variety did; if it took a longer or shorter time to grow, and whether the vegetable turned out to be tasty or not-so-tasty. Using these records, she was well prepared to

Garden Notebook

April 18

Lots of mixed sun and showers this month. Unusually warm all this week. Ground should be warm enough soon for early planting.

April 28

Had Junior spade up vegetable patch. Soil moist and crumbly. Will begin planting tomorrow. Moving corn and beans to N.W. corner this year opposite last year's.

April 29

Hill-planted corn and beans. Used Tender Crop stringless beans again—two packets. Tried one packet Marcross early corn along with my usual Golden Cross Bantam. Sarah Amos says it's the sweetest early variety. We'll see. Put in four rows of carrots (one more than last year.) Rows fifteen inches apart—one inch deep. Chantenay red core type—these did well last year. Junior raked in root crop maggot control before planting carrots, radishes and beets. Hopefully the cutworms will leave us alone this year!

June 2

Beets are nearly ready for thinning now. Very wet last 2 weeks.

decide what to plant the next year.

Another reason to keep records of the placement of each vegetable is so you will remember not to plant the same type of plant in the same spot next season. Grandma taught me all about crop rotation and that continued plantings in the same area take too many of the same nutrients from the soil. This makes the next planting weaker and much more susceptible to disease.

After several years of accurate record keeping, you, like Grandma Putt, will have a good idea of which plants do best in your garden, and when they should be planted. This is valuable information you'll never be able to get from any other source. So start keeping records during your first year of gardening and then keep up with good work!

TOOLS OF THE TRADE

Whenever I complained that I needed this or that tool to get a particular gardening job done, Grandma Putt always laughed out loud and said that most of the Indian tribes got by with a moose-antler rake, a clam-shell hoe, and a deer-horn planting stick. I didn't believe a word of it!

As I've learned since, you can plant and grow a beautiful garden with just three or four basic tools: a spade, a rake, a hoe, and a small hand trowel. Don't even begin to begin without the first three.

But if you're like me and most other folks, it won't be long before you begin to accumulate an impressive number of other useful, if less important, items. The list of garden tools is practically endless. The most important are:

- a vegetable fork for digging;
- plenty of garden hose, a bucket, a watering can, and a canvas soaker hose;
- a hose end and/or compression sprayer for cleaning and greening;
- a V-shaped hoe for easy furrowing; and
- several different sized baskets for harvesting.

If you're one of those bright-eyed American tool collectors who turn up in the garden center every spring, you might as well buy a wheelbarrow. If you really take to gardening in a big way, you may also want to purchase a mulching attachment for your lawn mower, or a rototiller. Whatever you do, do it gradually; let your tool collection grow as your enthusiasm for gardening does!

THE VICTORIOUS VEGETABLE GARDENER!

THE LAY OF
THE LAND

If, as I suggested in the last chapter, you deep-plowed or spaded your garden patch in the fall, and then worked the topsoil with a rototiller or a hoe and rake in the spring, then you're probably all set to plant. Grandma Putt used to say that the garden surface should have a slight crown at the top, and taper off on all four sides. That way, any excess water from heavy spring showers or summer thunderstorms will run off, away from the plants.

If you don't have much planting space, like I didn't in my first garden, then you'll need to make the most of what you have. Most folks will tell you that the best-growing gardens face east or south, with the rows laid out from north to south.

When you draw up your plan, be careful not to allow tall growing plants to block out the sun of those which grow close to the ground. Place corn, pole beans, wired peas, and staked tomatoes to the north of your garden. Low plants, like root crops and leafy vegetables, should be on the south. Lettuce and some of the leafy vegetables can stand some shade, but potatoes and tomatoes require lots of sun.

Space-Saving Tips

If your garden must be small, choose your veggies wisely. Select only those that make the most efficient use of the space available. Follow Grandma Putt's Space-Saving Tips:

Tip #1—Don't waste space on a vegetable no one will eat.

Tip #2—Potatoes, melons, vining squash, and pumpkins all take up a lot of space, so think twice before including more than a few plants.

Tip #3—Some vegetables, like potatoes, onions, and celery, are readily and cheaply available all year long; so don't waste the space.

Tip #4—Vegetables best-suited to a small garden are those that are at their best when served fresh from the garden—lettuce, tomatoes, peas, and sweet corn top the list.

Some plants are real space stealers. First and foremost among these are potatoes. If you don't have a very big planting area, the best advice I can give you is to forget them. They are susceptible to disease, and since they store well, they're almost always available at your local supermarket anyway.

A BARNYARD BOOSTER SHOT

Each spring, Grandma Putt gave her garden soil a dose of fertilizer to prepare it for those rough weeks ahead, much the same way we now give our kids a booster shot before flu season hits. You can do this by mixing up a batch of her old-fashioned 'Barnyard Booster Mix.'

Grandma Putt applied this mixture along with liberal quantities of leaves over each 100 square feet of garden area in the fall, winter, or very early spring. If she had any left over, she would throw it in a gunnysack, and soak it in a 55 gallon drum of water. Then she'd use this Barnyard Tea to water her garden plants throughout the year.

In most northern areas, this booster mix should be spaded into the soil in late April before you plant your garden. The timing of this application depends entirely on your local climate and soil temperature. If your garden is located in a valley, it will take several more weeks to be ready for growing than if it's located on higher ground, where the dampness and moisture can be baked out more quickly by the sun.

Barnyard Booster Mix

To make a batch of Barnyard Booster Mix, Grandma Putt mixed:

50 lbs. of manure,
50 lbs. of peat moss,
50 lbs. of gypsum, and
25 lbs. of garden food

in the biggest container she could find. Then she'd set it aside until she was ready to use it.

THE VICTORIOUS VEGETABLE GARDENER!

TO SEED, OR NOT TO SEED...

SEED PACKETS

When you plant a garden, you must always start with fresh seed. Sometimes the seed is old; usually it'll state on the packet where the seed came from, and how old it is.

Lots of folks swear that garden seeds stored for more than a year are worthless. This just isn't so; why, Grandma Putt kept her seeds for several years!

The longevity of seed depends on where you got it, and how it was stored. Keeping seeds in stoppered bottles in a cool, dry place like a basement will give them at least two years of life, and probably several more. If you're in doubt, test the viability of leftover seed by sowing a few in a container or wrapping them in a moist paper towel. Keep the temperature around 70° F, and check periodically to see if the seeds are sprouting. (Most seed will sprout in about a week, but some take longer—up to three weeks. So be patient.)

> ### Green Thumb Tip
>
> Vegetable seed longevity can be grouped according to:
>
> *Short-lived*—usually not good after 1 or 2 years; includes leek, onion, parsley, parsnip, salsify, and sweet corn.
>
> *Moderately long-lived*—good for 3 to 5 years under good conditions; includes asparagus, beans, Brussels sprouts, cabbage, carrot, cauliflower, celery, kale, kohlrabi, lettuce, okra, peas, pepper, radish, spinach, turnip, and watermelon.
>
> *Long-lived*—may be good for more than 5 years under good conditions; includes beets, cucumber, muskmelon, mustard, and tomato.

Seedling Buying Secrets

There's more than one way to skin a cat (namely you), so to make sure you don't get skinned when buying seedlings, remember these helpful secrets:

Secret #1—Purchase your seedlings between 10:00 a.m. and 11:00 a.m. because the garden center operator has probably just returned from the early produce market with fresh plants, or his grower has just delivered fresh flats to him.

Secret #2—Whenever possible, try to select your veggie packs from inside flats, since they have less damage from the truck ride.

Secret #3—Purchase very short plants with little or no flowers.

Secret #4—Never purchase tall, lanky, flowered plants because you'll only have to cut them back.

Secret #5—If at all possible, plant your veggies the day you bring them home.

SEEDLINGS

Instead of starting from scratch, you may want to buy your plants as partly grown seedlings, ready for transplanting directly into your garden. Buying seedlings is more expensive than growing your own plants from seed, but there are some advantages. One is that your plants will have a good healthy start *before* they go into your garden. Another is that you'll get a jump on Mother Earth's timetable.

Seedlings are especially economical when you only want a few plants. By using them, if you think before planting, you'll be able to eliminate the crucial (and for some, painful) thinning step for some of your vegetables.

Whatever you do, I can't emphasize this point enough—*don't buy bargains!* You get what you pay for, and cheap plants are usually a disaster waiting to happen!

VEGETABLE GARDENING AT-A-GLANCE

Vegetable	Seeds	Plants	25 ft. Rows	Spacing of Rows	Planting Time	Thin Row to	Harvesting Time	For Winter Storage Add
Beans, Lima	1/4 lb.	–	2	30-36"	May 20	8"	Sept.	Freezing/6-10 rows
Beans, Snap	1/4 lb.	–	2	30-36"	May 20 & June 20	6-8"	Mid July-Sept.	Freezing/3-5 rows
Beets	1 pkt.	–	1	30"	May 1	1"	Aug.-Oct.	Freezing/1 row
Brussels Sprouts	1 pkt.	(or 10)	1	36"	Plants—May 20	–	Sept.	Freezing/20 plants
Cabbage	1 pkt.	(or 25)	2 to 3	36"	Plants—May 20	24-36"	Sept.-Oct.	Dry storage/25 plants
Carrots	1 pkt.	–	1	30"	April 20	1"	Aug.-Oct.	Freezing/1 row
Chard	1 pkt.	–	1	30"	May 10	4"	July-Sept.	Freezing/no extra
Corn, Sweet	1/4 lb.	–	4	36"	May 20 & June 20	10"	Aug.-Sept.	Freezing/6-10 rows
Cucumbers	1 pkt.	–	1 or less	6 ft.	May 20	Hill of 3 at 4 ft.	July-Aug.	Pickling/2 rows
Eggplant	–	10	1 or less	36"	June 1	–	Aug.-Sept.	–
Kohlrabi	1 pkt.	–	1	30"	May 20	4"	Aug.-Sept.	Freezing/1 row
Lettuce	1 pkt.	–	1 or less	24"	April 20	3"	Late May & June	–
Melons	1 pkt.	(or 10)	2	6 ft.	June 1	Hill of 3 at 5 ft.	Aug.-Sept.	Freezing/no extra
Onions	1 pkt.	–	1	24"	April 20	1"	Aug.-Sept.	Dry storage/1 row
Onions, sets	1/2 lb.	–	1 or less	24"	April 20	–	May	–
Parsnips	1 pkt.	–	1	36"	April 20	1"	Nov.-Apr.	Freezing or fresh
Peas, wrinkled	1 lb.	–	4 double	36"	April 10-20	1 1/2-2"	Late June	Freezing/ 8-10 dbl. rows
Peppers, sweet	–	10	1 or less	36"	June 1	–	Aug.-Sept.	–
Radishes	1 pkt.	–	1	24"	April 20 & May 1-10	–	May-June	–
Squash, Acorn	1 pkt.	–	1	8 ft.	June 1	Hill of 3 at 6-8 ft.	Sept.	Dry storage/1 row
Tomatoes	1 pkt.	(or 30)	3 or 4	4 ft.	Plants—June 1	3 ft.	Aug.-Sept.	Canning or Juicing/30 plants
Zucchini	1 pkt.	–	1 or less	4 ft.	May 20	3-4 ft.	July-Sept.	Freezing/no extra

AT LAST...TIME TO PLANT!

A Little Squeeze... Please!

Grandma Putt taught me not to walk on or work with my garden soil when it was sopping wet. She said that this will compact the soil too much, drive out air, and make it unhealthy for the plant roots.

How can you tell if your soil is too wet or too dry to work? Scoop up a handful and squeeze it into a ball. Then open up your hand. If the ball stays together, the soil is too wet to work; if it crumbles, then it's rarin' to grow!

Grandma Putt's Words of Wisdom:

"Plant in the morning, harvest in the evening."

After I had gotten through with all of the preliminaries, and I thought I had my soil ready for planting, Grandma Putt had me give my garden a good and thorough soaking. No, it *wasn't* time to play in the mud!

Ideally, for planting, the soil should be moist clear through, but not cold and muddy. Pick up a handful. It should be moist enough to pack, but still dry enough to crumble easily through your fingers.

When it came time to plant, Grandma insisted that we do it in the morning, saying it was an ancient tradition. This bears up under close scientific study because plants *are* like people. You're asking a lot of them to begin work during the hottest part of the day. So, when planting, remember that only "mad dogs and Englishmen go out in the midday sun!"

There are several different methods of planting a garden. All are as old and as time-tested as the Ten Commandments themselves. You can choose whichever method suits the lay of your land and appeals to your sense of order and aesthetics. Here's a brief rundown on the most popular methods:

THE VICTORIOUS VEGETABLE GARDENER!

Surface Planting

Most gardens all over the world are planted at the surface level of the ground. This method is the quickest, easiest, and best for most beginning gardeners.

Raised-Bed Planting

This old-fashioned method of planting is where foot-deep furrows are dug between rows, with excess soil piled on either side of the furrows. If you live where it is generally dry, then don't use this method because the soil in the raised beds may dry out too quickly.

Single- And Double-Row Planting

This method is a compromise between surface and raised-bed planting. The furrows are hoed to a depth of only 4 to 6 inches, and the seed is planted toward the southern edge of the furrow bank. Double-row planting is just what the term implies—you put two rows of vegetables like carrots, radishes, turnips, or onions in parallel rows about 2 feet apart.

A Hill of Beans

Beans and corn have been planted in hills since Indian times. The Indians planted about a half-dozen kernels of corn in a two-foot circle around a dead fish. Even in pre-Columbian times, they were apparently aware of the beneficial and fertilizing qualities of decaying animal matter.

This method of planting will give you lots of room for interplanting the other members of the North American Indians' big four vegetable crops: beans, squash, and pumpkins.

Hill Planting

As the name implies, vegetables are planted in a hill, or more accurately, a circle. With this method, you'll have to thin your seedlings to the healthiest two or three as soon as they develop two leaves. Proper thinning will help you have a better harvest, so don't be timid about it!

Mound Planting

This Indian method of planting is similar to hill planting. Place corn, muskmelons, and watermelons in little mounds of soil that are about a square foot or more. Thin the seedlings out when they're up. Furrow around the mounds and keep the area well watered.

Contour Planting and Terracing

If you want to grow crops on slopes and mountainsides, then these methods are just what the doctor ordered. You may even need to use a variation of these systems if your garden area has a slope to it.

If the grade is gentle, plant across the slope following the contour of the land. If the slope is steep, then you'll probably have to make several flattened terraces, or steps, across the face of it to accommodate your garden. These steps can be several rows deep.

"WE ARE THE WORLD, WE ARE..."

Grandma Putt first taught me about companion planting or as she called it, "brotherhood gardening." She said the idea was very old, and mentioned in the earliest almanacs as "good influence" planting. She got the name "brotherhood gardening" from a local minister's sermon right after the 1919 race riots in Chicago. He was a local gardener of some renown, and he told his parishioners they would be wise to take a good, hard look at the example of certain dissimilar flowers, herbs, and vegetables which live together in a mutually beneficial way. They help each other out by supplying much needed nutrients or by warding off bothersome insects.

> ## ☺ Companion Planting Benefits
>
> When planted together, certain vegetables can provide a variety of benefits to their neighbors including:
> - ✔ **Increasing the harvest**
> - ✔ **Efficiently using nutrients**
> - ✔ **Pest protection**
> - ✔ **Conditioning the soil**
> - ✔ **Saving space and effort**

Grandma Putt explained that this good-neighbor system had been working in the world of plants long before we came to this country. The Indians taught the first colonists to plant corn with pole beans so the cornstalks could help support the beans. Now we know that the beans also supplied much needed nitrogen to the corn. Squash and corn are another good example—the squash leaves provide shade, reduce weeds, and make it tough for varmints (raccoons) to wander in the field. The corn, in turn, provides shade during the hot summer months. So it's a win-win situation for both varieties.

☺ GOOD NEIGHBOR PLANTINGS ☺

Plant	Good Neighbors
Asparagus	Tomatoes, parsley, basil, nasturtiums.
Beans	Potatoes, carrots, corn, cauliflower, cabbage, celery, cucumbers, most other vegetables and herbs.
Beets	Beans, kohlrabi, onions.
Borage	Tomatoes (attracts bees, deters tomato worms, improves growth and flavor), squash, strawberries.
Cabbage Family	Potatoes, celery, dill, chamomile, sage, thyme, mint, rosemary, and onions (deters cabbage worms).
Carrots	Peas, lettuce, chives, onions, leeks, rosemary, sage, tomatoes.
Celery	Leeks, tomatoes, bush beans, cabbage, cauliflower.
Corn	Potatoes, peas, beans, cucumbers, pumpkins, squash.
Cucumbers	Beans, corn, peas, radishes, sunflowers.
Dill	Cabbage (improves growth and health), carrots.
Eggplant	Green beans.
Garlic	Roses and raspberries (deters Japanese beetle); enhances herb production of essential oils; deters pests.
Horseradish	Potatoes (deters potato beetles).
Lettuce	Carrots, radishes, strawberries, cucumbers.
Mint	Cabbage family, tomatoes (deters cabbage moth).
Nasturtiums	Tomatoes, radishes, cabbage, cucumbers; plant under fruit trees (deters aphids and other pests).
Onions	Beets, strawberries, tomatoes, lettuce (protect against slugs), beans (against ants), summer savory.
Parsley	Tomatoes, asparagus.
Peas	Grow well with most vegetables, adds nitrogen to soil.
Petunia	Protects beans; beneficial throughout.
Pigweed	Brings nutrients to topsoil; beneficial with potatoes, onions, and corn.
Potatoes	Horseradish (as trap crop for beetles), beans, corn, cabbage, marigolds, lima beans, eggplant.
Pumpkins	Corn.
Radishes	Peas, nasturtiums, lettuce, cucumbers; general aid to repelling insects.
Rosemary	Carrots, beans, cabbage, sage; deters cabbage moth, bean beetles, carrot fly.
Sage	Rosemary, carrots, cabbage, peas, beans.
Spinach	Strawberries.
Squash	Nasturtiums, corn.
Strawberries	Bush beans, spinach, borage lettuce.
Summer Savory	Beans, onions; (deters bean beetle).
Tomatoes	Parsley, asparagus, marigold, nasturtium, carrots.

Herb Buddies

Grandma Putt taught me that herbs can be mighty defenders of your garden territory. Good, all-purpose repellent herbs include anise, borage, cilantro, dill, scented geranium, mint, rosemary, sage, and tansy.

Some good neighbors, like spearmint, tansy, garlic, and onions, should be planted near vegetables to repel aphids. They also deter rabbits who just love tender young beans and leaf lettuce. Spearmint and tansy, incidentally, are also good for warding off ants. Put some dried spearmint leaves at the back of your pantry shelves if this is a problem.

Helping herbs that enhance the growth of other plants include basil and thyme with tomatoes, savory with onions, borage with strawberries, sage with cabbage, and chervil with radishes. On the other side of the coin, there are hindering herbs which, as the name states, hinder the growth of plants. These include sage with onions, dill with tomatoes, garlic with beans, and marigolds with cucumbers.

The Lure of the Wild

Herbs have another good use in the garden, which is attracting beneficial insects like lacewings, lady beetles, and parasitic wasps. Grandma Putt planted these herbs around her vegetable garden to lure the good bugs into it, and they, in turn, fed on the bad guys:

Anise	Mint
Chamomile	Tansy
Dill	Yarrow
Fennel	

Flower Buddies

Four outstanding good-neighbor plants which can improve your vegetable harvest are old-fashioned **marigolds, nasturtiums, geraniums, and poppies.** Grandma Putt used all four in the border outside of her vegetable garden. Sometimes she chopped, squeezed, and then mixed them up with an old eggbeater to make an organic insect repellent. If you try this, be sure to dilute the flower pulp with at least 10 parts of water in your sprayer.

The Sacrificial Lambs

There may be times when it seems as though your garden is going buggy to the rabbits, moles, and other critters. If it is, don't give up! Old-time gardeners who shied away from chemical insecticides came up with what they called "trap planting." These plants lure the insects and varmints away from nearby vegetables.

They are the sacrificial lambs of the plant kingdom which leave themselves wide open to attack so that your favorite vegetables may survive. For example, Grandma Putt used dill to trap tomato worms, zinnias, and knotweed to attract Japanese beetles, clover to distract rabbits, and daffodils to protect her tulips.

Baa.

BAD NEIGHBORS

Just like some folks, there are certain plants that just can't seem to get along with others. It's not that they're mean or misguided, it's just that they both need the same nutrients from the soil or attract the same kinds of insect enemies. One plant in particular, the white potato, is a real "Archie Bunker"—it doesn't get along with anyone else in the vegetable patch! Here is a list of some bad neighbor vegetables, along with those to avoid:

☹ BAD NEIGHBOR PLANTINGS ☹

Plant	Bad Neighbors
Asparagus	doesn't get along very well with onions, leeks, garlic, and glads; neither do beans. Pole beans also have onion problems, as do bush beans (maybe it's their breath). Pole beans also have trouble with sunflowers, kohlrabi, and beets.
Beets	feel the same way about pole beans, so keep them on opposite sides of the tracks.
Cabbage	Most members of the cabbage family can't stand strawberries, dislike tomatoes, and would just rather not be anywhere near pole beans.
Carrots	just don't dig dill.
Chives	are not on speaking terms with peas.
Cucumbers	are not fans of potatoes or any of the members of the herb family.
Peas	share some of the bean family's prejudices against the onion and garlic guys.
Potatoes	are loners and bigots; they just don't like anyone to move into their neighborhood, especially pumpkins, sunflowers, tomatoes, or raspberries.
Pumpkins	don't like potatoes in their patch.
Strawberries	think certain members of the cabbage family stink.

If you match these natural prejudices against the Good Neighbor list (page 48), you'll be able to plant a garden that will soon break into a rousing rendition of "We Are The World!"

THE VICTORIOUS VEGETABLE GARDENER!

Interplanting

Some of the "good neighbors" can help save space in your garden. For instance, you can plant radishes between cucumbers and squash. And, of course, pumpkins between rows of corn. This space-saving system is sometimes called interplanting. You can also use interplanting to properly use space by planting fast-growing varieties in the same rows as slow growers.

Succession Planting

Never having gardened before, I thought I would do all of my vegetable planting at once, and that it would be the end of it. *WRONG!* Grandma explained that a smart gardener uses what she called succession planting. That is, she keeps taking out the spent crops, and putting in new ones throughout the growing season, right up to and including the fall.

Early corn, early peas, lettuce, carrots, radishes, broccoli, and turnips will finish maturing in plenty of time for successive plantings of other crops. It's even possible to plant in the early fall, before the first frost. Just follow the chart on the next page.

Leaders and Followers

Here's a list of good plant "leaders" and their "followers" to help you plan your succession planting:

- Cabbage is the starter, replaced by lima beans.
- Lettuce, followed by spinach.
- Onion sets, followed by tomatoes.
- Early peas, followed by early corn, then late snap beans.
- Late peas, replaced by corn, and then by radishes.
- White radishes start, snap beans finish.
- Spinach, followed by wax beans.

THE VICTORIOUS VEGETABLE GARDENER!

SUCCESSFUL SUCCESSION PLANTING

Spring and Summer Vegetables	Sown or Planted by	Will be over by	Succession and Fall Vegetables
Beans, Pole and Lima	Late May	Frost	Same crop bears until frost
Tomatoes set out from hotbed	Late May	Frost	Same crop bears until frost
Corn, Sweet, late or main crop var.	Mid-May	Sept.	Pumpkin and vine squash planted
mid-season varieties	Mid-May	Mid-Aug.	in corn rows by mid-June
early varieties	Mid-May	Early Aug.	will succeed the corn
Peas, late or main crop varieties	Apr. or May	Early Aug.	Rutabaga and late turnips
early and mid-season varieties	Apr. or May	Mid-July	Celery from seedbed
Potatoes, early varieties	Apr. or May	Aug.	Sweet Corn, early varieties
Beans, Dwarf or Bush varieties	Mid-May	July	Cabbage and cauliflower from seedbed
Cabbage and Cauliflower	Apr. or May	Aug.	Beans, dwarf or bush varieties
Lettuce and Endive	Apr. or May	Mid-July	Beets for fall and winter use
Kohlrabi, 1/2 row; Swiss Chard	Apr. or May	Aug.	Lettuce and endive
Carrot and Turnip, early varieties	Apr. or May	Aug.	Chinese cabbage and florence fennel,
Radish	Apr. or May	July	from seedbed or sown in radish row,
Onion Sets	Apr. or May	Aug.	will occupy the 3 rows in fall
Onions from seed	Apr. or May	Sept.	Spinach for early winter
Beets, early varieties	Apr. or May	Aug.	Spinach for fall use
Spinach	Apr. or May	Mid-June	Carrots
Squash, bush	Mid-May	Frost	Same crop bears until frost
Cucumbers and	Mid-May	Sept.	Kale and Brussels sprouts
Muskmelon			set between vines in July or Aug.
Eggplant and Peppers	Late May	Frost	Same crop bears until frost
Beans, Bush, and Lima	Late May	Frost	Same crop bears until frost
New Zealand Spinach	Late May	Frost	Same crop bears until frost
Leek and Parsley	Apr. or May	Frost	Same crop bears until frost
Parsnip	Apr. or May	Frost	Same crop bears until frost

Another method of succession planting that guarantees a steady supply of your favorite vegetable crops is to plant them several times in a series throughout the spring, and on into early summer. Make your plantings approximately ten days to two weeks apart.

Most seed packets tell you whether the variety is for early, midseason, or late planting. By using this information, and paying careful attention to the Good Neighbor and Bad Neighbor Planting lists, you'll be able to keep changing your garden, making it a comfortable place for your plant people to live all season long!

REVAMPING AN OLDER GARDEN

For far too many years, most folks have planted traditional vegetable gardens. They all look the same, like miniature model farms: rows of radishes, corn, carrots, and lettuce; they make sure that everything is separated from everything else in nice, neat, even lines. Then to compound the problem, they plant the same thing in the same part of the garden year after year after year.

When all is said and done, these folks wonder why their crop production gets smaller and smaller and smaller every year. The answer is simple—each plant extracts certain elements from the soil to help carry out the necessary chemical processes within its own system. After a couple of years in the same spot, the plants take all of these necessary nutrients from the soil. So if your garden is not new, and you've been working it for several years, then you need to think "outside the box," and renovate your garden.

Grandma Putt's Words of Wisdom:

"The soil is like a tableful of food—each plant that sits down and eats leaves less for those who follow."

ROTATE YOUR CROPS

The answer is as old as the Indians, and as sure as the Bible—you must rotate your crops! Grandma Putt said that I had to keep my vegetable plantings moving from year to year to avoid planting the same crops (or their relatives) in the same place each year. I didn't quite understand what she meant, but she said I had to choose a different bed or area to grow this year's vegetables, using succession planting methods.

Grandma Putt then sat me down, rounded up a stick, and drew a picture like that at right to illustrate what she meant by crop rotation. She said that she divided her garden into three main areas, and used a three-year crop rotation plan according to what was best for the plants' need for nutrition.

She divided her crops according to what they gave and took from the soil as follows:

Area 1: Root crops like beets, carrots, onions, and potatoes.
Area 2: Cabbage family crops.
Area 3: Heavy feeders like corn, melons, squash, and tomatoes.

Each year, she shifted the previous year's crop to the right, and prepared the soil accordingly. That's all there was to it!

THE VICTORIOUS VEGETABLE GARDENER!

TRANSPLANTING TIME

Transplanting Tips

Tip #1—Transplant seedlings to your garden on a cloudy day, or in the late afternoon or early evening. If this isn't possible, protect the plants from the sun with a newspaper tent, a shingle, or an inverted flowerpot.

Tip #2—Always water thoroughly before transplanting.

Tip #3—Dip the roots of the plants in soft mud, then water with a starter solution, like Vitamin B-1 Plant Starter.

Tip #4—Firm the soil around the roots gently. After lightly watering, cover the moist soil with dry soil.

If you start your plants indoors, or outdoors in a special seedbed, you will have to transplant them to their proper growing place in your garden. When you do, you must be very careful to avoid damaging the plants.

Be sure to move each plant with as much dirt around its roots as possible. Set them a little deeper than they were planted before. Water after setting, firm the earth well, and if it is an especially hot day, shade your transplants during the hottest part of the day. Do this for about a week, or as long as your tender young seedlings show any signs of weakness.

Veggies that *can* be transplanted successfully:

asparagus, beets, cabbage family, celery, eggplant, kale, lettuce, onions, peppers, potatoes, radishes, and tomatoes.

Veggies that *can't* be transplanted successfully:

carrots, garlic, Jerusalem artichokes, parsnips, potatoes, rutabagas, sweet potatoes, and turnips.

THE VICTORIOUS VEGETABLE GARDENER!

THIN IT OUT!

One of the worst mistakes new gardeners can make is to allow your vegetables to grow too close together, making them share the same soil and fighting each other for the same nutrients! That's a surefire recipe for disaster!

When Grandma first sent me out to thin my crops, I was downright mad that she wanted me to pull up and throw out so many healthy-looking plants. I could just imagine throwing my profits right out of the window!

Green Thumb Tip

To make the thinning process easier, Grandma Putt told me to water the plants, and let them set for about an hour or so before actually thinning them out. This makes the plants easier to remove, and keeps the soil disturbance to a minimum. If you don't want to replant the thinnings, simply cut the plants off at ground level, and you won't end up disturbing the soil (or the plant roots) at all!

Like most apprentice gardeners, I erred on the heavy side—leaving too many plants in each hill and row. What may look like plenty of room to the inexperienced eye will wind up being not nearly enough room when the plants are fully grown.

In the immortal words of Grandma Putt...**"Be brave, my son!"** Then she pushed me out the door. The lesson was to be strong-minded, even heroic about thinning. Grandma said Indian women thinned their crops "savagely." She probably meant it as a pun, but that's how you should do it anyway.

Thinning should be done when the plants are "well up" (usually when they have three or four leaves), and growing healthily. Each plant has a different growing and thinning schedule, so consult the seed catalogs or seed packets for the proper thinning times.

WILD WATERING

Grandma Putt really emphasized proper watering in the vegetable garden, particularly when I was first starting out.

Watering Tips

Grandma Putt never let anything go to waste, and that was especially true when it came to recycling "garbage" in her garden. Here's several ways she reused leftover "stuff" to help water her garden:

Tip #1—She took an ordinary rain gutter, capped both ends of it, and punched holes at each furrow. Then she placed the gutter at the high end of her garden. This allowed water to slowly flow down the gutter and evenly into each furrow.

Tip #2—To make a water bubbler, she took an old, worn out sock, and stuck it inside of another one, and then placed a rock in the toes. She tied the socks to the end of a hose, and used it in her vegetable garden.

Tip #3—She buried cans, with both ends removed, between her vegetable plants. She filled the cans with rocks, and watered directly into the cans; the water ran through to the roots.

When the first seedlings are up, it's important to keep the top two or three inches of the soil consistently moist. After that, we shifted to a less frequent, but more thorough watering schedule.

Grandma Putt's general rule was that most vegetables require about 1 inch of water per week; that's what they need to grow best. She said to always water early in the day because the foliage needs to dry out completely before nightfall. You don't like going to bed soaking wet, and neither do your vegetables!

Even during dry spells, one good, thirst-quenching watering per week is usually adequate. If you're experiencing a drought and you've got sandy soil, more frequent watering may be necessary. Adjust your watering schedule to the amount of rainfall.

Always give your plants enough water to quench their

THE VICTORIOUS VEGETABLE GARDENER!

thirst—soak the soil to a depth of 6 inches or more. But don't kill them with kindness—avoid keeping the soil soggy for several days at a time. This can cause roots to decay, leaves to turn yellow and drop off, growth to become stunted, and the plant may die.

There are many different ways to efficiently water your garden—a sprinkler or a soaker hose, by running it down the rows from a regular garden hose, a hose-end sprayer, or even a good old-fashioned watering can.

Most vegetables would rather have their roots watered than their tops. But this doesn't mean they don't appreciate you giving their foliage a shower from time to time. They do, and here's how to do it.

SINGING IN THE SHOWER!

To give her vegetables a decent shower, Grandma Putt put 1 cup of Fels-Naptha Soap Solution* in a large sprayer, and thoroughly sprayed her garden. This discouraged insects, and helped kill any hanky-panky that was going on. The soap also acted as a surfactant on the leaf surfaces, improved respiration, and increased the plants' ability to carry on photosynthesis.

Over the years, I've tinkered with this basic tonic, trying to make it better. I eventually came up with my **All Season Clean-Up Tonic** which uses liquid dish soap, antiseptic mouthwash, and chewing tobacco juice to deliver a knock-out punch!

All Season Clean-Up Tonic

To keep your garden in good health, wash it down every 2 weeks with this supercharged clean-up tonic:

1 cup of liquid dish soap,
1 cup of antiseptic mouthwash, and
1 cup of chewing tobacco juice*
per 20 gallons of water.

*See page 341 for instructions on how to make this solution.

FEEDING TIME

Grandma Putt said that if you feed your plants well and often, you will eat well and often after you harvest them. She used the "little bit, lots of times" feeding method, as opposed to "lots of food at one time."

Old-Time Fertilizers

Grandma Putt used everything she could find that had some nutritional value as fertilizer around her place. Here's a few old-time favorite fertilizers that she and others used to energize their soil.

Ashes—hardwood ashes were best, applied at the rate of 1 lb. per 20 sq. ft. of garden area. Ashes provided potash, which is essential for the development of strong plants.

Bones—known as bone meal today; in times past, it was used as crushed or ground bone. It provided many nutrients; a bucketful was applied to 200 row feet in a garden.

Eggshells—great for peppers and tomatoes; calcium is the main nutrient. Let crushed eggshells soak in water for 24 hours, then use it to water your garden plants.

Fish—any fish parts, buried and/or composted, are an excellent fertilizer.

Hair—either animal or human, worked into the soil or the compost pile, provided many nutrients including oil, iron, manganese, and sulfur.

(cont.)

There are several ways you can take your own vitamin supplements, and there are several ways to give your vegetables theirs— their fertilizer, that is. You can feed them before you put them in the ground, on the first day of the season (planting time), or while the growing season is in progress.

Different methods of application are best at each of these times. After experimenting a little bit, you'll probably use two or more of Grandma Putt's methods outlined on the next two pages at different times during the growing season.

THE VICTORIOUS VEGETABLE GARDENER!

STRAIGHT AND NARROW ROW APPLICATION

Placing fertilizer in narrow bands alongside the rows makes the most efficient use of small amounts of fertilizer. If you use this method, use a mild, slow release fertilizer like bone meal. To do this correctly, follow these simple steps:

Step #1—Make 2- to 3-inch deep furrows about 3 inches from each side of where your row of vegetables are going to be growing.

Step #2—Apply the fertilizer in furrows, using 1 to 2 lbs. per 100 feet of row.

Step #3—Level off the soil, and make a row between the bands of fertilizer.

Step #4—Then sow your seed in the rows, and forget about them for a few days.

Old-Time Fertilizers (cont.)

Hooves—horse hooves were best; a bushelful of "clippings" was put into a barrel of water, and let to set for a week. The water was then used to fertilize the garden.

Leather—since it's originally from an animal, small bits of leather were worked into dry soil to perk it up.

Manures—all forms—cow, horse, sheep, and pig—were used primarily to enrich the soil. Most of the time, it was composted first.

Mud—pond mud was used as fertilizer because of the rich accumulation of nutrients. Grandma's neighbor, Roy States, drained his pond every spring to grow crops in it.

Rags—cloth rags were okay, but linen or wool was preferred. They took a while to compost, so Grandma Putt chopped them into little pieces first. One bushel was used over 1,000 sq. ft. of garden area.

Sawdust—this was generally composted with manure or vegetation as a good source of carbon, especially when mixed with fresh grass clippings.

Soot—"soot tea" was much sought after as a liquid fertilizer. To make this brew, Grandma Putt placed a peck of soot in a half barrel of water, and scooped it out as needed. Soot worked into the soil by itself also increased color, thickened stems, and strengthened roots.

BROADCAST SPREADING

After plowing or spading up your garden plot in the spring, broadcast the prescribed amount of fertilizer from a pail or with a hand-held fertilizer spreader. Then spade or harrow the soil to work the fertilizer in.

Melon Growing Secrets

Here's Grandma Putt's secrets on how to grow the biggest, sweetest melons in town:

Secret 1—Dig a hole 1 foot deep and 3 feet wide. In center of this hole, dig a second hole that is 1 foot wide by 2 feet deep.

Secret 2—Fill the deeper, smaller hole with good rich compost. This will act as a water well, and the compost will draw moisture up to the melon plants.

Secret 3—Fill the larger hole with 2 parts sand, 1 part compost, and 1 part planting mix. Mound the soil so that the center is about 6 inches above ground level. Several days before planting, soak the hill thoroughly. Then plant when the soil is dry enough to work.

HILL APPLICATION

If you don't want to use either of these methods, then you can directly apply fertilizer to the holes in which transplants, like cabbages and tomatoes, are to be planted. Dig the holes 2 to 3 inches deeper than the plants require, place about 2 tbsp. of fertilizer mix in each hole, and cover it with 3 inches of soil. Then set the plants in as usual. This method is particularly good for cabbages, tomatoes, cucumber, melon, and squash plants.

Use a gentle fertilizer (like fish emulsion) to get transplants off to a good start. Mix well and pour about 1 cup on the soil around the roots of each plant after transplanting.

THE VICTORIOUS VEGETABLE GARDENER!

A Side Order of Nitrogen, Please

Most vegetables like a side dressing of a high nitrogen fertilizer, especially if they are not growing well or if they don't have healthy, dark green color. To side-dress your plants, simply scatter any all-purpose fertilizer on both sides of the row, several inches from plants, and work it into the soil. Don't get any fertilizer on the leaves—it will burn them, and never side-dress when the leaves are wet. Adding a pinch of Epsom salts to the mix will really boost your plants to new heights.

WEED-FREE, AND PROUD OF IT!

Grandma Putt said that one of the surest signs of a good job of preparing the soil was the army of hostile weeds that seemed to spring up overnight. She said it was very important to pull them all out before they choked out the seedlings. She also warned me how amazingly quick weeds are able to go to seed.

Unfortunately for us gardeners, hot, sunny days are the best ones for killing weeds! Weeding is one of the best ways I know to get a sunburn and a backache, so try not to kill yourself the first day.

There are two different areas where weeds can be a problem in the garden—in among the crops themselves, and between the rows. For those in the crops, the surest way to get rid of them was to get down on your hands and

From the Kitchen Cupboard

To relieve the pain of sunburn after a long day in the garden, Grandma Putt soaked a hand towel in a cool garlic tea (chopped cloves in boiling water, simmer for 5 minutes, cover, and steep for 45 minutes), wringed out the excess liquid, and applied it to the sore area. She'd leave it on for 20 minutes, and replaced it with a fresh compress until relief was obtained.

The Facts of Life

When weeding, the best way to make sure you are removing a weed and not a valuable plant is to pull on it. If it comes out of the ground easily, you know that it's a valuable plant!

knees, and pull them out using the old-fashioned "Armstrong" method. I tell you, it seemed like I spent weeks on my knees, searching for and pulling out these invaders!

Pull weeds carefully as you get close to each side of a row of vegetables. Too many folks are in too big of a hurry, and pull up half of their crops along with the weeds! Be careful to pull them away without disturbing the roots.

HOE, HOE, HOE!

After I had cleaned up the rows by hand, Grandma Putt handed me a hoe, and said to go to it. I ran it up and down the rows, once in each direction, doing my best to avoid damaging any roots.

"Stir the soil"—that was the catch phrase of old-time vegetable gardeners. In addition to keeping weeds out of the garden so they won't compete with your vegetables for essential nutrients and moisture, stirring also loosens the soil, and improves aeration. For these reasons, it's especially good for heavy soils which tend to pack or form crusts.

Stirring should be shallow—particularly around plants, and late in the growing season. When you're using a hoe, make short, shallow, scraping motions instead of chopping deeply into the soil. Soon, the area will be spotless. If you hoe thoroughly two or three times after planting, you and your plants won't have much trouble with weeds all summer.

Weeding, however, is a never-ending battle in the garden. Why, one good spring shower is all it takes, and soon you'll be up to your elbows in the wild and woolly weeds! Just remember Grandma

THE VICTORIOUS VEGETABLE GARDENER!

Putt's words of wisdom…"Don't get discouraged; if you stick it out, you'll win the war, even if the weeds seem to win a few battles!"

MULCHING IS A MUST!

To give my vegetables a real advantage over their rivals—weeds—and to save me many tedious hours of weeding, Grandma Putt introduced me to the wonderful world of mulch. As I later learned, mulching is just a fancy term for covering the soil with a protective material.

Besides controlling weeds, a good mulch conserves moisture, cools the soil, and helps keep your low-growing vegetables (like squash, beans, and melons) from getting dirty and water spotted. Mulching tomato plants prevents blossom-end rot by regulating the supply of moisture, which results in a longer growing season and bigger yields. Okra, eggplant, peppers, and all other long-season vegetables grow best when their roots are cool and moist during the hot, dry summer months.

One of the best things about mulching is that the material can usually be obtained for FREE. That's right, you can use grass clippings or fallen leaves raked from your yard—and maybe from some of your neighbors' yards as well.

Mighty Mulch!

Mulch does so many things for your garden:

- ✔ Controls weeds
- ✔ Conserves moisture
- ✔ Cools the soil
- ✔ Keeps plants clean
- ✔ Prevents evaporation

The best mulches are:
> Straw
> Leaves
> Grass clippings
> Leaf mold
> Pine needles
> Processed manure
> Redwood shavings
> Sawdust

The best time to mulch your vegetable garden is after your plants have had a chance to get started—usually when they're about 6 to 8 inches tall. If weeds are already showing their ugly little heads, then cultivate the soil before you mulch. And never mulch when the ground is dry—if you do, the mulch will absorb water, and allow it to evaporate before it can soak down into the soil.

GET THE BUGS OUT!

As far as Grandma Putt was concerned, the best program for fighting off bugs and disease in her garden was summed up by two words—**PREVENTION FIRST!** She used time-tested, cultural practices—making sure her plants got plenty of sunlight, water and food, regular weedings, effective mulches, and an occasional soapy shower. If you do all of these things, chances are, your plants will be so healthy that they'll be able to fight off most bugs and shake off any disease without any additional help from you.

Grandma Putt's Words of Wisdom:

"Garden enemies are born bullies; they almost always pick on plants that are weaklings."

When you begin to garden, you'll be bombarded with tons of literature containing claims and counterclaims by those in favor of or opposed to the use of chemical controls for insects

An Ounce Of Prevention...

An invasion of insects or disease can seriously damage your garden and dampen your enthusiasm. To handle these problems, do the smart thing—keep them from arising in the first place! Here's Grandma Putt's preventative maintenance rules:

Rule #1—Buy healthy plants and seeds from a reliable source to be sure that they are insect- and disease-free.

Rule #2—Rotate crops so the same (or a related) crop is not in the same area every year; this helps control soil-borne diseases.

Rule #3—Feed early in the day, using enough fertilizer to promote vigorous growth.

Rule #4—Disease thrives in damp conditions, so water early in the day so that leaves can dry off before night.

Rule #5—Don't handle plants when they're wet, and don't handle tomato, eggplant, or pepper plants after smoking, which can spread tobacco mosaic virus.

Rule #6—Keep your garden weed-free; weeds hide insects and diseases, and interfere with spraying or dusting crops.

Rule #7—Watch closely for insects; pick them off by hand, knock them off with water, or apply a clean-up tonic or insecticide before they get out of hand.

Rule #8—Promptly dispose of all plant remains to prevent the spread of insects or disease. In the fall, plow up the remains, leave the roots exposed for several days to destroy nematodes, and then plow everything under.

and diseases. I have always followed Grandma Putt's no-nonsense, common-sense methods. She practiced insect, weed, and disease control in what she explained as her letting "the punishment fit the crime method." She never needlessly used a strong chemical control unless it became absolutely necessary, and only after all other methods had failed! She started out with the mildest solution possible, then worked her way up.

THE VICTORIOUS VEGETABLE GARDENER!

BE DIPLOMATIC—ENLIST SOME ALLIES!

Grandma Putt used a war analogy when she talked about fighting the battle of the bugs—one country (or person) couldn't do it alone, but if they were allied, they would eventually win the war. So her secret was to enlist the help of every creature, great and small, in her garden.

She tried to attract as many birds to her garden as she could. She said a couple of robins are worth their weight in berries and cherries. They prefer a meat diet, and that means look out bugs, grubs, and worms! She put up lots of birdhouses and feeding stations, especially to attract finches, who eat lots of weed seed. But she cautioned me, don't overfeed your allies with birdseed—leave some room in their stomachs for a few bugs!

She also encouraged me to catch toads to put under her shady plants, and ladybugs for the tomatoes. She was not the slightest bit squeamish about encouraging me to bring home a garter snake or two. She even had me place a pile of sticks near the corn where these bug-eating snakes could live. These allies played an important part in controlling insect pests in and around Grandma Putt's garden.

Grandma Putt would also mix a little molasses with axle grease, and band the trees to trap the insects; place bottle caps of honey near the peonies to discourage the ants from crawling on them, put out pans of beer to drown slugs, and dusted

The Facts of Life

My Uncle Art was a real cut-up; I remember one time being on a scavenger hunt with him, when he told me that if you eat one live toad first thing in the morning, nothing worse will happen to you the rest of the day! I hope he was saying that with his tongue-in-cheek!

THE VICTORIOUS VEGETABLE GARDENER!

her lawn with bone meal to chase out ants. Looking back, I'm proud to say that my Grandma Putt was a practicing ecologist years ahead of her time.

So, if you follow Grandma Putt's old-time gardening wisdom, you, too, can become a shining example for the rest of your neighborhood. And that's a mighty big step in the right direction toward finding the solution to pollution!

IF AT FIRST YOU DON'T SUCCEED...

My Grandma Putt was the best and most successful gardener I've every known. She was more in touch with nature and the natural way of things than anyone I've ever met. But as much as she emphasized the natural way of doing things, she never hesitated to use sprays, dust, or any other preparation in her garden that would get rid of her garden enemies.

Grandma Putt's Ten Spraying Commandments

Most folks think that applying controls to their garden is difficult or too time consuming. But it doesn't have to be if you follow these rules:

 Select the right sprayer for the job, buying the best you can afford.

 Before you spray, read all of the sprayer directions, and "test drive" it to see how it works.

 Mix all spray materials exactly according to instructions.

 Choose the right pressure—high pressure for a fine, penetrating mist, and a lower pressure for heavier, wetting, nondrift spray.

 Spot spray to the point of run-off; don't broadcast. Avoid drenching and wasting material.

 Spray only where the trouble is, especially on the underside of leaves.

 For maximum effectiveness—not to mention less wear and tear on you— spray in the cool of the day.

 To prevent drifting of spray to non-target areas, don't spray when the wind is blowing.

Dress sensibly; that includes wearing gloves, a hat, and shoes.

Thoroughly drain and clean your sprayer when finished.

She knew that chemicals could be used wisely and carefully to help us work with nature. Grandma Putt said that Mother Nature can lose control once in a while, and the Bible is full of examples of locusts, plagues, and pestilence. Sure, we've made some mistakes and overused some chemicals that have left harmful residues, but they have been relegated to the waste dump. No one in his right mind would suggest that we get rid of penicillin, Aureomycin, or the polio vaccine. The important thing to remember is… <u>use chemicals for the right job, wisely, safely, and carefully</u>. And always follow the directions on the package to the letter.

THE DIRTIEST DOZEN (OR SO)

There are literally thousands of bugs and thugs that can (and will) attack your vegetable garden in search of a free meal. As Grandma Putt said…"It's time to haul out the heavy artillery only after everything else has failed." So on page 71 is a handy compilation of the dirtiest dozen or so garden pests, along with how to get rid of them with some light, and not so light, artillery.

ELECTRIFY YOUR GARDEN!

After many a thunder-and-lightning storm, Grandma Putt would haul me out into the garden and point out how the plants seemed to turn green on the spot! She said that these elements have an extremely beneficial effect on your garden because storms' are electrically charging the atmosphere which turns oxygen into almost pure nitrogen.

Grandma Putt created this same condition in her garden

BUG CONTROL CHART

Pest	Old-Fashioned Remedy	New Modern Control
Ants	Boric acid, vinegar, cucumber peels, corn meal, and borax	Diazinon, Dursban
Aphids	Fels-Naptha Soap Solution, lime, mint, citrus rind, alcohol, Diatomaceous earth	Diazinon, Malathion, Total Pest Control pyrethrin, rotenone
Beetles	Hand picking, drop in kerosene, Fels-Naptha Soap Solution, garlic, and onions	Carbaryl (Sevin), Diazinon, Malathion
Borers	Moth balls, nicotine sulfate, nutshells	Carbaryl, lindane
Caterpillars	Dead bug brew, aluminum foil wrap, and axle grease	Carbaryl, Diazinon, Malathion, Dormant oil spray, rotenone
Cutworms	Twigs, nails, newspaper, cards, drain tile, or cups around plants	Carbaryl, Diazinon, Dursban
Fleas, ticks	Fels-Naptha Soap Solution, rosemary	Carbaryl, Diazinon, Dursban
Grasshoppers	Fels-Naptha Soap Solution, salt water, nicotine sulfate, fall plowing	Carbaryl, Diazinon, Malathion
Japanese beetles	Hand picking, garlic/onion spray, Fels-Naptha Soap Solution	Carbaryl, Malathion, pheromone lures
Leaf hoppers	Fels-Naptha Soap Solution	Diazinon, Malathion
Mites (red spider)	Fels-Naptha Soap Solution, fall plowing of the soil	Diazinon, Dicofol (Kelthane), Malathion, All Seasons Oil Spray
Mosquitoes	Fels-Naptha Soap Solution, Pine Sol Soap Solution	Malathion, pyrethrum, pyrethrin
Snails, slugs	Hand picking, beer, grape juice, cider vinegar, Diatomaceous earth, aluminum foil, ashes	Metaldehyde
Scale insects	Mix of tomato leaves, garlic, onions, and alcohol; rubbing alcohol	Carbaryl, Diazinon, Malathion, All Seasons Oil Spray
Thrips	Water, vinegar, and water food, aluminum foil	Carbaryl, Diazinon, Malathion, rotenone
Worms (bag, web)	Hand picking, dormant spray	Carbaryl, All Seasons Oil Spray, Malathion

by practicing "electroculture." This, she explained, was gardening by using metal objects like copper wire, metal trellises, and tin cans. They can attract static electricity to the atmosphere surrounding a vegetable garden, supercharging and stimulating the flow of elements to increase the size, health, and yield of the crops.

Grandma Putt said that back when Great-Grandpa Coolidge was a young man, electroculture was the rage in all of the agricultural journals of the day. This growing method was first discovered and practiced in Europe; when it was brought to our shores, it spread like wildfire among the faddist farmers. Then, like many good things that are overpraised and overpublicized, electroculture fell into disrepute. Well, all things old are new again, and that goes for this type of gardening. If you approach it carefully, and use it properly, you, too, will get outstanding results!

Recycling Roundup

Metal objects you can use in and around your yard and garden include:

- ✔ Tin cans
- ✔ Copper wire
- ✔ Pie plates
- ✔ Bedsprings
- ✔ Chicken wire
- ✔ Bicycle rims
- ✔ Kitchen utensils
- ✔ Electrical conduit
- ✔ Aluminum foil

ELECTRIFYING TIPS

To use electroculture in my garden, Grandma Putt had me stretch a piece of fine copper wire over the top of my vegetables, fastening it to metal stakes at each end of the row. I placed the wire high enough so that it didn't touch the tallest plants. Then, I hung old tin can lids and pie plates here and there to attract more electricity while at the same time keeping the birds away.

THE VICTORIOUS VEGETABLE GARDENER!

Another trick Grandma Putt taught me was to bury the bottom two inches of tin cans every 12 to 10 inches apart in my rows, with the tops and bottoms removed, and fill them with stones to secure them in the soil. I used these "portals" to get fertilizer directly to the roots of my crops.

Other ways to use this method of gardening is to place a peony ring around roses, evergreens, and shrubs to give them a better start. Besides giving them vital support, you'll be boosting them to new heights.

To keep rabbits and other varmints away from our cabbage patch, and supercharge the air at the same time, we made wire huts, and put them over our cabbage plants. You can also make short, sturdy fences out of chicken wire; just be sure to slant the fence outward to thwart any would-be climbers. This kept our furry friends out, while still letting the electric energy in.

Tomato yields can also be improved by training them to grow on metal poles rather than wooden stakes. When you do this, the sky's the limit! As an added bonus, tie them up with nylon panty hose strips; then they'll really benefit from the static cling.

IS THAT YOU, BLANCH?

When Grandma Putt first started talking about blanched vegetables, I thought that she was talking about one of the neighborhood ladies. I quickly discovered that blanching is a technique that is used to get rid of the green coloring of certain plants (asparagus, cauliflower, and celery in particular) which comes from the sun during photosynthesis.

To get rid of the color, all you need to do is block off the sun. Here's how Grandma Putt got rid of the green:

Asparagus…she mounded up mulch around the shoots, or used boards to block out the sunlight as they developed.

Cauliflower…she tied up the leaves around the heart or flower with soft twine, rubber bands, or tape.

Celery…she used boards, soil, large inverted clay pots, a drain tile, or cardboard collars around the plants to keep the sunlight out.

HARVEST TIME

Grandma always picked her vegetables early in the evening or when it was cloudy and overcast. In the case of sweet corn, she would always have the water boiling before sending me out to pick it. She said the less time spent between the stalk and your mouth, the better the corn will taste. She was right—today, scientists know that an ear of corn begins losing its sugar about ten minutes after it's picked. That should make it pretty obvious that no corn you buy at the store will taste as good as the corn you grow in your own garden, and eat immediately after picking!

Modern research also supports the practice of picking leafy vegetables in the evening. During the day, the sun burns up a lot of the vitamins and minerals stored in the plant leaves. As soon as the sun starts to set, the plants begin to replenish and refortify themselves.

Grandma Putt also taught me not to store vegetables in the hot sun after they've been picked. If you do, Ol' Sol will work hard and fast to diminish their nutritional value even after you've brought them out of the hot garden sun. Put them in the dark, where it's cool. If you don't have a cool, dark storage room or root cellar, use the basement laundry room or a dark corner of your garage. As a last resort, keep them in a closed paper bag in the crisper drawer of your refrigerator.

Those were the days...

The best memories I have of growing that first garden with Grandma Putt have to do with the cool part of the afternoon and early evening, just before suppertime. That was when we would take a deep, old picnic basket and go out to the garden to pick our evening meal. Crisp leafy lettuce, crunchy carrots and radishes, bright red tomatoes, and tender string beans would join each other in the basket for the trip to the kitchen. Of course, there was plenty of sampling done right on the spot. For a young boy, brushing the dirt off a fresh picked carrot and biting off a hunk has got to be one of the real delights of summer!

TALK TO YOUR PLANTS!

That's what made me famous many, many years ago, and I still strongly believe in that philosophy today! Psychiatrists and psychologists have endorsed and recommended the therapeutic benefits of gardening for quite some time, and today, it's the number one hobby in America!

Believe you me, talking to vegetables, shrubs, grass, trees, and flowers is not a kooky or crazy thing to do. Any doctor worth his degree will tell you you're *not* a nut if you talk with the living, growing things in your garden. Getting to know each plant in your garden, personally, through good conversation, will help you become more observant of its general health and well-being. By stopping to talk to a bean, a row of carrots, or a tomato plant, you may notice that one is beginning to yellow at the leaves, another needs thinning, and a third could use a little support.

Grandma Putt's Words of Wisdom:

"Talking to your plants is fine, but listening to them is even more important."

Grandma Putt said anyone who has been gardening for a very long time has to be a great plant communicator. Why? Because they are most likely reaping as much news from their gardens as there is in the newspaper they use for mulch!

So, if you want to have green-thumb growing success, get out there and start gabbing with your plants…the minute they stick their heads above ground!

HEY! Over Here!

THE VICTORIOUS VEGETABLE GARDENER!

THE "COMPLETE" VEGETABLE GARDENER?

Not me, or anyone I know! Like medicine or cooking, you can never learn everything there is to know about gardening. I firmly believe that there is no such person as "The Complete Vegetable Gardener," although, my Grandma Putt certainly came close.

If you're anything like me, it'll take you many, many years to become an accomplished vegetable gardener. Sometimes, you'll have successful crops and harvests; other times, you will find that you and Mother Earth are marching to the beats of different drummers.

Gardening should be a labor of love; each year, it should offer some new delights and new surprises. There will always be a new vegetable to try and grow or a new hybrid variety of one of the old standbys. Above all else, have fun; gardening is a pastime you should enjoy!

GRANDMA PUTT'S GARDEN CALENDAR

JANUARY-FEBRUARY-MARCH

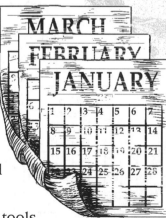

In January, Grandma Putt used to send away for the new seed catalogs and nursery stock offerings. That way, she would have them in plenty of time to sit down with a piece of paper and a pencil and prepare that year's garden.

February was the month to take to stock of her tools,

making sure they were clean, sharp, and ready to grow! Buy any new tools you think you'll need for the season.

Grandma Putt always checked her supply of vegetables she stored, canned, or froze at this time. Did she grow enough vegetables to keep her well-stocked through the winter? Did she over/under do it? If so, then she made the proper adjustments in the year's garden plan.

In March, we started some seedlings indoors under glass for our early crops. Almost any vegetable can be started indoors, but many have to be planted in individual peat or newspaper pots so that they can be transplanted outdoors successfully. Sow fast growers four weeks before setting out, and slow growers up to eight weeks.

The lesson was…whatever you do, **DON'T RUSH SPRING!**

APRIL-MAY-JUNE

April was the time to spring into action and get out into the garden! Grandma Putt dug up a spadeful of her soil, and checked its texture. If it crumbled easily and was not soggy, she began her plowing or roto-tilling, setting the blade for its deepest cut. Since she always plowed her garden deeply in the fall, her garden was easy to work with in the spring. She also spaded in her **Barnyard Booster Mix** of gypsum, peat, manure, and garden food (see page 40).

THE VICTORIOUS VEGETABLE GARDENER!

A week or two after tilling, Grandma checked her soil and the temperature again. If the last hard frost seemed to have passed, and the days were starting to get sunny and warm, she planted her early or cool-season crops like asparagus, artichokes, rhubarb, lettuce, turnips, radishes, and cabbages.

Ten days to two weeks later, she planted peas, corn, and beans. She wasn't in a hurry to plant tomatoes and peppers, holding those until late May. Grandma and her neighbors had a tradition of planting pole beans after the longest day of the year—they said they were better bearers and more disease-resistant.

If there was a late frost warning, Grandma Putt headed for the newspaper piles. She spread them over her young shoots to protect them, taking them off the next morning.

At this time of year, she began her regular feedings, cleanings, and waterings. Also, she got a jump on the weeds before they jumped all over her garden!

Then remember the "savages"—thin your crops with determination! Grandma made sure there was enough growing space between her plants on all sides. Some crops, like beets, required two thinnings—we ate the early ones she pulled, and saved the others for later.

Green Thumb Tip

Grandma Putt used to plant her tomatoes sideways, in trenches! That's right—on their sides in a shallow trench! First, she'd strip off all the leaves except the top two sets, then she'd place the plants in a deep trench, firming the soil around them. The plant would quickly straighten itself out, while the buried stem would develop lots of life-giving roots.

Grandma transplanted her seedlings when there were 5 to 6 leaves on each plant. She gave her transplants plenty of soil—a good-sized ball, and she didn't disturb the delicate root hairs in the process. That ensured their health and survival.

JULY-AUGUST-SEPTEMBER

In early July (or late June), Grandma planted her vegetables for the autumn harvest: eggplant, cabbages, melons, radishes, and pumpkins. Also, she made a second sowing of carrots, radishes, corn, beets, lettuce, and greens by the middle of the month.

Grandma didn't overwater her garden during the long, hot summer because of root rot. She watered from below, not on the tops of plants. She also gave her garden a weekly shower with the Fels-Naptha Soap Solution. This kept the insects and diseases at bay.

Summer was also the time to prop up tomatoes and pole beans. Grandma made her own cages out of heavy-duty wire mesh; they later came in handy when we had to cover the plants to protect them from the fall frost. Staking will also help inhibit disease and insects, and the electroculture worked wonders on her tomatoes. Have you ever seen a 5 lb. tomato? Neither have I—got'cha!

Grandma showed me how to prune tomatoes by pinching off the tops in late summer. This kept the plants short, bushy, and easy to care for.

THE VICTORIOUS VEGETABLE GARDENER!

After they started to bear fruit, we pinched off all of the suckers. These worthless branches feed heartily, and don't produce a thing, so we got rid of them as soon as we discovered them.

Fall was the time to watch out for bugs and thugs. Late summer/early fall tomatoes and corn were highly susceptible, as were peppers, potatoes, and squash. Always check your beets, carrots, parsnips, turnips, and other root crops for maggots.

Most of the work from hereon in was keeping the bountiful harvest picked. Grandma Putt never let any food go to waste; if she had too much, then she either gave it to neighbors or a local needy family.

OCTOBER-NOVEMBER-DECEMBER

As the year was winding down, Grandma Putt plowed up her garden, adding gypsum, manure, peat, garden food, etc. to it. She left all vegetable foliage and green fruit on the soil, and then plowed it under along with grass clippings and maple leaves. Of course, all ripe fruit and vegetables were removed.

Fall Garden Tonic

To prep the soil for the coming spring, the last thing Grandma Putt did in her garden in the fall was apply this tonic:

1 bottle of beer,
1 bottle of soda pop, and
1 cup of ammonia

per 20 gallons of water. She thoroughly applied it until the ground was saturated.

In November, Grandma added some late falling leaves to her vegetable garden, spreading them out on top of the spaded or plowed soil. Then she sprayed her **Fall Garden Tonic** over them, making sure they were saturated.

December was the time to relax, gardenwise. There wasn't a whole lot going on, and the winter brought a moment of welcome respite from the outdoor hustle and bustle.

Of course, Grandma Putt was so busy with the holiday happenings that she never really got a chance to relax. But I never heard her complain, and I'm sure she didn't want it any other way!

3

You Want Me To Eat...<u>Weeds</u>?

Just turn a small boy loose in a field or woods where there are apple trees or wild huckleberry bushes, and you will soon discover traces of that insatiable, inquiring appetite that got Adam into so much trouble in the Garden of Eden! A ten-year-old boy with a sharp knife will eat (and sometimes overeat) just about anything! This often resulted in what Grandma Putt jokingly referred to as "The Green Apple Shuffle."

Most of the time though, she didn't seem to mind ministering to my bellyaches. As a matter of fact, Grandma encouraged me to taste almost everything growing wild near her place. That kind of encouragement was all I needed to become an eager forager and expert explorer of Mother Nature's by-ways and boy-ways.

In the fields and woods, I quickly learned about the relationships and interactions between plants, animals, and humans, and how they help each other survive and propagate. Speaking of propagation, on a good day's jaunt, between blowing dandelion parachutes, carrying cockleburs on my pants, shaking nuts and other fruits from trees, "thinning" the wild berry crops, and robbing honey from a wild bee's nest—why, I probably did more for plant reproduction than Luther Burbank *ever* did!

Those were the days...

During my forays, I also learned that the greatest danger to my safety and well-being in the woods came just after dark. That was when the mosquitoes appeared like hungry little vampires to drink my blood! But thanks to Grandma, and one of her recipes using **fresh crushed parsley, bruised fresh basil leaves, honeysuckle vine juice, spirits of ammonia, meat tenderizer, or a dab of toothpaste,** my mosquito scars and chigger bites were reduced to next-to-nothing.

Our neighbor, Sam McGee, would often get a small bottle of Grandma's mosquito repellent to take along on our fishing trips. He said (out of earshot of the women) that since it was the female mosquitoes that caused all the trouble, it was only right that a woman should brew up the repellent! Imagine that!

Grandma Putt also taught me that Mother Nature takes care of her own, that some plants didn't need any help from me. She showed me how violets and touch-me-nots were able to shoot their seeds some distance, and how water cress released a few stems which would soon find a new place to root and grow a little distance downstream.

During the day, when I was off on my own catching grasshoppers or chasing butterflies, I would find all sorts of plant specimens to gather for food or bring home to have identified. At the end of each day, Grandma Putt would sit down with me and examine that day's treasures. Here's some of what I found:

FAST FIELD FORAGING

Besides their fascination for youngsters and curious adults, the wild plants that are found in the fields and woods have been, and can be, put to many beneficial uses. It's *amazing* what you can learn from even the lowliest weed…like the dandelion, of course!

"DANDY-LIONS"

The lowly dandelion, which is the bane of many a homeowner, had many health-related uses around the old homestead. Here's a few of Grandma Putt's favorites:

Salads: Young, tender dandelion leaves (called greens) taste a lot like chicory, and were used in salads. The older leaves were steamed or sautéed like spinach. The bright yellow flowers were minced, and added to butters and spreads for color. The flowers were also used as garnishes, and to lend color to herb vinegars.

Baths: Dandelions were also used in herbal baths and facial steams, and the flowers were used to make yellow dyes for wool. If you use the whole plant, the dye will be magenta in color.

Spring Tonic: For a fabulous spring tonic, Grandma Putt took 2 tsp. of dandelion juice (pressed from the leaves), and added it to milk, once a day. It got her motor jump-started in a hurry!

Dandelion Health

Diabetes—a tea made of dandelion root and/or leaves will help alleviate the symptoms; dandelion greens in a salad will help do the same thing.

Indigestion—roasted dandelion root coffee will help ease gas and stomach acid pains.

Kidneys—a dandelion greens salad along with powdered dandelion root is one of the best remedies for kidney problems.

Liver Problems—the best liver treatment the Amish have used for hundreds of years is…guess what? Dandelions!

All-Purpose Dandelion Cure

Grandma Putt made her famous All-Purpose Dandelion Cure by mixing up:
2 tsp. of fresh root and leaves, and 1/2 cup of spring water.
She boiled and let the mix steep for 15 minutes. Then she took half a cup, morning, noon, and night to cure whatever ailed her!

Grandma Putt's Dazzling Dandelion Wine

This sparking, golden wine looked like champagne, but tasted entirely different, with a lovely flavor all its own!

This recipe will produce about five gallons of light, dry wine. If you prefer a sweet wine, add an artificial sweetener before bottling. You will need to gather these ingredients:

12 pounds of sugar,

4 diced oranges,

4 diced lemons,

4 gallons of water,

4 gallons of dandelion flowers,

and 1 ounce of bakers' yeast

To make the wine, put the 4 gallons of flowers in a large plastic pail or crock. Pour 4 gallons of water over them, cover with a sheet of polyethylene, and let the mixture soak for seven days, stirring frequently.

Green Thumb Tip

When gathering dandelions, pick only fresh flowers, and remove every bit of stem because they are very bitter. The best dandelion wine is made from the flower petals, but you can use the whole flower heads.

If you can't gather all of the flowers at one time, try one of Grandma's favorite tricks: wash out a gallon milk carton, and dry it thoroughly. Then, as you gather your dandelions, press them down in the milk carton, and stick them in the freezer. They will stay perfectly fresh until you have enough to make the wine.

On the seventh day, pour the liquid into a sterilized 5 gallon jug or bottle. To make sure you get every last drop out of the flowers, put them into a clean sieve, and squeeze all of the liquid into your jug or bottle.

Then boil half of the sugar (6 pounds) in a quart of water for about 2 minutes. Cool to lukewarm, and add it to the "must" (strained liquid). Also, add the diced oranges and lemons, and crumble in the bakers' yeast.

Boil the rest of the sugar for about 2 minutes in a quart of water. Let cool, and add that to the "must." Put on a fermenta-

YOU WANT ME TO EAT... *WEEDS?*

tion lock, and let it ferment until all fermentation stops. Once the wine clears, siphon it into your bottles, and cork 'em up!

MILKY MILKWEEDS

The common milkweed that so many folks try to keep out of their flower beds and vegetable gardens is another good example of weeds we take for granted. The young shoots or stalks of this plant can be boiled and eaten like asparagus, and are about as tasty a vegetable side dish as you will ever set on your table! Grandma Putt said that the Indians also cooked and ate the buds, pods, and roots.

Like most youngsters, I was curious to see the "milk" that gives this plant its name. So one day, Grandma broke a stem and the sticky milky substance gushed out. She said this was not the sap, but a special "juice" or secretion which the plant uses to heal itself when its stems are partially cut or broken.

Saved By…Weeds?

During World War II, the U.S. government found two additional uses for milkweed: as the stuffing for Navy life preservers, and in the linings of Army/Air Force flight jackets. Scientists discovered that the milkweed silk was more buoyant than cork, and several times less heavy, but just as warm as wool. This common weed was an uncommon hero—it probably saved countless lives during the war!

PLAIN PLANTAIN

This hardy green weed grows so well that it is a nuisance in most lawns, so most folks don't appreciate its medicinal value. Grandma Putt used the wet leaves as a poultice to treat snakebites, poison ivy, and other minor wounds. She also crushed the fresh leaves, and rubbed them on to treat a variety of ailments including "breaking out," minor scrapes, and I hate to say it, rectal itch.

 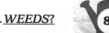

A Sweet Afterthought

One kind of natural food that Grandma Putt and I occasionally came across on our nature walks was wild honey. While honey isn't exactly a plant food, it is a by-product of plant reproduction.

Following a "Bee-line"

Grandma showed me how to make a "bee-line box" so I could follow the bees back to their hive. First get an old wooden matchbox, and fill it with cornstarch soaked in honey water. Set it in a conspicuous spot near where the bees are working on flowers. As the bees come again and again to the box, they will pick up some of the color of the cornstarch. You can follow the "colored" bees home; just keep moving the box in the direction they are flying.

You'll be surprised to find how far bees will go from their hives in search of nectar, so be very patient in tracking them. You'll also discover that they are very sneaky about how they enter their hive; if you want to strike pay dirt, you'll have to be alert and very observant!

As the bees move from blossom to blossom to drink the nectar and gather "bee glue" from the trees, shrubs, and wildflowers, they carry pollen with them. At each blossom, some of this pollen is accidentally left behind, fertilizing the plant.

Bee...utiful

Grandma used honey for many of her "medicines", and for cooking. She said it was good for soothing sore throats, calming the nerves, and helping induce sleep among other things.

When I lived with her, I learned to tell the difference between plain old bees and "honeybees." While most bees only drink the nectar from the flowers, honeybees take it back to their hive, and store it. They're not as efficient pollinators as the more familiar bumblebees, which are one of the few species of native

North American honeybees. The small honeybees you see swarming around hollow logs in the woods are probably descendants of bees that were introduced to this country by the very first colonists.

OTHER WILD EATABLES

Nowadays, it doesn't matter whether you live in the city or the country, there are literally thousands of plants worth looking at and eating within walking distance of your home. So don't be shy, get on out there, and see what you can find. The list could go on forever; here are a few of my favorites:

Blessed Bee Relief!

Vinegar has thousands of uses around the house, and one of the very best is pouring a little on a bee sting to soothe the irritation and relieve itching! Another remedy Grandma Putt used was to gently rub the sting with either a freshly sliced white onion or potato, whichever was handier.

Asparagus...make a sack out of your shirt, snap off the young stalks, and carry as many home as you can. Believe you me, you'll be a hero at suppertime!

Bugle...or carpenter's bugle as we called it, was used on cuts and scraps to stop the bleeding. Grandma Putt also made a dynamite tonic that cured bronchitis almost overnight.

Catalpa trees...nothing much here worth eating, but my Uncle Art and I smoked many a catalpa cigar. As "sophisticated" as we were, we thought they were much better and more fun than corn silk!

Those were the days...

Walking along the road toward the woods one summer day, I came across some big white flowers with maroonish-looking eyes. Thinking they were wild morning glories, I picked as many as I could, and brought them home. When Grandma Putt saw them, she told me to get the vegetable fork and a gunnysack, and show her where I had found them.

When we came to the field, she had me dig in the dry soil below one of the plants. Before long, I had unearthed a huge root as big around as my thigh and about a foot and a half long! Grandma said the Indians called these plants "Man-in-the-Earth," which they roasted or boiled the roots.

That evening, we had some boiled Man-in-the-Earth. Even though Grandma changed the water several times when she cooked it, the root was bitter tasting, like day-old turnips.

I remember eating "the whole thing" very manfully, except for a taste I gave my Aunt Jane. She wrinkled up her nose, and said that it tasted like *dirty socks!* Now that I think of it, that was a pretty good description!

Chicory...some states have laws against picking wild-flowers along the roadside. If yours doesn't, chicory is great to spice up a salad (blanch the leaves), or use it as they did in the Great Depression—dry and grind up the roots to brew with coffee. Grandma Putt used it as a tonic and mild stimulant, and to treat jaundice, gallstones, and stomach and sinus problems.

Groundnuts (Indian potatoes)...look for the telltale purple-brown flowers and twining vines. The older plants have the largest tubers. Grandma said they were good for eating raw, frying, baking, and roasting; I, myself, thought they were good for nothing!

Honey locust trees... Grandma showed me the sweet pulp between the seed pods...she said these were the "locusts" John the Baptist ate (but be careful; some black locusts are poisonous).

YOU WANT ME TO EAT...*WEEDS?*

Jack-in-the-pulpit…nowadays, they are scarce; but back then, they were everywhere! Grandma said the Indians boiled and ate the roots. (Be careful because other parts are poisonous.) After a couple of attempts to eat both young and old plant roots, I decided to pass them by. Try boiling some (change the water at least twice to get the acid out), and see what you think.

Jerusalem artichokes…they look just like hairy sunflowers. When you spot some, remember where they're located. Then come fall, go back and dig up the tubers—they're better tasting than potatoes!

May apples (American Mandrake)…you'll smell them before you see them. The plants have a two-inch, white flower, and a big, single leaf. They appear in the early spring, but the fruit (which looks like small golden eggs) isn't good until July or August. Put them in a large container when they're golden-yellow.

Mustard…wild mustard and Indian mustard were the most common types we found, although I often mistook them for radishes when they were small. The leaves were edible, although they were spicy and slightly bitter. The older folks considered the green, unopened flowers to be a tasty treat.

Wild Mustard Tea

Grandma Putt made a tea from wild mustard leaves to keep cabbageworms, loopers, and potato beetles out of her garden. She'd steep:

1 handful of wild mustard leaves,
1 clove of garlic, and
4 whole cloves,

in 1 cup of boiling water. After it cooled, she'd spray it on her garden so that the egg-laying moths would stay away.

Paw-paws...grow on trees, mostly in thickets. You'll have to acquire a taste for the fruit, which look like short, stubby bananas. After a while, they aren't so bad.

Peppermint...you'll probably disregard Grandma Putt's advice about wild onions (page 93) anyway, so chew on some peppermint leaves to hide the smell. Or, better yet, bring them home to make a perky peppermint tea.

Persimmon Beer

Grandma Putt used to make a tasty "brew" from these fruits. She took 1 gallon or so of ripe persimmons, mashed them well, and added 1/2 cup of corn meal. She put it in a large container, and added 2 cups of sugar and 5 gallons of water. She put it in a cool, dark place, letting it set until the fruit rose to the top. Afterwards, she strained, bottled, and sealed it. The brew was clear, light colored, and fizzy. Oh...by the way, she only filled the bottles two-thirds full—otherwise, she said they might explode!

Persimmon...don't try 'em when they're not ripe, or you'll be puckered up for a week! Grandma Putt's homemade brew was pretty good once you acquired a taste for it.

Pokeweed...you'll find it along fences, or growing as a weed in the spring-spaded soil of your garden. Grandma used the shoots for potherbs; I used the berries for "ink" to write secret messages; but don't eat the berries or the roots—the berries can cause a terrible burning sensation in your mouth, and the roots are poisonous.

Skunk cabbage...believe it or not, this foul-smelling plant can be delicious (just make sure you change the water when you boil it, or you'll soon find out why it's named after Pepe Le Pew!)

YOU WANT ME TO EAT...*WEEDS?*

Wildflowers…Nasturtiums were my favorite—Grandma would brush the petals with egg white mixed with a little water, then sprinkle them generously with granulated sugar. After they dried, we'd eat 'em like…well, like candy!

Wild onions…the bulbs were tough, but Grandma Putt used them to add a fresh flavor to her soups. She also was fond of saying…"An onion a day keeps the doctor away." Kind of catchy, don't you think?

Nasturtium Capers

To make these tasty treats, get:
> 1 lb. of nasturtium seeds,
> 1/2 inch of cinnamon bark,
> 4 whole cloves,
> 1 qt. of white wine vinegar,
> 2 blades mace, and
> 1 tsp. of salt

Put the seeds, cloves, mace, and cinnamon bark in an earthenware crock. Bring the vinegar and salt to a boil, and pour it over the seeds. Then cover the crock tightly, and let it stand one month before using.

Ginger (American wild ginger, that is)…was another wild root we gathered in the woods. A little bit of the ground root of this plant goes a long, long way. On a cold winter day, a cup of ginger tea was warm and invigorating. Although Grandma also used ginger in her "medicines," she had another use for it that I preferred a whole lot more—homemade root beer!

Other good-eating things I found that Grandma Putt made me try were the bark from **sassafras trees** for tea, **elder leaves** for cough syrup, **daylily bulbs** (which are used today in Chinese cooking), **sweet flag** for calamus candy, **wild spinach, bloodroot, horseradish, sunflowers, wild rice, golden thistle nettles, chickweed, wake robin, Solomon's seal, slippery elm** for chewing, **field sorrel, Johnny jump-ups, cowslips,** and…well, the list goes on and on and on!

YOU WANT ME TO EAT…_WEEDS?_

FUN FOREST FORAGING

Going out with Grandma Putt to pick roots and bark in and around the woods was one of the best adventures I've ever had! We would criss-cross the area that skirted the woods with our eyes peeled for our next "victims." Grandma carried a garden trowel, and I had my trusty jackknife and an old flour sack. We looked for dandelion roots, burdock and yellow-dock roots, wild cherry bark, and some birchbark. Then we scoured the fields until we found elecampane, sarsaparilla, and spikenard.

Grandma Putt's Words of Wisdom:

"Once you get to know poison ivy and poison oak, there aren't too many plant people in the woods you need fear."

Up in Grandma's hot attic, she had a small gunnysack full of hops that had been hanging there to dry since last autumn. We'd gather all of this together, and combine our treasures into the meanest root beer this side of Amarillo, Texas, *pardner!*

Grandma Putt's Old-Fashioned Root Beer

To make this tasty brew, you'll need these ingredients:

1 oz. of burdock roots

1 oz. of dandelion roots

1 oz. of yellow-dock roots

1 oz. of elecampane roots

1 oz. of sarsaparilla roots

1 oz. of spikenard roots

1 oz. of wild cherry bark

1 oz. of birchbark

1 oz. of hops

1 lb. of sugar

YOU WANT ME TO EAT...*WEEDS?*

25 drops oil of sassafras or spruce

8 tbsp. of liquid yeast, or a dissolved dry yeast cake

2 gallons of cold water in a large kettle

Wash the roots and bark very clean. Then bruise them so the oils and juices will cook out easily.

Put the cold water into a cleanly scoured kettle. Add your roots, etc., and bring to a slow boil. Simmer for about half an hour. Toward the end of the half hour, add your sugar, and 20 to 25 drops of the oil of sassafras or spruce.

Pour the mix slowly into an earthenware crock, and let it cool to lukewarm. Stir in the yeast, cover, and set it away in a cool, dark place to ferment.

The beer will be drinkable in three to six hours, or you can seal and store it. Fermented, the beverage is slightly alcoholic, and very delicious!

We spent many a hot summer afternoon, sittin' on Grandma's back porch, and drinkin' a tall, cool glass of homemade root beer, just watchin' the world go by.

But there are many more good reasons to take nature walks other than just to feed your appetite, or heal your body. And, there are plenty of plants worth talking to just to find out what they are like, and what they are up to.

MISTLETOE AND OTHER PARASITES...

As we were walking in the woods, Grandma Putt used to tell me stories about the plants we were looking for. Mistletoe was one of her favorites.

She said (with her tongue-in-cheek) that armed with a sprig of mistletoe, a person could **ward off lightning, treat everything from mumps to wounds, crack a safe without a blowtorch, prevent nightmares, drive out witches, unearth**

You Don't Say...

Long ago, folks thought that any plant which grew without any apparent roots must have supernatural powers. In all probability, they just picked on whatever kind of trouble bothered them the most, and hoped that whatever magic was available would work a charm against it.

Luckily, none of these superstitions surrounding mistletoe is of any concern to the gal who gets caught (or wants to get caught) under it. If she wants to play the game according to Hoyle, however, she should know that the tradition says that the lucky fellow must pluck a berry from the Mistletoe sprig for each kiss he steals, and stop when the berries are gone. As I recall, this didn't stop Grandpa Putt from stealing an extra kiss or two, nor did Grandma Putt protest too much!

buried treasure, put out fires, and increase the harvest. I used to get such a kick out of these stories!

Actually, mistletoe is a partial parasite that sucks the sap from its host tree, causing it to eventually die. Its seeds are carried up onto tree limbs by birds who have just dined on their sticky, pale-white berries. There was plenty of mistletoe growing in the trees around Grandma Putt's place, and I was always looking for a reason to climb trees; collecting mistletoe is still one of the best ones I ever came up with!

There are several other plants that take their meals at the expense of other living plants. You are likely to come across some of these not far from your home, or in local woods and parks. Among these are **dodder, beechdrops, Indian paintbrush, and fungi.**

A ROLLING STONE...

If you live in the southeastern part of the United States, you are well-acquainted with Spanish moss, which can be

seen hanging from the trees arching most streets. This plant is a real pain in the "you-know-what," growing on trees, other plants, and on wires and posts.

It is an air plant, but makes its own food from the atmosphere, rain, and debris around it, not drawing on its host at all. Spanish moss is not true moss, anyway—it belongs to the pineapple family! Most folks probably wish it was edible because it's not good for much of anything else!

MUSHROOMS AND TOADSTOOLS

Over the years, I've learned that most gardeners eventually come up against certain fungi that are worth watching and eliminating. The word fungus gives most folks the "heebie-jeebies," and makes them run for the nearest fungicide and sprayer! And no wonder, too; these parasitic fungi include "bad guys" like potato blight and wheat rust, and the real nasty guys that cause diphtheria and typhoid fever in people and animals.

But out in the woods, you'll find fungi that are not parasites. They are hard workers for Mother Nature

Those were the days...

I always found plenty of mushrooms in the woods near Grandma Putt's. They were especially plentiful all summer long when there was a warm, wet spring. Grandma said God provided for small boys by making them dislike mushrooms, and I think she was right. Loving them as I do now, I really feel twinges of regret that I didn't harvest any of the thousands that I came across that first summer.

Once in a while, Grandma would go with me to gather mushrooms, and she'd soon fill a bag to overflowing. That night, all the adults would be "oohing" and "aahing" over fresh mushrooms sautéed in Grandma's special herb butter. I wish I could spend some of those dinnertimes over again now! I didn't know it at the time, but I was missing out on enjoying some of the very best "wild eatables" Mother Nature had to offer!

and Mother Earth; they live and feed off dead and decaying matter like fallen branches and tree stumps. They help speed up the decaying process, thereby returning valuable minerals to the soil. Among these are the plants we know as mushrooms and toadstools.

Harvesting these delectable edibles is quite a tricky proposition, so I don't recommend it for the beginning field and forest forager. I always went with Grandma Putt to pick mushrooms, and _**she never let me do it by myself!**_ So if you're interested, pick up a book and study it so that you can learn which mushrooms are poisonous "toadstools," and which are among Mother Earth's finest delicacies.

While you're at it, don't put your faith in old wives' tales that claim to show which species are poisonous. (No, poisonous mushrooms don't turn silver spoons black!) The best way to get a treat instead of treatment is to carefully study up on which ones are good eating; use a book with accurate photographs, or take along a knowledgeable guide who has been gathering and eating mushrooms from the wild for many years.

GRANDMA PUTT'S FIELD & FOREST REMEDIES

Grandma Putt's Words of Wisdom:

"Mother Nature's medicine cabinet can be found right in your own backyard."

Grandma used a lot of the things we found in the nearby fields and forests to cure what ailed her friends, family, and neighbors. Drawing on her Indian background and upbringing, she seemed to have a homemade remedy for just about everything, plus an ailment for just about anything we found on our little adventures. Here's a sampling of a few of her favorites:

YOU WANT ME TO EAT..._WEEDS_?

For Bad Breath: On those particularly "bad" mornings, Grandma would give Grandpa Putt and me anise seed, nutmeg, orris root, or cloves to chew on. This seemed to work because we seldom heard about our "morning breath" again.

For Baldness: Grandma used to recommend rubbing the area with a mixture of onion juice and honey every morning and night. Grapevine sap, castor oil, and strong sage tea was also said to work.

To Stop Bleeding: Grandma would grab the nearest handful of spider web she could find, and slap it on and around the wound. Witch Hazel also did the trick if she had it available.

For Bruises: Grandma applied marigolds (as a tincture), wild alum, Lily of the Valley (roots), and warm vinegar compresses.

For Burns: This was a touchy subject (ouch!); she used aloe vera leaves (which were growing in her kitchen), butter, honey, and/or one of her homemade salves, not necessarily in that order!

For Clean Teeth: Grandma used to get a sweet gum or dogwood twig, soak it in water (the older folks liked brandy), and had us chew on it until it was soft.

From the Kitchen Cupboard

"Fresh aloe is the best aloe," Grandma Putt always used to say. The best (and the freshest) way to use aloe is to simply break a leaf off of the plant, slice it lengthwise, and apply the gel directly to the skin. If I had a major burn, Grandma Putt would apply a simple poultice by placing the cut off leaf directly on the burn, wrapping a piece of gauze around it, and taping it in place.

The Great Healer

Grandma Putt firmly believed in the healing powers of garlic, so she kept enough of the stuff hanging around to kill all of the vampires in Hollywood! She knew it was great for treating a whole host of ailments, as an antiseptic and to fight infection. Here's a few of her favorite old-time remedies:

To treat asthma—She boiled a large quantity of bulbs in water until they were soft, then added as much vinegar as there was water left over. She added some sugar, and boiled again until a syrup formed. She recommended taking 2-3 teaspoons a day, as required.

To lower blood pressure—She made this remedy by soaking 1/2 pound of peeled cloves in 1 quart of brandy for 2 weeks, shaking the mixture a few times a day. She strained it, and took up to 20 drops a day as needed.

To treat coughs—She poured a quart of boiling water on a pound of fresh sliced garlic. After letting it steep for 12 hours, she added sugar until it was like syrup. To improve the taste, she also added a little honey and vinegar.

For earaches—Grandma would place a few drops of warm garlic oil in my ear, which she made by slicing one garlic clove, adding a small amount of olive oil to it, and heating them briefly. She strained the mixture before using it.

For sore throats—Grandma chopped up several cloves of garlic, and let them steep in 1/2 cup of water for 8 hours. She made me gargle garlic tea, and swallow it if I had the flu.

For Coughs and Colds: She rubbed my chest with a salve she made of arbor vitae, pine, or cedar, and then wrapped me in a piece of flannel that she had been warming up near the fireplace.

For Fevers: Grandma used any one of several hot teas to break up a fever. She made them from aspen (leaves), dogwood (leaves and bark), tulip trees (roots and bark), and willow (leaves and bark).

To Remove Freckles: Grandma recommended rubbing raw cucumber, strawberries, buttermilk, and oatmeal or corn paste on the area. Also, she said that catching a frog and rubbing it on the freckles would do the trick!

YOU WANT ME TO EAT...*WEEDS?*

For Minor Wounds: She made and kept many salves on hand for minor cuts, scrapes, and bruises. These salves were made of balsam fir pitch, sweet gum (roots), plantain (leaves), hollyhocks, water lily (powdered root), and calendula (flowers and leaves).

For Poison Ivy and Poison Oak: As soon as I came in contact with poison ivy, Grandma Putt would rinse the area with cold water, then cut open a green tomato, and pour the juice on the area. If a rash appeared, she mixed equal parts of buttermilk, vinegar, and salt, and rubbed it over the skin. This helped stop the itching and soothed my skin. She also rubbed jewelweed (touch-me-not) or sweet fern on the area.

Grandma Putt's Words of Wisdom:

"Leaves of three, let it be."

For Sore Throats: Grandma made a mean garlic tea that I had to gargle for a sore throat, and swallow if I had the flu. The recipe is listed on the previous page.

For Toothaches: Oil of clove or a clove of garlic applied directly to the gum above or below the tooth seemed to take the pain away enough to get into town to see the dentist.

For Warts and Moles: She treated these by applying milkweed juice, castor oil, chigger weed (sap), and wood ashes to the area until the unsightly blemish was gone.

YOU WANT ME TO EAT... *WEEDS?*

4

AH, THE SPICE OF LIFE—HERBS!

Back in Grandma Putt's day, the many wondrous powers of and uses for herbs were not as well known or documented as they are today. Most folks, if they gave them any thought whatsoever, had some vague knowledge that they were used for cooking, but few ever guessed the wide range of medicinal and healing properties that many plain old, garden-variety herbs possessed.

Grandma Putt, however, was way ahead of her time. She always had an outdoor herb garden filled with basil, chives, chamomile, garlic, and thyme, as well as aloe vera, rosemary, and sage potted up in the house. If you had a problem, more often than not, Grandma had the cure—just a few steps away from her back door!

Nowadays, herbs and their healing powers are a multi-billion-dollar a year business that pervades every aspect of our society; in fact, you can buy just about any processed herb you can think of down at the local Wal-Mart. But no matter how hard big business tries, you just can't beat the flavor, vitality, and satisfaction that comes from growing your own herbs.

In general use, *herb* is a term applied to plants that are used as aromatics. They can be used as food flavorings,

Spicy Ladies

There is no real clear-cut distinction between herbs and spices. How can you tell which is which? Well, in general,

✔ Stems, roots, etc. are spices, while leaves are herbs.

✔ Spices come from the tropics, while herbs grow in the more temperate regions.

✔ Spices are brown, black, or red, and have dramatic tastes, while herbs are generally green, and have subtle flavors.

beverages, deodorizers, and pesticides. The list is practically endless; the herbs in common usage really depends on where you happen to live.

If you've never tried your hand at growing herbs, don't worry—they're easy to grow. In fact, they're much less demanding than a vegetable garden. And as Grandma Putt taught me many years ago, they're also very rewarding. Here's how she got hers growing:

GRANDMA'S OUTDOOR GROWING SECRETS

SELECTING A SITE

Grandma Putt's herb garden was located just to the side of her back porch, facing south. A hedge shielded the garden from the north, while the house and garage protected it on the west. Little did I know back then, but this was the ideal location.

Grandma Putt's Words of Wisdom:

"Herbs need sunlight to produce their essential oils."

Herbs need a sunny, protected area to grow well; as a matter of fact, most herbs need full sun for at least six hours each day. Grandma Putt said that herbs needed the sun to help them produce their essential oils which gives them their unique flavors and fragrances. I've subsequently found out that if your herb garden is in the shade, you'll be disappointed—herbs grown in shade have a lower oil content which decreases their value for cooking and potpourris.

SOIL PREP IS ESSENTIAL!

Most herbs prefer well-drained soil; an ideal site is a gentle slope with sandy soil. If your site is less than ideal, then before plant-ing, you should condition the soil so the herbs have some-thing to grow on. For smaller areas, mix up a batch of **Grandma Putt's Soil Booster Mix,** and work it into the soil to a depth of 12 to 18 inches. After spading this material into the soil, let it set for seven to ten days. Then you can begin planting your herbs.

Soil Booster Mix

Grandma Putt made her herb Soil Booster Mix by combining:
**5 lbs. of lime,
5 lbs. of gypsum,
1 lb. of 5-10-5 garden food, and
1/2 cup of Epsom salts**
She'd work this amount of mix into each 50 sq. ft. of herb garden area.

For larger areas, Grandma Putt mixed up the following:

**2 yards of sand,
2 yards of peat moss,
2 yards of shredded bark,
5 lbs. of ground limestone,
5 lbs. of 5-10-10 fertilizer, and
1 lb. of iron sulfate**

This gave her about 5 inches of soil in an area measuring 25 sq. ft. She worked it into the soil, and then let it set.

Grandma Putt showed me how to remove a plant from a pot until I got it right. Yes, there is more to it than simply pulling on the stem. To remove an herb from its container, follow these steps:

Step #1—Soak the plant's roots 30 minutes before transplanting so that it holds together.

Step #2—Hold the pot with the stem between 2 fingers.

Step #3—Tip the pot upside-down, and gently tap it on a table to loosen the soil.

Step #4—Lift the pot away, holding onto the herb.

PLANTING THE GARDEN

Planting always provided Grandma Putt with some serious quiet time, when she could get in touch with the land. When planting herbs, she dug a hole slightly larger than the plant's root ball. She gently loosened the roots, placed the plant in the hole at the same depth as it was in the container, and firmed the soil in around the roots.

If your herbs are in peat pots, you can break off the rim, and plant them directly in the ground. Cover the peat pot with soil. Once your herbs are planted, water them thoroughly. Then place labels near each plant so you know exactly what's growing where.

KEEP 'EM THIN!

Overcrowding in the herb garden can be a problem if you're starting your plants from seed. So we always thinned out overcrowded areas when the little plants had formed two pairs of true leaves. You can use the thinnings in food, or transplant them to another part of your garden. Since you will only want a few plants, it may be best to buy your herbs from an herb nursery rather than grow them from seed.

WATERING AND FEEDING

Herbs need a deep soaking that penetrates the ground at least 12 inches deep. Avoid overwatering, but never let the soil dry out!

Feed your herbs in the spring with a side dressing of a good 5-10-5 fertilizer. After that initial feeding, Grandma Putt fed her herb garden every six weeks, before noon, with her **Herb Booster Tonic.**

Herb Booster Tonic

Grandma Putt made her Herb Booster Tonic by mixing:

1 bottle of beer,
1/2 cup of Fels-Naptha Soap Solution,
1 cup of ammonia, and
1/2 cup of corn syrup

in 20 gallons of water. Then she sprayed all of her herbs until they were good and full.

She was quick to point out that you needed to avoid heavy or frequent applications of fertilizer during the growing season. This can cause low oil production or leggy, stretched growth, which doesn't do anyone any good.

INSECT AND DISEASE CONTROL

The essential, fragrant oils in herbs that make them attractive to us help repel insects and make the plants disease-resistant. Nevertheless, every now and again, Grandma Putt's herbs needed a helping hand. So at the first sign of trouble, she mixed up this tonic:

1 cup of Fels-Naptha Soap Solution*, and
1 cup of chewing tobacco juice*

in 20 gallons of water, and gave them a nice, gentle bath when things started to get out of hand.

*See page 341 for instructions on how to make these tonics.

ANNUAL MAINTENANCE

There really is nothing to it. To maintain plant size and encourage branching, Grandma Putt pinched off the growing tips of her herbs periodically during the growing season. She began pinching when the plants were 6 inches tall, and continued to pinch after every 4 to 6 inches of new growth. This helped the plants remain compact and bushy, which resulted in more abundant harvests.

Grandma Putt's Words of Wisdom:

"Take care of your herbs, and they'll take care of you."

To help retain soil moisture and control weeds, she also mulched them well with an organic material like shredded bark, pine needles, or chunky peat moss.

Finally, after the leaves on Grandma Putt's perennial herbs faded in the fall, she cut all stalks and stems down to ground level. She brought evergreen perennials and annuals indoors before the first frost. Then, during the severe winter weather, she protected the plants by covering them with straw, pine bark, or evergreen boughs.

GRANDMA'S INDOOR GROWING SECRETS

I tell you, Grandma Putt's kitchen was filled with an air of earthly delights. The many different fragrances would literally hit you the minute you stepped through the door, and could send even the most insensitive sniffer into a tizzy!

She taught me that besides being very rewarding, growing herbs indoors is fast, fun, and easy to do! Here are a few of her indoor growing secrets:

AH, THE SPICE OF LIFE—HERBS!

PICK A POT!

Grandma Putt preferred the natural look of clay pots, although she often used any container that had good drainage and enough room for the plants' roots.

Perfect Soil Mix

Grandma Putt's perfect blend of soil for her indoor herbs was made by mixing:

1 part sand,
1 part clay loam,
1 part compost, and
1 part topsoil

Then per peck of soil mixture, she would add a pinch of Epsom salts, a handful of dried coffee grounds, and some eggshells, dried and crushed into a powder.

Among the more popular containers nowadays for indoor herbs are plastic pots, colorful glazed ceramics, wooden planters, tubs and half-barrels, clay strawberry jars, coffee cans, and other kitchen containers. If there's one thing I've learned, it's to use your imagination!

Don't forget to put the right type of saucer or tray under indoor containers! Moisture seeping through unglazed clay can damage tabletops and floors, so you're better off with plastic, glass, rubber, china, or other nonporous catchers. A layer of small pebbles in the saucer will keep the container's drainage holes above water.

THE KITCHEN WAS KEY

Like everything else, Grandma Putt knew that location was the key to growing herbs successfully indoors. The best place in her house was the kitchen window; it got four to five hours of sunlight each day, and the higher humidity near the sink definitely gave her plants a boost. For other areas of her house, she added artificial light and a humidifier. Also, remember that:

 Large, shallow trays filled with gravel and water are great for holding lots of pots.

 Nighttime temperatures should be at least 50°F.

 Turn your herbs each week to keep them shapely.

 Never allow your herbs to flower indoors.

DON'T KILL 'EM WITH KINDNESS...

Indoor herbs need to be watered regularly, but don't overdo it! Grandma said to water them when the soil half an inch below the surface dries off. All too often indoor herbs, like all indoor plants, are killed with kindness. So water your herbs thoroughly until the watering mix runs through to the saucer. Wait a half hour, then pour off the excess, and use it outdoors in your garden.

Healthy Herb Tonic

Grandma Putt kept her herbs healthy by mist spraying them with this tonic:
**1 tbsp. of Fels-Naptha Soap Solution,
1 tbsp. of mouthwash,
1 tbsp. of ammonia, and
1/4 cup of tea**
in 1 quart of warm water. Her Healthy Herb Tonic took care of insects and disease, while giving the plants a gentle nutrient boost.

REVIVE THAT SUCKER!

Grandma Putt wasn't perfect, and occasionally, some of her indoor herbs took a turn for the worse. In treating her sick plants, she first removed all dead or dying foliage, and in doing so,

AH, THE SPICE OF LIFE—HERBS!

examined each for aphids or other insects. If any were found, she gave them a gentle bath with her **Healthy Herb Tonic** (see page 110).

If they were tall, slim, and anemic-looking, they needed more light, but without high temperatures. So she stuck them in her "herb hospital"— a storm window sash that was converted into a tiny window "greenhouse."

In a nutshell, then, Grandma Putt's rules for health in the windowsill herb garden were sunshine, cool temperatures, no insects and disease, light, rich soil, regular mistings with her **Happy Herb Tonic,** and moderate, but regular waterings. Of course, the plants also need fresh air without direct drafts, and as much humidity as they can get. That should about do it!

From the Kitchen Cupboard

Belly up to the bar! Indoor herbs can't reach out like their outdoor brethren to grab their own food. So, feed them during the growing season, early spring to mid-fall, with Grandma Putt's Happy Herb Tonic.

Happy Herb Tonic

This tonic was made by mixing:

1/2 tbsp. of bourbon,
1/2 tbsp. of ammonia,
1/2 tbsp. of hydrogen peroxide,
1/2 tbsp. of dish soap, and
1/4 cup of tea

in 1 gallon of warm water.

HARVEST TIME

For Grandma Putt, the greatest joy (and most fun) in herb gardening was in the harvest. Snipping, clipping, pinching, gathering, and cutting were all part of the process.

SNIP AND CLIP!

We used most herbs throughout the season because the flavor was already there. All we did was get a small pair of scissors, and as we used to tell the barber, "take a little off of the top." Grandma Putt said we had to be careful so that we didn't rob any one stem of all its foliage. In cutting chives, for instance, we clipped a few stalks here and there, without shearing them away whole-sale. That way, we had enough to "come and pick another day."

There are a number of different ways Grandma Putt used to preserve her herbs, depending upon when they were ready for harvest, and what she was going to use them for. The most common methods of preserving herbs she used were **drying, freezing,** or **refrigerating** them.

From the Kitchen Cupboard

Two other ways Grandma Putt kept herbs was by making butter and mustard. Here's how she used to do it:

Herb Butter—soften 1/4 pound of butter at room temperature. Add about 4 tbsp. of dried herb leaves, and just a dash of lemon juice. Beat with a blender until the mixture is light and fluffy. Store in the refrigerator in a covered container.

Herb Mustard—mix 8 tbsp. of dry mustard, 8 tbsp. of flour, 4 tbsp. of salt, and 1 tsp. of sugar. Add enough vinegar to this mixture to make a smooth paste. Divide into 4 equal portions, and into each portion mix 1 tbsp. of your favorite herb.

TIMING REALLY IS EVERYTHING

Grandma Putt said that if you're going to dry herbs, do so early in the season so that you can also take later cuttings. If you wait too long, the

AH, THE SPICE OF LIFE—HERBS!

flavor won't be as strong, and there's always a chance that you'll lose the plant as well. Herbs that are harvested need a chance to regrow if they're to survive the winter!

Grandma Putt always harvested her herbs early in the morning because the oils in the plants were strongest at that time. As the sun becomes hotter, a chemical change takes place in the plants, and the oil's potency diminishes. Also, she said that if you're going to use the herbs for cooking, then you must pick them just *before* flowers appear on the plant. The reason for this is that the plant contains the most oils, and has the greatest flavor and fragrance at this time.

As soon as she cut her herbs, Grandma Putt got them ready to dry. If the leaves were dirty, she thoroughly washed and dried them. On heavier-stemmed herbs like lovage, the tops and leaves were picked off the stems. Picking the leaves off also shortened the drying time, and provided better flavor and color. For herbs like parsley, leave most of the stems on until after they are done drying.

Harvest Tips

The right time to harvest herbs depends upon which part of the plant you want to use. Here's a few of Grandma Putt's helpful harvest tips:

Tip #1—Pick flowers when they blossom, and are still only half open.

Tip #2—Pick stems and leaves before the plants flower because their essential oils are strongest at that time.

Tip #3—Pick seeds when they are slightly hardened.

Swapping Herbs

I've talked to a lot of great (and not-so-great) chefs over the years, and learned that dried and fresh herbs can be swapped in most recipes. Depending upon the strength of the herb, use 3 to 5 times more fresh than dried. And if you want to develop the flavor of dried herbs, soak them in an oil, vinegar, or lemon juice that is used in the recipe.

One other thing to remember about using herbs is that dried herbs are much stronger, and more "insistent" than fresh ones. So only use about half to one-third as much dried herbs as you would fresh ones.

DRY THEM OUT!

There's a right way and a wrong way to dry herbs. Grandma Putt said that you shouldn't cut and dry them in the sun because you'll dry out the herb's peculiar oil or fragrance. Another bad move was to tie them up under some kind of cover, which may cause them to discolor, get moldy, or ferment.

Grandma Putt used the most common method of drying herbs, which conjures up visions of French chateaus, bottles of wine, and loaves of fresh baked bread. That's right—she dried bunches of herbs by hanging them from an overhead nail in her kitchen!

If you want to dry them this way, simply gather them together, and tie them in small bundles. Hang them in a warm, dark place for about two weeks, or until they are completely dry. To keep them from getting dusty while they're "hanging around," put the herbs in a paper bag. The only problem with this is that the paper bag tends to lengthen the drying time by several weeks.

The paper bag method is good for drying seed heads like anise, caraway, coriander, dill, and fennel. Be careful when gathering these herbs so that you don't scatter them to the wind. A trick that Grandma Putt taught me was to gather the seed heads just as they were turning color.

AH, THE SPICE OF LIFE—HERBS!

We put the seed heads in a large paper bag, cut the stems, and then tied them into the neck of the bag so the heads hung freely.

Another drying method we used involved an old window screen. We got one from out in the garage, set it on some boards (to allow the air to circulate freely), and then spread the herbs on top of it in a cool, dark place.

If, for some reason, Grandma Putt was in a hurry (and she *rarely* was), she'd oven-dry the herbs. She'd take sheets of brown kraft paper, cut slits in them (to allow air to circulate), place the herbs on the paper, and then put them in the oven (on the lowest setting) for up to six hours. After a few hours, she'd remove the leaves from the stems, and then dry them some more, making sure that they were completely dry before storing them away.

PROPER STORAGE

After drying, we'd strip the leaves from the stems, and store the herbs in airtight containers. Grandma Putt stored hers in a cool, dark pantry off of the kitchen to preserve their natural color. Sunlight fades the leaves, and destroys some of their flavor. So store them in the dark!

We'd periodically check the containers to make sure there was no moisture build-up on the inside. If there was, then we'd have to remove the herbs, and redry them.

When storing air-dried herbs, Grandma Putt would always leave the foliage whole to retain the flavor longer. Then she'd simply crumble the leaves as she needed them.

Dry Dock

Drying works well for:
**Basil
Dill
Fennel
Lovage
Mint
Oregano
Parsley
Rosemary
Sage
Tarragon
Thyme**

FREEZING — IT'S COLD!

Frozen Delights

The best herbs to freeze are:
- **Chives**
- **Dill**
- **Mint**
- **Oregano**
- **Parsley**
- **Sorrel**
- **Sweet Marjoram**
- **Tarragon**

Freezing herbs was one of Grandma Putt's favorite ways to use them. To prepare them for freezing, she'd harvest the herbs, wash them (if necessary), shake off the excess water, and then place them in containers that have been properly labeled. Then she popped them into the freezer. Now do you see why this was her favorite method?

The best part was she didn't have to defrost the frozen herbs before using them. For minced herbs, she'd chop them while they were still frozen, and they'd easily break apart.

Another way Grandma Putt froze herbs was to chop up the herb into a million tiny pieces, put them into ice cube trays, and pop them into the freezer. After they were frozen, she'd place the cubes into labeled containers, and store them in the freezer. Then when a recipe called for a certain herb, she'd just pop an ice cube into the mix, and away she went!

I've since discovered a simple way to make herbs into a paste for freezing. First, puree them with oil until they're like a pesto. The herb flavor blends with the oil, and the oil protects the mix from being freezer damaged. Then pack the paste into airtight, freezer-proof containers. Use the paste like dried herbs, but be careful because the flavor is a lot stronger! This method works well with basil, chervil, chives, dill, lemon balm, parsley, sorrel, and tarragon.

AH, THE SPICE OF LIFE—HERBS!

COOKING RIGHT WITH HERBS

Herb	Type	Harvesting and Preserving	Cooking Use
Anise	A	Cut the green leaves whenever the plants are large enough. Harvest the seeds when they turn brown. Wash the seeds in warm water; drain thoroughly.	The leaves can be used in salads, soups, beverages, meats, game, and poultry. Use the seeds to flavor cakes, breads, and cookies.
Balm, Lemon	P	Fresh leaves can be picked any time. For dry leaves, harvest just before the plant flowers.	Use in herb teas and as a garnish. Adds taste to lettuce or fruit salads.
Basil, Sweet	A	For fresh use, harvest the leaves as they mature—about 6 weeks after planting. For dry use, harvest leaves just before the plant blooms.	One of the most popular herbs, used mainly with tomato and egg dishes, stews, soups, and salads, but also with many poultry and meat dishes.
Caraway	B	Harvest the seeds after they turn a grey-brown color. Scald the seeds in boiling water, then dry thoroughly.	Use the seeds in breads, cakes, cookies, and potato salad. Also can be used in coleslaw, sauerkraut, cheese spreads, and meat stews.
Chervil	A	For fresh use, pick the tips of stems once a month. For dry use, harvest leaves just before the blossoms open. Dry on trays.	Use fresh leaves the same as you would parsley—in salads, salad dressings, soups, egg dishes, and cheese souffles.
Chives	P	Leaves can be harvested any time during the growing season. Cut them off close to the ground. Can be pureed with water in a blender, and frozen in ice cube trays.	Chives add a mild onion-like flavor to dips, spreads, soups, salads, omelets, casseroles, and many kinds of vegetables.
Coriander	A	The leaves, which are only used fresh, can be cut for seasoning as soon as the plants are 4 to 6 inches tall. The seeds can be harvested when the heads turn brown.	Coriander seeds smell and taste like a mixture of sage and orange, use them in baking, poultry dressings, and salad dressing. Used in Chinese, Middle Eastern, and Latin American dishes.
Dill	A	The fresh leaves can be harvested as needed and used as seasoning. Seed heads should be harvested when the seeds ripen to a light brown color.	Used in making dill pickles. The leaves also add flavor to salads, cottage cheese, soups, fish dishes, omelets, sauces, and casseroles.

COOKING RIGHT WITH HERBS

Herb	Type	Harvesting and Preserving	Cooking Use
Fennel	TP	The leaves can be harvested and used fresh. Fennel seeds are harvested when the seed heads turn brown. Dry in a paper bag. Florence fennel is harvested when the bulbs are large enough.	The leaves and seeds are widely used in fish dishes, cheese spreads, and vegetable dishes. Use the leaves and stems like celery.
Lovage	P	Harvest young, tender leaves and use fresh. You can dry or freeze the leaves for later use.	Use the celery-flavored leaves in soups, stews, potato salads, and vegetable dishes. Seeds can be used in salads, breads, and cakes.
Marjoram, Sweet	A	Cut back to 1 inch above the ground just before flowering; a second crop will form for later use. Easily dried or frozen.	Use leaves with meat, poultry, vegetable dishes, potato salad, and egg dishes.
Mint	P	Harvested before flowering and use fresh or dried. Cut off near ground level. A second cutting can be harvested later on.	Used primarily for flavoring. The leaves are often put into teas, as well as lamb, sauces, and jellies.
Oregano	P	Harvest and dry before flowering occurs.	Used to season spaghetti sauces and tomato dishes. Flowers are attractive in summer arrangements.
Parsley	B	Snip young leaves just above ground level as needed.	Use as a garnish in soups, salads, meats, and poultry.
Rosemary	TP	Harvest the young, tender stems and leaves, but avoid taking off more than one-third of the plant at one time.	A gourmet seasoning for meats, poultry dishes, and potatoes.
Sage	P	Harvest when just starting to flower and use either fresh or dried.	Use for meats, stuffings, soups, and salads.
Summer Savory	A	You can gather young stem tips early, but when the plant begins to flower, harvest the entire plant and dry.	Used to flavor fresh garden beans, vinegars, soups, stuffings, and rice.
Tarragon, French	P	Harvest tarragon in June for steeping in vinegar. For drying, harvest in early to mid-July.	Used in various sauces, like tartar and white sauce, and for making herb vinegar.
Thyme	P	Cut leafy stem and flowers when plants are at the full flowering stage. Use fresh, hang-dry, or freeze.	Used in combination with other herbs. Leaves can be used with meats, soups, sauces, and egg dishes.

A=Annual   B=Biennial   TP=Tender Perennial   P=Perennial

AH, THE SPICE OF LIFE—HERBS!

FRESH STORAGE

The final way Grandma Putt stored herbs was to harvest them as usual, place them in special crisper boxes, and then refrigerate them. Don't wash them beforehand because the herb foliage lasts longer when it is washed just prior to being used. This method of storage was especially useful in late fall; we always had plenty of fresh, outdoor herbs available for the winter holidays.

USING HERBS

Grandma Putt knew that herbs have wonderful healing powers from her many years of experience in and around the garden. She also knew that like anything else, too much of a good thing can cause problems. For example, chamomile tea can help settle your stomach or make you sleepy, but for those folks who have asthma, it can cause a severe allergic reaction.

Whenever we were discussing any kind of homemade herbal remedy, Grandma Putt always cautioned me that

Those were the days...

Grandma Putt was a great believer in the medicinal properties of herbs and other plants. She said it was a shame that the Indian medicines were mostly lost or perverted because they were way ahead of the shoddy kind of medicine practiced by the first white settlers in this country.

These early settlers believed in what was called "The Doctrine of Signatures." This doctrine believed that whatever a plant looked like, that was the ailment it was good for. For example, an herb like eyebright was used for eye ailments because it was white with a dark, pupil-like spot on the flower, resembling an eye; lungwort, whose leaves were spotted, was used for treating lung ailments; etc. Imagine where we'd be today if that was how medicine was still practiced?

Herbal Precautions

"Safety first" is what Grandma Putt always used to say, particularly when it came to any of her home remedies. I want you to be safe, so please, use all herbal remedies cautiously. Follow these general guidelines to good health:

- Always consult a doctor if you're having any painful or chronic symptoms.

- Don't mix medicines and/or prescriptions.

- Always identify the herb first, and know exactly what it can and can't do for you.

- Grow your own herbs, so you're sure of the purity and quality, and properly label and store them.

- Stop using any herb if you're experiencing any side effects (like headaches, dizziness, or an upset stomach).

- Don't give any herbal medicines to small children, and don't take them if you're pregnant or nursing without a doctor's consent.

there are many unknown variables that can affect an individual herb's healing powers. The type of soil it was grown in, other plants that may have been growing nearby, when it was harvested, how it was stored, and the potency of the dose all have an impact on its effectiveness.

So, to be safe (and not sorry), she always gave me a dose that was half of what she felt the "normal" dosage was until she was absolutely certain of its effects.

I saw Grandma Putt use many different herbs in many different preparations around her homestead over the years with varying degrees of success. Here's a brief overview on the different ways she prepared herbs for use:

CONSERVES AND MARMALADES

Grandma Putt combined the fresh leaves, shoots, or flowers of herbs, or a pulp made from rinds of the fruit with an equal amount of sugar and boiled until it was thick. She kept the resulting conserve in jars.

DECOCTIONS

Grandma Putt used this method of preparation for those herbs or parts of herbs (such as roots, seeds, and bark) from which it is difficult to extract the active ingredient. She cut 1 oz. of the fresh or dried herb into small pieces, and let it stand covered for several hours in 1 pint of cold water. Then she heated it slowly, allowing it to simmer for 20 to 30 minutes. She thoroughly strained the mixture while it was still hot, and added sugar, honey, or wine to taste.

From the Kitchen Cupboard

Herb Alert! If you spot any bugs crawling around the kitchen when you're washing your herbs, dip them in a mild vinegar water solution (1 tbsp. per cup of water) to get rid of the creepy crawlies in a hurry!

JUICES

We often had fresh herb juice made from the leaves, roots, and stalks of the plants we gathered. Grandma crushed that part of the herb which contained the most juice, pressed it through cheesecloth, clarified it by simmering it, and skimmed off the residue. She allowed thick juices to settle so that they were more palatable. She also added sugar, orange juice, and a touch of wine to any not-so-good-tasting herb while it was being crushed, mixing all of the ingredients well.

OINTMENTS

Ointments were used a lot on the burns around the kitchen, so Grandma always kept some on hand. She used ordinary lard or solid cooking fat, combining it with the fresh chopped and bruised leaves of an herb. She boiled the mixture until the leaves felt crisp, and then strained off the lard or fat. To increase the strength of the ointment, she repeated this process.

Poultice Power!

Grandma Putt used poultices to draw out infection and relieve muscle pain. She found the best herbs to use for poultices were:

> **Burdock**
> **Comfrey**
> **Coriander**
> **Flax Seed**
> **Slippery Elm**

She didn't use hot, spicy herbs like cayenne or mustard because they can actually burn the skin. So be forewarned!

POULTICES

Poultices provided moist heat, and so they were frequently used on sores or to soothe inflamed areas. To make a poultice, Grandma Putt would steep a mixture of herb and oatmeal (1 part herb to 4 parts oatmeal) in water for a short time, and then spread it out on a piece of cloth. She'd apply the poultice for anywhere between 1 and 8 hours, replacing it as soon as it lost its heat.

Grandma Putt also used a thick paste made from powdered herbs which had been mixed with hot water over a double boiler. Ground or granulated herbs worked best. To use the mix, she completely covered the area with the poultice, and wrapped a towel around it to prevent the heat from being lost.

PRESERVATIVES

These were relatively easy to make—1 or 2 ounces of glycerin, honey, or sugar syrup, and 1/2 tsp. of baking soda were added to a pint of a hot, strained decoction.

SYRUPS

Herbal syrups were made like preservatives—to every pint of herb juice, infusion, or decoction, Grandma Putt would add a half a pound of sugar. She'd boil the mixture, skimming it constantly to remove any residue that accumulates, until the liquid was reduced by half. Then she'd add some honey, cool, bottle, and store in the refrigerator.

INFUSIONS—TEAS

Teas were my favorite, and I sure drank a lot as a boy! They tasted mighty good, and Grandma said that they were good for me too! To make an infusion, she'd take the delicate leaf, flower, or part of the plant that gave up its essence easily, and poured 1 pint of very hot water over an ounce of it. She covered the mixture and let it steep for 5 minutes, stirring occasionally. If you're doing this, don't let it steep for more than 10 minutes, or the tea may be bitter. And don't boil it because if you do, the herbal benefits will be destroyed. Then Grandma Putt would strain the infusion, and serve it, adding sugar or honey to taste. For a single cupful, steep 1 to 3 tsp. of the herb in 1 cup of (covered) very hot water for about 5 minutes.

Timely Teas

Try any of these herbal teas for a timely pick-me-up:

Borage
Catnip
Chamomile
Lemon Balm
Lemon Verbena
Rose Hips
Rosemary
Sage

HEALING HERBS

There is no substitute for experience, which is by far and away the best teacher. Grandma Putt had many, many years of it, so she knew and grew an awful lot of herbs. The following is a "down and dirty" overview of some of Grandma Putt's favorite herbs and their uses, both cooking, medical, practical, and otherwise.

Anise *(Pimpinella anisum)*

Smells and tastes like licorice. The seeds are used in flavoring baked goods. Anise promotes digestion, alleviates nausea, and relieves cramps. Fresh leaves rubbed on clothes repel insects. Grandma Putt used a strong tea spray to repel aphids and other bugs in her garden.

Balm, Lemon *(Melissa officinalis)*

The lemon scent of this herb makes a good tea of the same flavor. The leaves are used in herbal medicine to reduce fevers, calm nerves, and gladden the heart and mind. It is also a good general bug repellent which is helpful throughout the garden.

Basil *(Ocimum basilicum)*

This herb is an anti-spasmodic and general stomach cure-all. Basil tea, sweetened with honey, was often used for coughs. And it repels most common pests, including flies and mosquitoes. In the kitchen, basil was a favorite for

Green Thumb Tip

Always plant basil, bee balm, and borage near your tomatoes —they're the best neighbors your tomatoes will ever have, and will boost your plants to new heights!

flavoring tomatoes, pizza, salads, dressings, vegetables, chicken, and cheese dishes.

Bay *(Laurus nobilis)*

The leaves and fruit are used as an astringent and digestive. It was used to flavor soups, chowders, meats, stews, chicken, turkey, and vegetables. Grandma Putt said the leaves repel many pests of flours, cereals, and grains, so she always placed a few leaves in each container.

Bayberry *(Myrica pensylvanica)*

The bark and roots are used as astringents, tonics, and stimulants. The leaves make a tea good for sore throats and bronchial congestion, and are used in flavoring meats, and added to soups and stews. A word of caution, though— use this herb sparingly!

Bee Balm *(Monarda didyma)*

The citrus-tasting leaves make a pleasant flavored tea. Grandma Putt used it to induce sleep, and clear up pimples. It also improves the growth and flavor of tomatoes, as well as being a good general garden repellent.

Borage *(Borago officinalis)*

This herb was the old-fashioned remedy for snake and insect bites, and other infections. It was also used as a gentle laxative and blood cleanser. In the kitchen, use fresh, dried, or frozen borage in soups, tea, stews, and sauces. In the garden, it attracts bees, and deters tomato hornworms.

Insect Repellent Herbs

Grandma Putt used all of the following herbs to do double duty—indoors, for cooking, and outdoors, to repel bugs, slugs, and other thugs:

Basil	Lavender
Bee Balm	Oregano
Borage	Pennyroyal
Catnip	Peppermint
Chive	Rosemary
Coriander	Savory
Dill	Spearmint
Fennel	Thyme
Garlic	Valerian
Horehound	Woodruff
Hyssop	Wormwood

Burnet (Poterium)

The fresh, young leaves are added to drinks, salads, soups, cream cheese, and vinegar. Way back when, it was used as a menostatic (to stop bleeding), and to stop diarrhea.

Caraway (Carum carvi)

Has a warm, aromatic odor, and adds flavor for cooking pastries, cheeses, sauces, and soups. Once used in poultices for colds, and as a tea to relieve gastric troubles and aid digestion.

Catnip (Nepeta cataria)

This herb was used to treat chronic bronchitis and diarrhea. It is a mild stimulant, nervine, and anti-spasmodic. A favorite of all cats, it also repels flea beetles and other insects. Grandma Putt made up a tea, and used it as a repellent spray in her garden.

Chamomile (Matricaria recutita)

This is a good flea repellent for use around dogs and cats; you can add it to pet pillows for this purpose. It is one of the best plant "buddies," having earned a reputation for healing sick plants when grown nearby. A delightful tea is made from the flowers, and it's considered by many to be antispasmodic, antiseptic, and anti-inflammatory.

AH, THE SPICE OF LIFE—HERBS!

Chervil (*Anthriscus cerefolium*)

Has a sweet, mild anise-like flavor. Way, way back when, it was used to prevent plague. In more modern times, a poultice of chervil leaves was used for bruises and rheumatism. Outdoors, it improves the growth and flavor of radishes. Indoors, use it as garnish, like parsley.

Chives (*Allium schoenoprasum*)

These onion relatives stimulate the appetite and aid digestion. They also have healthy amounts of iron. The mild onion flavor is useful in dishes where you'd use onions, like salads, baked potatoes, omelets, etc.

Comfrey (*Symphytum officinale*)

The allantoin in this plant is used to reduce inflammations, both internally and externally. It's the only vegetable source of Vitamin B-12, and has more protein than beefsteak. Imagine that!

From the Kitchen Cupboard

Whatever was bugging Grandma's plants didn't do it for too long—she'd mix up a batch of her potent "Knock 'Em Dead" Insect Spray, and they'd soon be gone. She'd strain out the particles first, and then let 'er rip in a mist sprayer!

Knock 'Em Dead Insect Spray

To make this potent brew, Grandma Putt would mix:

6 cloves garlic (chopped fine),
1 small onion (chopped fine),
1 tbsp. of cayenne pepper, and
1 tbsp. of dish soap

in 1 quart of warm water. She let it sit overnight, then she'd mist spray her plants.

Coriander *(Coriandrum sativum)*

This herb was used as a poultice for rheumatism. The seeds are also used as a flavoring for other medicines. By itself, it is an anti-spasmodic and stomachic. It also repels aphids and other harmful insects.

Dill *(Anethum graveolens)*

Dill is used to stimulate appetites, settle stomachs, and relieve colic. The seeds are used in pickles, relishes, breads, etc., while the leaves used in salads, soups, fish, meats, etc. It's a good companion plant to cabbage.

Eucalyptus Lemon
(Eucalyptus citriodora)

Has a strong lemon odor. The oil is considered a very strong antiseptic, and is a repellent to most insects.

Honey, Can You...

Attract bees to your garden? *You sure can!* Among the best herbs for this job are:

Borage
Coriander
Hyssop
Lemon Balm
Rosemary
Sage
Thyme

If you've got a large enough plot of them, and an industrious beekeeper, they all make very tasty honey, too!

Fennel *(Foeniculum vulgare)*

The leaves are used as a flavoring in salads, stews, and vegetables. It removes the fishy odor from seafood and fish. Powdered fennel makes a great flea repellent for your pets.

Garlic *(Allium sativum)*

One of the most widely used medicinal herbs. Good for high blood pressure, it was used to treat colds, fever, flu, coughs, earache, bronchitis, shortness of breath, sinusitis,

AH, THE SPICE OF LIFE—HERBS!

stomachache, diarrhea, dysentery, gout, pneumatism, ulcers, snakebites, and clogged up kitchen sinks—just 'kidding!' In the kitchen, it's great in tomato dishes, soups, sauces, salads, meats, etc.

Hops *(Humulus lupulus)*

Herb has a mild sedative effect which is helpful with stomach cramps, and as a general digestion aid. Beer drinkers also know—they're used in flavoring beer!

Horehound *(Marrubium vulgare)*

This herb is considered to be the premiere remedy for coughs and bronchial problems. It was also used to restore the normal balance of secretions of various organs and glands. Horehound is a good companion to tomatoes since it seems to improve their yield and quality, and it's a good general bug repellent.

Horseradish *(Amoracia rusticana)*

This herb has a strong, bitter flavor. Use it to season soups, sauces, stews, and meat. It's also a very good repellent in the garden.

Hyssop *(Hyssopus officinalis)*

This cleansing herb is valuable in treating chest infections, reducing blood pressure, and improving circulation. It's used externally for healing wounds and ulcers. Outdoors, it repels cabbage moths, and is a great companion to cabbage and grapes. Indoors, the young shoots are often used in salads, soups, meats, poultry, fatty fish, and stews.

Love That Sachet!

Grandma Putt was the master mixer when it came to making up potions and lotions. To make her favorite sachet, she'd mix:

**3 cups of lavender petals (dried),
1 cup of calamus root (ground),
1/2 cup of caraway seeds,
1/2 cup of marjoram,
2 tbsp. of cloves,
2 tbsp. of rosemary,
1/2 cup of thyme,
1 cup of mint (dried), and
2 cups of rose petals (dried)**

in a large container, and let it age for 2 weeks. Then she'd package it neatly, and give it to someone she loved!

Lavender
(Lavandula angustifolia)

The sweet smell is used in perfumes and potpourris. Lavender is said to reduce acne and puffiness of the skin. It's useful for nerve disorders, hoarseness, and sore throats. It's used externally for toothaches and sore joints. In the garden, the scent repels mosquitoes, flies, moths, etc.

Lovage
(Levisticum officinale)

As its name implies, it's a love potion ingredient. Once used for stomach problems and colic in children, now it's used to flavor salads.

Marjoram (Origanum majorana)

Scattered throughout the garden, marjoram improves the flavor of many herbs and vegetables. In the kitchen, use it to season meats, poultry, vegetables, and legumes.

AH, THE SPICE OF LIFE—HERBS!

Oregano (*Origanum vulgare*)

This herb is very helpful when planted near vine crops like cucumbers and melons. It repels cabbage butterflies from broccoli and its kin. Outdoors, it's a good ground cover for steep slopes. Indoors, use it to spice up pizza, spaghetti, and other tomato sauces.

Parsley (*Petroselinum crispum*)

This herb is a vitamin shop in and of itself, containing Vitamins A, B, C, and calcium and iron. Indoors, use fresh, dried, or frozen in soups, salads, stews, and vegetable dishes with meats, poultry, and seafood. In the garden, it repels asparagus beetles.

Pennyroyal (*Mentha pulegium*)

Used medicinally in Europe as a diuretic and for itchy, burning skin; recent research had indicated that *it should never be taken internally*. In the garden, it repels fleas and other insects.

Peppermint (*Mentha piperita*)

This herb is noted for its stimulating properties. It's an excellent alternative to caffeine, and it relieves most upset stomachs. Outdoors, it repels ants and most crawling insects. In the kitchen, use it to flavor candies, frostings, etc.

Grandma's Beauty Secret

Grandma Putt used to make a fabulous herbal facial steam bath by pouring 1 quart of boiling water over 1 cup of herbs in a large bowl. Her favorite was a mixture of peppermint, sage, and linden flowers.

If you're going to try this, hold your head approximately 4 inches above the bowl, and cover it and the bowl with a towel to retain the steam. Remain over the bowl for ten minutes or less. This will cleanse your pores, and soften and moisturize your skin.

Pineapple Sage *(Salvia rutilans)*

Its oil was used as an antiseptic, astringent, and irritant. Use it fresh in iced tea or to flavor chicken, cheese, jams and jellies; dry for potpourris.

Bath Time for Bonzo!

I had to give old Charley, Grandma's "Heinz-57" variety dog, a bath every now and again. Before I did, Grandma had me add 1 cup of rosemary (fresh or dried) to 1 quart of boiling water. She covered it, let it cool, and then strained the mixture. After I washed Charley, I would pour the rosemary tea on him, work it in well, and then let it dry. The rosemary took care of the rest, repelling fleas, bugs, and anything else Charley came in contact with!

Rosemary
(Rosmarinus officinalis)

This herb is used in many natural cosmetic products, and as a poultice. Rosemary's sweet and savory flavor complements many meat and vegetable dishes. In the garden, it repels bean beetles, carrot flies, and cabbage pests.

Rye *(Ruta graveolens vulgare)*

In European folk medicine, rye was used to treat

gas pains and colic, as well as improve digestion. Grandma Putt planted it in her garden to deter Japanese beetles.

Sage *(Salvia officinalis)*

Grandma Putt made up a tea we used as a mouthwash and gargle for sore throats. It also reduces perspiration. In the kitchen, use it in preparing meats, fish, and poultry; particularly fatty meats and game to lighten their taste.

AH, THE SPICE OF LIFE—HERBS!

Savory *(Satureja hortensis)*

This herb is used in flavoring beans, and said to be an aid to the well-known brown bean/gas problem. It mellows the strong flavor of cabbage and turnips. In the garden, savory repels bean beetles and other pests, and improves the flavor and growth of beans.

Spearmint *(Mentha spicata)*

A stimulant, carminative, and antispasmodic. It is useful for children because it is milder than peppermint. Outdoors, spearmint repels flies, rats, and cabbage family pests.

Tansy *(Tanacetum vulgare)*

This herb has a reputation as a spring tonic. Way back when, it was used in flavoring old-country Easter cakes; it was also sometimes substituted for pepper. Tansy is a very effective insect repellent, chasing away Japanese beetles, squash bugs, striped cucumber beetles, and ants.

Tarragon *(Artemisia dracunculus)*

Although it is primarily a cooking herb, it has been used to stimulate appetites, relieve colic, and cure rheumatism. It has a mild anise-like flavor, and is used for flavoring fish, meats, eggs, and salad dressings.

Natural Moth Repellent

Here's another one of Grandma Putt's secrets— a natural moth repellent made out of equal parts of dried **sage, rosemary, and thyme** leaves in a mixing bowl. She'd place half a handful of the mixture in a loosely woven cotton bag, and then sew the bag shut. She'd hang the bags in closets, or lay them in the drawers among our clothes to keep these pesky little critters away.

Thyme *(Thymus vulgaris)*

Grandma Putt used it as a local anesthetic pain killer. Thyme tea was also used as an antiseptic, carminative, antispasmodic, stimulant, and diuretic. It is one of the most common culinary herbs. Thyme helps eggplant, potatoes, and tomatoes grow better, and repels cabbage-worms and whiteflies.

Valerian *(Valeriana officinalis)*

This herb has a reputation as a natural tranquilizer, useful in treating many sorts of nervous conditions. It's also a mild sedative and nervine. It can be used everywhere in the garden as an overall repellent and good companion. On the flip side, it's said to attract earthworms.

Cats and Rats!

That's what valerian attracts, so use it to your advantage. Cats go crazy whenever they're around it, and will roll all over it if allowed to do so.

Rats will do the same, which is a good reason *not* to plant it if they're around. Legend has it that the Pied Piper of Hamlin secretly used valerian to rid the city of rats. So there's no telling what effect it has on small children!

Wintergreen
(Gaultheria procumbens)

Its chief ingredient is methyl salicylate, which is a precursor of aspirin. Grandma made a tea from the leaves as a sore throat gargle. In the garden, it's a good ground cover for wooded sites.

AH, THE SPICE OF LIFE—HERBS!

Woodruff *(Galium odoratum)*

This herb was used as an antispasmodic, calmative, and diuretic. It helps migraine headaches, and relieves conditions such as restlessness and insomnia. Indoors, it repels insects from clothing and linens.

Wormwood *(Artemisia absinthium)*

This is a powerful stomach remedy for indigestion and gastric pain. Grandma Putt made a wormwood tea to treat sprains and bruises. It's a well-known animal and insect repellent, repelling fleas from pests, and moths from wool.

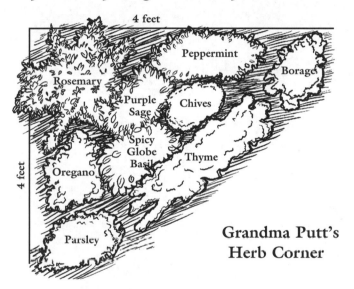

Grandma Putt's Herb Corner

Here are some other variations you might want to try, depending upon your personal preferences:

Medicinal Herbal Garden	*Fragrant Herbal Garden*
Aloe	Blue Wonder Catmint
Chamomile	Garlic Chives
Comfrey	Hidcote Lavender
Echinacea	Lemon Balm
Feverfew	Lemon Thyme
Lobelia	Nasturtium
Valerian	White Flavored Rosemary

AH, THE SPICE OF LIFE—HERBS!

5

A BERRY, BERRY GRAPEFUL GARDEN

Grandma Putt had a strawberry patch out back, along with her raspberries growing wild along the fence, and her prized grapes and their stately arbors in front of the garage. After having all of this luscious fruit available during my childhood, I think you're missing the boat if you don't try to grow at least one of the small fruits in your backyard.

Grandma Putt said that small fruits were the teenagers of her garden, difficult to manage if you allow them to get out of bounds. They grow rapidly, tend to sprawl lazily, and are full of prickles. But these youngsters are full of sweetness, too, so be patient with them—good care, the right diet, plenty of water, and early training will pay off. They will try their best to get ahead of you, so think in advance, and guide them with a firm but gentle hand.

Like most gardening projects, raising small fruit is easy and fun if you know what you're doing. Don't think you don't have enough room, because you do. You can incorporate small fruit crops into your landscaping plans whether you live on a farm, in suburbia, or even a city apartment. Here's how to get the best out of them using Grandma Putt's great growing tips and tricks.

Those were the days...

It just may be, as someone once suggested, that the best-looking and most perfect-tasting strawberries grow only in our memory. They're the ones you may recall gathering and eating right from the berry patch on a sunny spring day. Or, they may be the ones you ate with shortcake and heavy cream at a Country Corners' Annual Strawberry Social long ago. No matter how much truth there is to the idea, it isn't a good enough reason *not* to grow your own strawberries. Believe you me, these taste-temptin' treats will create the same kind of memories for your family as they did for you.

SUPER STRAWBERRIES

Most small fruits are relatively easy to grow, but strawberries are among the easiest. They can grow in just about any part of the country... and they usually do!

Strawberries are native to most parts of the world. No one knows who first cultivated wild strawberries, or even how they got their name. Grandma Putt told me that Anglo-Saxon children used to string them on straws and sell them.

Regardless of who cultivated them first, American gardeners have inherited a tradition of growing them from the English. They are, hands-down, our favorite berry fruit. In Izaak Walton's famous classic, *The Compleat Angler*, Dr. William Butler says, "Doubtless God could have made a better berry, but doubtless God never did." Those are my sentiments exactly!

GRANDMA'S STRAWBERRY PATCH

Grandma Putt's strawberry patch produced big, fat, juicy berries year after year. Her secret?

She said most folks go wrong raising strawberries because they expect too much of them. Don't assume that just because strawberries are perennials they will go on producing good fruit forever! And don't expect them to develop new plants from runners indefinitely. These secondary plants tend to produce small and harder berries after a few years. The plants will also be more susceptible to disease.

Grandma Putt's secret to raising the best strawberries in town was to keep rotating her stock—introducing new plants into her patch every year, and eliminating the older plants every two to three years. Here's how to do it:

LOCATING YOUR PATCH

As I said, strawberries will grow almost anywhere. They grow best in cool, moist climates, but can do well in warmer areas if you select suitable varieties.

Grandma Putt taught me that the key factors in selecting a site for a strawberry patch are full sun, adequate air and water drainage, the slope of the land, and orientation of the patch. It's best to avoid planting them where water stands above the ground in the winter, or stays beneath the surface too long any time of the year. If you have a drainage problem, you can correct it by adding plenty of organic material to the soil, or by planting your berries in raised beds. Just be sure to keep the soil moist.

Strawberry Delight

The ideal site for your strawberry patch has:

- Full sun
- Well-drained, fertile soil
- Good air circulation
- Rich soil with a pH between 5 and 6.
- A southern exposure

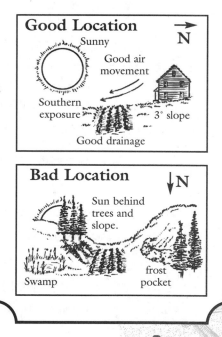

Good Location

N

Sunny

Good air movement

Southern exposure

3° slope

Good drainage

Bad Location

N

Sun behind trees and slope.

Swamp

frost pocket

When you choose the location of your patch, keep it clear of frost pockets, and away from the roots and shade of large trees. Tree roots rob the soil of moisture and block out much needed sunlight. A good southern exposure on a slight slope with no trees nearby is an ideal location.

PREPARE TO PLANT

Grandma Putt always prepared a new strawberry bed in the fall, before the snows came. That way, it was ready to plant come spring. She'd till the soil, then apply her special **Bed Prep Mix** to the area, letting it loosen and condition the soil during the long, cold winter.

Then when spring came, she turned the soil again, and graded it off into 6 foot high, 3 foot wide, slightly raised beds to allow for good drainage. Then she'd apply a mix of 3 lbs. of high nitrogen lawn food and 1 lb. of Epsom salts per 100 sq. ft. of bed area.

Bed Prep Mix

For every 100 sq. ft. of berry patch, Grandma Putt worked:

50 lbs. of manure, and
50 lbs. of shredded leaves

deep into the soil. Afterwards, she'd top-dress the bed with 25 lbs. of gypsum, and let it set for the winter.

Strawberry plants are like my grandson, Zachary—they have big appetites, and just love to eat! So, you need to feed them with this same mix several times during the growing season. Just don't feed them during their fruiting time in the spring, or the plants will be so busy growing, they'll forget to produce quality fruit.

A BERRY, BERRY GRAPEFUL GARDEN

THE ALL-IMPORTANT "FIRST PICKING"

No, I'm not talking about picking the berries, I'm talking about picking the variety you're going to plant! Selecting the right varieties depends entirely on your wants and growing needs.

There are two types of strawberries: **Springbearing** (also called Junebearing) and **Everbearing**. Both are quite hardy and easy to grow, but there are some important differences you need to know.

Springbearing varieties produce a single crop over a short period of time in late spring. They produce the most and largest fruit, but you must wait until the second year for your first crop.

Everbearing varieties, on the other hand, bear two crops each season, one in spring, and a second, smaller crop in fall. When planted in the spring, Everbearing varieties produce berries in late summer or fall of the same year.

Whichever varieties you choose, make sure you buy one-year-old plants with single crowns that have lots of light-colored roots. Also, make sure that they're resistant to such diseases as gray mold, leaf spot, and powdery mildew; strawberries are easily attacked by diseases, so it's best to always buy your plants from a reputable dealer.

Variety is the Spice...

There's a strawberry for everyone, and everyone for a strawberry. Take your pick among these favorite varieties:

For edging beds:
Alpine

For flavor:
Fairfax
Midway
Ozark Beauty
Pocahontas
Redglow
Red Rich
Sparkle
Sunrise

For firmness:
Dixieland
Pocahontas
Surecrop

For high-yields:
Catskill
Midway
Sunrise
Surecrop

PERFECT PLANTING

Grandma Putt always set her plants out in the spring, as soon as the soil could be properly prepared. But don't attempt to plant *anything* until the soil is dry enough to work.

Try to plant strawberries as soon as you get them. If that's not possible, store the plants in wet peat or a trench dug in moist soil. Trim the bare-root plants so that the roots are about three inches long. Before you plant, soak them in Grandma Putt's **Strawberry Starter Solution** to give them a boost.

Plant your strawberries so the crown is just at surface level. *This is absolutely critical!* I don't know how many times Grandma Putt had to show me, but I finally got it right. If the crown is too high, the roots will dry out; if it's too low, the crown will rot.

Spread the roots out like a fan, and pack the soil firmly around them. Place a good layer of straw around the plants; and then pour a little of the Starter Solution around it to settle the soil. Then keep your newly planted strawberries well watered until you're sure they are doing okay.

Strawberry Starter Solution

To ensure that her plants got off to a great start, Grandma Putt soaked them in a batch of this timely tonic:
> 1 tbsp. of Fels-Naptha Soap Solution,
> 1 tbsp. of Epsom salts, and
> 1/2 cup of tea

in 1 gallon or so of warm water.

Too High

Too Low

Just Right

A BERRY, BERRY GRAPEFUL GARDEN

Grow-in-the-Know

Remember what Grandma Putt said about berry plants being like teenagers? Well, if you don't keep your strawberries under control, they'll grow so quickly that they'll literally party themselves to death! Back in Grandma Putt's day, there were basically two different training systems to keep them in check: the matted row and the hill system.

The Matted Row System

In the Matted Row System, you allow the plants to produce runners freely. Plants are set 18 inches apart in rows that are at least 3 feet apart, and mulched well with straw. Thin out excess runners at the end of each season to prevent the patch from becoming overgrown. By using this system, you'll harvest more fruit per square foot than from the Hill System, but the fruit will be smaller.

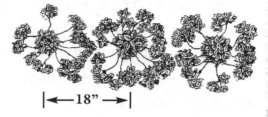

|←— 18" —→|

The Hill System

The Hill System requires more plants and attention, but Grandma said that we'll get larger fruit with it. Plants are set 12 inches apart in rows that are 12 inches apart. If you use this system, cut off all runners as soon as they form, and don't allow any new plants to grow. As I found out, plants grown using this system will continue to produce for six years or more.

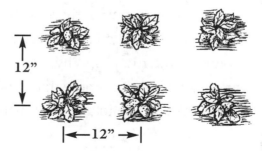

12"

|←— 12" —→|

A BERRY, BERRY GRAPEFUL GARDEN

Whichever method you decide to use, don't let any fruit develop the first year because the plants won't have a large enough root system to support both fruit and runner formation. So, pick off all blooms as fast as they form. Everbearing strawberries are an exception. Their blooms should be kept picked until midsummer the first year, but from then on, the plants can be allowed to flower and develop fruit naturally.

MULCH IS A MUST!

Strawberries must be heavily mulched. You can plant them through soggy newspaper, black plastic, or landscape fabric, or mulch them with clean straw. The mulch will hold down the weeds, conserve moisture, and inhibit runner growth.

Mulch also is a security blanket that'll protect the plants during the long, cold winter. In late fall, just before the first frost, build up the mulch around the plants to 3 or 4 inches between rows, and cover the plants with it. If you live in an area with mild winters, leave some of the foliage showing through the mulch.

MAKING BABIES

Strawberries reproduce by forming runners from the parent plant. These runners are an extension of the strawberry stem, and will produce roots and leaves when they touch soil. Each rooted runner can produce more runners. Why, a single parent plant of some varieties can produce more than 1,000 runners in a single season! That's a whole lotta' babies, baby!

A BERRY, BERRY GRAPEFUL GARDEN

To create new plants from those you previously planted, Grandma Putt showed me a simple layering system. We used to take the long runners, and cover them with soil, allowing several inches on the end to stick out above ground. When the buried portion takes root, clip it off! Then take up a good portion of the soil around it when you replant.

HARVEST TIME

Ah—this is the time to look forward to—when you can enjoy the fruits of your labor! But labor it is because picking strawberries still is a job that must be done by hand. I want to warn you though, the most natural way to grab and pull is not the best way to pick them. This bruises the berry, and opens it up to decay.

The secret to picking berries is to grab the stem close to the cap, twist and pull, leaving as short a stem as possible attached to the cap. Then as you put them in your harvest basket, don't pile them too high because these berries crush and damage easily.

Strawberries should be picked early in the day. They are firmer then, and easier to handle in the morning than later on in the heat of the day. Strawberries should be harvested at just the right stage of ripeness. Overripe berries are soft, easily damaged, and lose their flavor and appearance.

Renovation Reminders

If you renovate your strawberry beds each year, you'll have better harvests for many years to come. You should:

Step #1—Mow off the leaves and stems, and bag the clippings.

Step #2—Dig up wayward runners and weeds.

Step #3—Apply compost, fish fertilizer, and then cover the bed with straw. That's all there is to it!

If the berries you pick are dirty, chill them for an hour or two, then wash them in cold water.

Weather conditions can play a big part in how frequent you can pick your strawberries. They ripen fast in warm weather, and more slowly in cool weather. At a minimum, you should pick berries every two to three days.

OLD-FASHIONED STRAWBERRY BARRELS

If space is a problem, and you still want to grow strawberries, you can make a super hi-rise berry patch. Even though space wasn't a problem at Grandma Putt's, she still had a strawberry barrel sitting on her back porch that grew the sweetest berries in the yard.

To make your own old-fashioned strawberry barrel, get a barrel that's made of either cedar, oak, or redwood. About a foot above ground, cut 3 or 4 inch holes, spaced every 10 inches or so. Drill a good-sized hole in the bottom of the barrel for drainage.

Then make a cylindrical collar (out of hardwire cloth) about 4 to 6 inches in diameter, and place it down the center of the barrel. Fill this collar with sand and gravel. Surround the collar with a mix of equal parts of peat, cow manure, and good workable topsoil. Soak to settle it with each 6 inch layer of soil.

Plant your strawberry plants, one per hole. Don't put any plants on the ground level if the soil is poor. Choose Everbearing varieties so you'll have strawberries in April-May. Then make sure you clip off any runners.

Set your barrel in a sunny spot; it's a good idea to place it on some sort of castered platform so you can turn it every so often toward the sun. Add small amounts of well-rotted manure or a handful of complete fertilizer every two to three weeks if the plants look like they need it. Come winter, protect the barrel by bringing it inside, or by wrapping it in 6 inches of straw or other mulch to prevent excessive drying out or freezing injury.

THE BRAMBLE BERRIES

I remember one day, as Grandma Putt and I were out gathering fixins in a nearby field, I wandered into a patch of wild blackberries. They were mighty tasty, but I think I probably carried away as many scars as berries! That didn't stop me though; I went back time and again to gather these delectable delicacies.

Anyway, I'm wandering away from the point—which is those delicious (but dangerous) bramble berries that include: blackberries, boysenberries, dewberries, loganberries, and raspberries. They all make for some mighty good eatin'!

BEAUTIFUL BLACKBERRIES

Although most Europeans considered black- berries to be worthless weeds, Grandma Putt said that we Americans were probably the only people with enough fortitude to cultivate them. If you had ever tasted Grandma's blackberry flummery made with fresh-picked Darrows, you'd appreciate their true worth as a small fruit!

Blackberries come in two main types: erect or semi-erect, and the trailing type. This last type is more commonly known as dewberries.

Site Selection

Grandma Putt told me that the best soil for the bramble fruits is sandy loam, with lots of organic matter worked in deeply because their roots go down two feet or more. Annual applications of compost or manure are needed if you want the plants to keep on producing.

The soil must be able to retain moisture through the summer, yet have good drainage above and below for excess water. A pH of 6.0, slightly on the acidic side, is fine. Open, sunny places are the preferred location near some trees where strong winds won't buffet the long canes. A gentle south facing slope is also good if it is available.

Planting Tips

Whenever we bought new blackberry bushes, we planted them 3 inches deeper than they were grown in the nursery. Grandma Putt cut the tops back to 12 inches, and placed the plants at least 3 feet apart. You'll probably want to plant at least a half-dozen plants if you have a large family because each blackberry plant produces about a quart of berries per year. Keep the soil well cultivated until July.

What's Your Pleasure?

The erect and semi-erect types of blackberries include the following varieties:

Bailey
Darrow
Early Harvest
Early Wonder
Humble
Smoothstem
Thornfree

Trailing varieties include:

Jerseyblack
Lucretia
Young or Youngberry

A BERRY, BERRY GRAPEFUL GARDEN

Don't expect berries the first year, but you should have plenty by the second. On average, blackberry bushes live about ten years, and should produce well from the second year on.

Proper Pruning

From the second year on, we kept Grandma Putt's bushes well pruned. The best time to do this is in early spring. We used to snip off the weakest canes, and any dead lateral branches.

A procedure called "pinching off" was necessary in the summer. This involved pinching off the growing tips of all shoots that were over two-and-a-half-feet long. This will cause them to branch out, and be ready to bear fruit. After the fruit has been completely picked, we cut out the canes that bore berries, and then we were all set for next year.

In the case of the trailing-type berries, spring pruning is minimal. All you have to do is remove the weak canes, and cut the healthy ones back to five or six feet. After the harvest, cut out the ones that bore fruit.

Mulch, Mulch, Mulch...Your Plants!

To eliminate weeds, we mulched our berry plants with pine needles or bark. We put the mulch on as soon as the hot weather, weed-growing season began. Then we drew it away from the plants before the cold weather because they

Anatomy of a Weakness

Aside from brittle, breakable canes, the bramble fruits have bark that is very thin and prone to injury; airborne disease spores enter bruised and torn spots very easily. Mother Nature goofed in providing these plants with spines and prickles; tough tissue should have reinforced the skin instead. How sensitive is their skin? Well, even the motion of the wind can cause severe abrasive injury from the spines.

retain frost too long in open winters. At that time, you should remove it anyways to cultivate around the plants.

Brambles are least winter hardy of all bush fruits in the North. Beginning with red raspberry, in increasing tenderness are black, purple, amber, and white raspberries, blackberries, dewberries, and the hybrids: boysenberries and loganberries. You can increase winter hardiness by withdrawing nitrogen from the soil in late summer; to do this, you should plant a cover crop of rye or oats over all open soil.

We always fed our blackberries with a capful of high nitrogen (10-6-4), liquid lawn food in a quart of water for each plant every spring. Then we'd add a handful of an all-purpose dry fertilizer in mid-August, and that would be it for the year.

RAMBLIN' RASPBERRIES

Red, yellow, black, and purple raspberries come in either **Summerbearing** or **Everbearing** varieties. Although you can find varieties suited for almost any region of the country, the ideal growing conditions for raspberries are where there are long, cool springs.

Grandma Putt prepared her raspberry beds the same as she did for strawberries and blackberries. She found an area that was sheltered, yet got lots of sun. She planted them as early in the spring as possible. Since raspberries don't tend to spread as much as blueberries, she only allowed

☹ Bad Neighbors

Grandma Putt said that we had to keep red raspberries and black raspberries apart by at least several hundred feet. This was because these plants are all susceptible to some of the same rust and virus diseases. Also, she said to avoid using soil where potatoes, tomatoes, eggplant, and melons had been grown in several years, or any brambles (including roses) had grown in the last twenty years. Otherwise, your patch will produce zip in the way of berries!

A BERRY, BERRY GRAPEFUL GARDEN

3 to 4 feet between her plants.

These plants can take a little late frost, and, if planted early enough, will be ready to bear fruit in the fall. Most nursery stock is about one year old. Grandma Putt fed and mulched her raspberries like her blackberries.

Growth Habits

The two main varieties grow differently:

Group 1—red raspberries reproduce themselves by suckers in ever expanding circles; blackberries and dewberries do the same.

Group 2—purple and black raspberries form tight clumps for life.

With the first group, set the plants closer together, 2 to 4 feet in the row, with rows 10 to 12 feet apart. If you maintain a cultivated strip or path between rows,

Controlling Insects and Disease

Grandma Putt had a few no-nonsense rules when it came to growing bramble berries. They were:

Rule #1—Buy only certified, disease-resistant varieties; avoid "free" plants which may carry disease.

Rule #2—Plant in soil you've been cultivating for few years.

Rule #3—Keep the area weed-free, and eliminate any wild brambles.

Rule #4—Prune out all productive canes immediately after harvest.

Rule #5—Dig out sickly plants as much as possible, and destroy them.

Rule #6—Prevent problems by following a balanced spraying program:

✔ Dormant spray when leaves are a quarter mature.

✔ Apply a fungicide/insecticide mixture every two weeks during the growing season.

✔ Bees must pollinate plants, so don't spray during bloom.

Rule #7—Don't damage thin-barked canes because disease will enter the wound.

Rule #8—Replant your bed every five years or so.

Rule #9—Fertilize in spring with manure and a 5-10-5 fertilizer.

suckering is limited to form a solid bed no more than 5 feet wide for easier picking.

With the second group, plants should be 6 to 8 feet apart in the rows with cultivation possible in both directions for several years. Though new plants may be guaranteed to be disease-free, they may carry harmful spores; use the tops as handles for planting, then cut them to the ground at once and burn them. Replace the ones with temporary wood stakes if you need markers.

Raspberries will need some support—especially when they're producing fruit. Grandma Putt staked them up with metal poles, or, if she planted them in rows, with stakes at the ends of each row, running wires down either side of the plants.

Proper Pruning

With raspberries, don't expect fruits the first year; flower buds on new canes of Summerbearing varieties should be nipped off new plants. Raspberry canes are biennial; that is, they grow one season, fruit the next, and die. So, your first

pruning should be done as the last fruit is picked—don't wait! Cut canes cleanly down to ground level, leaving no visible stubs. Never cut new canes back in late summer; wait until cold weather to shorten them, the same as for staking and tying.

The second pruning should be done in late winter or very early spring. At this time, any winter kill

A BERRY, BERRY GRAPEFUL GARDEN

can be noted, and the damaged canes can be cut out. Thinning should be done to remove the smallest canes, and aerate the clumps. With bedding or suckering types of plants, prune the plants to allow canes that are no less than 8 or 9 inches apart.

At this time, you should shorten raspberry canes to 5 feet if they're larger than a pencil at that length, to 4 feet if they're less. Seal all cuts with lipstick, or spit and dirt to keep stem borers out. Burn all cuttings.

Finally, Grandma Putt said that you've got to be ruthless in eliminating suckers that spring up between plants, unless you want to transplant the more healthy of these as new plants. After harvesting the Summerbearing varieties, cut off the canes that bore fruit at ground level. If your plants are the Everbearing type, cut off the tips of the canes that bore fruit. These same canes may bear heavier fruit next season.

THE BUSH BERRIES

There are several kinds of sweet and spicy berries that are grown and cultivated on bushes. Among the best known are blueberries, huckleberries, currants, gooseberries, elderberries, and serviceberries (or shadbush plums). All are perennials, which can provide you with plenty of plump, juicy berries for many years to come.

OH SO BLUEBERRIES

Blueberries were once so common all over the world that people just took them for granted, and never grew them in their gardens. They are probably the easiest wild fruit to name because they seem to be native to every part of the world.

Blueberries are much more easily grown in a home garden than most folks ever suspect. Even when I lived with Grandma Putt, it was very common to let your blueberries simply grow wild near the wood. And most folks did their pickin' (and found their thrill) on Blueberry Hill!

Location and Soil Prep

Blueberry plants are pretty easy fellows to cope with… so plant some bushes, and enjoy the luscious results! Grow blueberries in full sun. Too much shade results in spindly growth, lower yields, and poor quality fruit. They require moist, acidic soil (pH between 4.5 and 5.5) that has plenty of organic matter and good drainage.

Grandma Putt prepared her soil in the fall with well-rotted manure and humus as I described for strawberries. In the spring, two weeks before planting, she'd apply a commercial fertilizer with a high nitrogen content, or use an evergreen fertilizer that was recommended for azaleas.

Planting Tips

Blueberries should be planted 1 to 2 inches deeper than they were in the nursery, and 4 to 6 feet apart in rows that

A BERRY, BERRY GRAPEFUL GARDEN

are spaced 8 to 10 feet apart. Place the plants in the hole, fill it three-quarters full of a compost-peat-sand mix, and fill it with water. After the water seeps out, pack the hole with the soil mix, water the plant thoroughly, and then mulch around the plant.

You'll need to plant enough bushes in close proximity to each other so that they will cross-pollinate. Plants are usually sold in bunches of six or more for just this reason.

Feeding Time

Grandma Putt used a blood meal, cottonseed meal, and well-rotted manure mixture to feed her blueberries. She made the first application about a month after planting, spreading the fertilizer around the plant in a broad band at least 6 inches, but not more than 12 inches away from its base. She repeated this application in early July.

If the plants appeared weak, she'd fertilize again in the fall after the leaves dropped. If you have mulched around your bushes, double the rate of the first application, and skip the second.

You should increase the rate of fertilizer each year until mature plants (after six to eight years in the field) are receiving about one pound of food per plant, two-thirds applied just as they're beginning to bloom, and the other third applied approximately six weeks later.

Proper Pruning

At planting time, you need to remove all weak, diseased, and broken wood, and all flower buds. After one year, limit your pruning to any diseased or broken wood. Allow your most vigorous plants to bear up to a pint of fruit from 20 to 30 flower buds. Remove any additional buds.

Before

For the next two to five years, you should continue similar pruning practices. Your emphasis should be on producing healthy bushes, and not on producing fruit. If the plants seem to be doing fine, then don't remove any more flower buds than are absolutely necessary during pruning.

For mature bushes (after six to eight growing seasons), you should remove all dead and diseased wood, and then thin out the bush by removing one-quarter of the main branches. Cut the canes at an angle slightly above ground level or to a low, vigorous side shoot. You should do this each year, always removing the oldest canes.

After cutting out the main branches, you should thin the remainder of the bush, removing weak lateral shoots, twiggy, bushy growth clusters, and interfering branches. Be vigilant because unpruned bushes will soon develop into a thick, tangled, twiggy mass of worthless wood.

After

A BERRY, BERRY GRAPEFUL GARDEN

HARDY HUCKLEBERRIES

In the Midwest, from Michigan to Mark Twain country, kids grew up calling blueberries, "huckleberries" and huckleberries, "blueberries." Actually there is a difference—huckleberries grow only in the wild. They are just a little bit smaller than true blues, and have large, hard seeds. I still can't tell the difference between wild blueberries and wild huckleberries. I wonder if Huckleberry Finn could?

GREAT GOOSEBERRIES AND CURRANTS

Grandma Putt made gooseberry pie and currant jelly, which are two of the best reasons I know to consider growing gooseberries and currants! These spicy bush berries grow well in the northern part of the United States and in Canada.

Growing Tips

These bushes can be planted just about anywhere—sun or shade, it doesn't seem to matter. They're not particular about soil either, but the pH needs to be at or near 6.5.

Gooseberries and currants are self-fruitful. If you can, buy two-year-old plants, cut the long roots off, and set the

Those were the days...

Gooseberries are great for pies. I remember that from my childhood; but once, my wife decided to "give me a treat" and bake one. The berries seemed a little sour while she was preparing the filling. By the time she was finished, she had used about two pounds of sugar, and still the pie turned out so sour, even my kids (who would eat just about anything labeled "dessert") turned it down...and so did the dog! There must be a secret to baking a delicious gooseberry pie. If you find out what it is, please let me know.

plants 6 feet apart in rows. The new plants should be set one to two inches deeper than they were previously planted in the nursery, which means about a half foot deep. Cut the tops back to 6 inches. Your two-year-old cuttings should bear fruit the following year.

Keep currants pruned; February or early March is the best time to do this. Then each winter, thin the plant, leaving the younger shoots, and cutting out any wood that is more than three years old.

Giving your gooseberries and currants a good soapy water shower twice a month, from spring to autumn, will help them fight off fungus and other pests and diseases. Spade some wood ashes in and around the base of the bushes in late fall to give them a real boost. Otherwise, both gooseberries and currants are usually very disease-resistant, and don't need much more of a helping hand.

EDIBLE ELDERBERRIES

Next to blueberries, the elderberry is the most common wild fruit-bearing shrub in America. During Prohibition, elderberries became very popular as a cultivated shrub. They have very pretty blossoms which appear in June and July, which have been known to make a very tasty wine. The berries are also used for making delicious jams and jellies.

Elderberries tolerate a wide range of soils, and can be planted in sun or shade. The bushes are easy to grow.

These plants are partially self-fruitful, but you'll get more berries and a bigger harvest if you plant at least two bushes.

Pruning should be done in winter, removing any suckers and all wood that is more than three years old. If you don't prune on a regular basis, your crop will be smaller the following year.

You can expect your first edible elderberries the year *after* planting. You'll know the fruits are ready to be harvested when they're soft and dark purplish/black.

JUNEBERRIES OR SHADBUSH PLUMS

I'd be remiss if I didn't at least mention these berries in passing. These bushes grow all over New England and out in the northwest where they're known as serviceberries. The berries themselves range in color from red to purple, and can be eaten uncooked. Some eastern varieties grow into good-looking, blossoming trees that rival the white dogwood for beauty.

These plants grow in most any type of soil, in either sun or shade. The only real care they need is a light winter pruning to shape. The berries can be harvested two to three years after planting; they'll be pink to purple in color, and taste a little like blueberries.

GREAT GRAPES!

Grandma Putt wasn't what you'd call a wino, but she sure knew how to make a mean wine! Her favorite was made from Concord grapes; she always said it made a better dessert than a main course.

The Psalm says, "Wine maketh glad the heart of man," and there have been glad hearts somewhere in the world every night for more than six thousand years. Wine is known to have been used in the earliest records of man. The Greeks first brought the grape to the Western world, and the Egyptians were the Gallo Brothers of ancient times.

If the bubonic plague hadn't wiped out the people in Iceland in the fourteenth century (and with them, the memory of North America's discovery), we all might be "Vinlanders" instead of Americans. The early Norse voyagers saw so many huge grapevines growing along the Canadian and New England coast, they dubbed this continent "Wineland." Just think, if the name had stuck, today we might be a nation of winos!

But more than wine, there were plenty of other culinary delights connected to Grandma Putt's grapes. One of my favorites was Concord grape pie, not to mention grape jelly and, of course, a luscious bunch of grapes for eating on a crisp September day!

GRANDMA'S GRAPEVINES

The four cedar-post trellises for Grandma's grapes ran parallel to each other for about 20 feet out back of the house, opposite her vegetable garden. Behind them was the garage. Her grape-yard, as she called it, was a tiny, thriving vineyard in its own right. Her trellises ran north and south in good fertile soil, but I have since learned from several authorities that grapes prefer a southern exposure in soil that is moist and slightly acidic.

Grapes can be propagated from cuttings which you buy from a nursery, from a spring pruning of established vines, or by layering one-year-old shoots. In any case, plant them as soon as possible; if you can't, then store them in wet sand until winter, and then plant them in the spring.

PERFECT PLANTING

Grapevines grow best in soil that has a loose texture like sandy loam or light clay loam topsoil. Grapes must have good drainage. Open space and sunlight are also beneficial because they stimulate the air movement that'll help control grape diseases.

Dig the planting hole at least 18 inches wide and 18 inches deep. Mix equal amounts of soil with peat moss, and add some manure; use this mix to plant each vine. Set it to the same depth as it was before, and water it well every week that first summer.

FERTILIZING

The first season, feed each vine 1/4 lb. of ammonium nitrate in late May. Spread it evenly on the ground in a circle with a 2-foot radius around the vine, and work it into the soil.

The second year, use 1/2 lb. of fertilizer in a circle with a 3-foot radius. The third year, use 1 lb. of good, all-purpose (12-12-12) fertilizer in a circle with a 4-foot radius.

From the fourth year on, instead of chemical fertilizer, Grandma Putt worked in rotted manure at the rate of 20-30 lbs. per vine each May. She said the fruit will be less acidic and much tastier if you follow this routine.

Viva Variety!

Selecting the proper varieties of grapes is crucial. Since the first settlers, growers have learned, much to their dismay, that climate is the key to growing certain types of grapes.

For instance, Thomas Jefferson tried and failed to grow European wine grapes at Mt. Vernon. Hundreds of doubting Thomases since then have tried the same thing with the same dismal results. In general, bunch grapes grow best in the North, Midwest, Southeast, and far West; wine grapes do well in northern California; and muscadine grapes do well along the Pacific Coast and down into Texas.

WATERING

Established grapevines are deep rooted, and as a result, they are not affected by minor droughts. In prolonged dry spells, soak the ground every two weeks with a six to eight hour sprinkling (3-4 inches of water); try to keep the foliage dry. You should not water from mid-September on to allow the fruit to ripen and finish.

PRUNING

You can incorporate grapes into your landscape plan by espaliering them against a sunny wall of your house or garage (I even saw a vine-covered outhouse once). Or, you can train them to an arbor. But if you want grapes for eating and preserving instead of grapes for looking at, build a grape trellis.

How-to Hint

You don't want your vines to work overtime, so if they produce an especially heavy crop, you need to thin out the excess bunches. Do it while the fruit is still small and hard, leaving one bunch per cane on young vines, and two bunches on more mature ones.

The best time for pruning grapes is in late winter or early spring, while they are still dormant. As with most pruning, be ruthless! Grandma Putt said that this pruning must be done before the sap rises or your vines will bleed. If you must wait until later, allow the leaves to grow to the size of the palm of your hand before cutting.

Several pruning systems are now in use which are designed to produce the maximum amount of quality fruit from the vines. Four Arm Kniffin, Umbrella Kniffin, and Cane Pruning are the most popular of these systems. The Kniffin systems are used for American grapes, while the Cane Pruning System is used for European hybrids.

A BERRY, BERRY GRAPEFUL GARDEN

The Four Arm Kniffin System

If you're going to use this system, plant the vines 8 to 10 feet apart in rows. You'll need to set sturdy, 7 ft. long <u>untreated</u> cedar or redwood posts 2-1/2 ft. into the ground between every other vine. Fasten a wire to the post 30 inches above ground, and another one to the top. Stretch the wires good and tight.

The First Spring: Right after planting, cut the vine down to two or three buds. Don't worry, it'll do just fine.

The First
Spring

The Second Spring: Tie the strongest of the new canes (shoots) straight up to the top wire. This will become the trunk. Clip off all the other canes at the source.

The Second
Spring

The Third Spring: Choose four well-placed side branches, and tie them down along the wires, one in each direction. These branches are this season's fruiting arms. Cut these arms back to six buds each. Next, choose another lateral close by each wire, close to the trunk, and cut it back to two buds to form the renewal spur. These spurs will produce the following year's fruiting arms.

The Third
Spring

From The Fourth Spring on: You need to replace last year's fruiting arms with new canes from the renewal spurs. Select four new renewal spurs, then cut off all other wood. If the prunings weigh less than 1 lb., cut the new fruiting arms back to 30 buds or less. Add 10 buds for each pound of prunings, so for 2 lbs. of prunings, leave 40 buds, for 3 lbs., leave 50 buds, etc. This is what is known as "balanced pruning."

The Fourth Spring

Four Arm Advantages

This system has several advantages over the others, primarily in that the vines produce:

- heavier crops, up to 5 lbs. more per vine;
- better quality fruit with higher sugar content; and
- balanced crops, the same size each year.

The most productive canes are those that are of pencil thickness between the 5th and the 6th bud. Thicker canes are called "bull canes." They won't produce fruit, so cut them off. If bull canes are the only ones available, use them as arms, but don't remove the little seed branches because they will produce some fruit. If your vines only produce bull canes, then switch to the Umbrella System.

The Umbrella Kniffin System

This system is used for vines that are too productive to be restricted to only four arms. The arms and renewal spurs are allowed to form near the top of the trunk, just below the top wire. Then they are looped over this wire, bent down to the lower one, and tied down. You can leave as many as six or seven arms if need be.

The Cane Pruning System

Cane pruning for European hybrids is just like both Kniffin systems, except it leaves 25% fewer buds. The vines are much more productive, and the fruit grows closer to the trunk. The bottom wire should be 3 feet, and the top wire 4-1/2 ft. above ground.

It is possible to train European hybrids in espalier fashion on an arbor or trellis. In this method, the arms are permanent. Many fruiting spurs pruned back to three buds each are kept along the length of the arms. These fruiting spurs should be spaced about 12" apart, and should be replaced each spring.

PEST PATROL

Grandma Putt kept the insects and diseases under control by spraying her grapevines four times a season according to the following schedule, starting in the spring:

Spray #1—When the new shoots on the vines are 6-10 inches long.

Spray #2—Two weeks after #1, *just before the vines bloom.*

Spray #3—Two weeks after #2, *after* blooming is done.

Spray #4—Two weeks after #3.

She used her Fels-Naptha Soap Solution, and followed that up with sulfur and rotenone as recommended.

Learn the Leaves

Grandma Putt taught me a couple of important things about grape leaves. First, don't make the mistake of pulling all of the leaves off to expose hidden bunches of grapes to the sun. The grapes need sunlight, but the leaves manufacture much of their sugar. When you pinch off the leaves, your grapes may become acid-tasting. Second, ask anyone from the Middle East or Greece, and they'll tell you that grape leaves are gooood eating! So check your cookbooks!

FRUITFUL FIGS

Grandma Putt grew figs as small, ornamental trees. They need constant sun, good drainage, soil that has pH in the 6.0 to 8.0 range, and protection from cold, wet weather. Fig trees can be grown from 8- to 10-inch cuttings similar to grapes. Root the cuttings in sand, or you can layer them like raspberries.

If you live in the North, then you should plant figs in tubs, and take them inside over the winter. If you have to leave them outside, tie the branches together, and mulch them heavily with straw. Then take a big, plastic trash bag, turn it upside down, and cover the plant, mulch and all.

Figs usually produce fruit after the first year. New fruit appears on new growth like the berries and grapes. In season, check them daily for fruit that's soft and almost full colored. Let it ripen at room temperature for a day or so, and then refrigerate for longer storage (up to one week). You must prune figs severely after harvest to guarantee another good harvest next year.

Rhubarb Tonic

To get her rhubarb growing, Grandma Putt made up a batch of this tonic:

**1 tbsp. of Epsom salts,
1 cup of tea, and
all of the table scraps she could find**

in 1 quart of water. She mashed all of these ingredients, then poured the mushy mix over her plants in both the spring and fall.

ROBUST RHUBARB

I don't know why, but rhubarb isn't classed as a small fruit, although we certainly treated it like it was. Grandma Putt called it "pie plant," and she stewed it or mixed it with strawberries to make some of the tastiest pie this side of heaven!

A BERRY, BERRY GRAPEFUL GARDEN

SOIL AND SITE SELECTION

Grandma Putt grew her rhubarb in full sun, although it will also grow well in rather heavy shade. Rhubarb prefers deep, fertile soil which will give it large, juicy stems. It's a perennial plant, so you need to plant it in a fairly permanent place. To prevent shading of other plants, it's best planted on the north or east end of a garden.

PROPER PLANTING

Bare-root plants are available in spring, and potted plants can be planted anytime of year. Plant rhubarb 3 inches apart in rows that are 5 inches apart. Work organic material like peat, compost, rotted manure, etc. into the soil when planting.

These plants will really take off if you mulch them well with straw, hay, and compost. Mature plants can be divided in spring when they're dormant, and replanted for vigorous growth.

HARVESTING

Grandma Putt said to let rhubarb grow the first season without harvesting it. After that, you can harvest by gently pulling leaves from the crown as cut stems. Stubs encourage disease problems. Harvest only lightly after the end of June, and *never* remove all the leaves from a plant.

Against Its Will!

You can force rhubarb to grow indoors all winter long. We did it at Grandma Putt's, and it was pretty darn good. If you want to try it, dig up a few crowns after the first frost, lay them on the ground, and cover them with a few inches of sand. After 7 weeks, dig the frozen clumps up, and plant them indoors in large buckets, baskets, or even plastic bags. The leaves will be yellowish, but the stems will be red. Then harvest all winter long.

Remove seedheads as soon as they are visible to encourage growth. Fall rains sometimes produce a lush crop of new foliage, so enjoy!

One word of caution—never harvest the leaves because they are poisonous. Only use leaf stalks. Pets avoid the foliage with no problem.

FOR THE BIRDS? *NOT!*

Although birds are of tremendous value around the yard because of the hordes of insects they consume, some birds also include your ripening fruits in their diet, much to your dismay. These birds seem to know a good place for nesting is near a future food supply, or right in it! Here's what Grandma Putt showed me to do to keep some of those delights for ourselves.

STRAWBERRIES

Ah, strawberries—"Plant enough for thee and me," the robin may be heard to say. To make sure we got our fair share, we'd cover the beds before the berries began to color; once the wise robin had a taste, he was persistent, and I even saw one squeeze berries through a net! We didn't drape regular bird netting loosely over or along edges of a strawberry patch; instead we built an 8 inch high frame around the bed, and stretching netting over the top.

A BERRY, BERRY GRAPEFUL GARDEN

We looped it over nails for quick removal at picking time. A word of caution: don't tear the netting when removing it because you'll use it elsewhere in the garden almost immediately

BLUEBERRIES

A lot of our fine-feathered friends flock to this feast; when these berries are ready, they seem to forget all about the insects! Pressure on the blueberry harvest can be relieved by cherries early in the season, and raspberries later on. As your bushes grow to about 6 feet tall, it's best to make a light, wood frame structure, and cover it with netting, securing it around the base.

CHERRIES

Dwarf, tart, or sour cherries are fairly easy to cover with large sections of netting. Sweet cherries, however, are too large to cover economically. So, here's a simple trick that Grandma Putt taught me to keep birds away: use a large spool of number 4 black thread, unreel it over the tree, back and forth, distributing it all around. Once discovered, birds seem to fear getting entangled, and will avoid the tree at all costs!

Green Thumb Tip

If you can't beat 'em, fool 'em! Grandma Putt had me paint some rocks to look like strawberries, and scatter them around her strawberry patch before her berries ripened. The birds got so disgusted pecking at the rocks that they soon took their act elsewhere. Try it, it worked for me!

BLACKBERRIES AND RASPBERRIES

Prickles, spines, and frequent removal or shifting for picking makes plastic netting hardly last a season, unless you can support it well above the foliage on tall stakes. So we used cheesecloth to save our harvest.

GRAPES

These fruits brought the small fruit season near the end. For small harvests, we used paper bags to protect our grapes. We cut a small hole in the bottom of the bags for drainage, and then slipped the bags over the bunches of developing grapes. We secured the top around the stem, and made sure the fruit had room to grow! For larger harvests, we draped large sections of netting over the trellis, and fastened it to the ground to protect against the invaders.

I want you to remember that these are all short-term solutions to the problem. A long-term, practical approach for diverting fruit snatchers that Grandma Putt used was to plant ornamental shrubs which produce berries at the same time as her small fruits were ripening. Nanking (bush) cherry and shadblow (serviceberry) are good for early crops. Mulberry is a great favorite, fruiting later, and for much of the summer. Late fruiting shrubs are more numerous, and few are more palatable to the birds than the Mountain Ash.

A BERRY, BERRY GRAPEFUL GARDEN

GRANDMA PUTT'S SMALL FRUIT GROWING CALENDAR

SPRING

As soon as the severe frosts were over, we began preparing the soil, and plant our small fruit-bearing plants. Don't plant them on a windy day… especially a cold windy day. If you can, get your plants in before the spring rains. They'll benefit greatly from the extra moisture and nitrogen. Remember, the planting soil should be moist, not wet and soggy!

If you're having an extremely dry spring, soak your berry patch thoroughly in the morning, and then plant that evening. Sporadic watering is worse than no watering at all! Never let the roots dry out or shrivel up. If the roots are frozen, let them dry out in the garage or basement before planting.

In spring, watch your plants carefully, just as you do young children. This is when unexpected cold and heavy rains or frosts can bring on sickness. Turn your back on your living young plants too long, and you may find them wiped out when you turn around!

Root Revival Tonic

Before planting any bare-root plants in spring, soak them in a mix of:

**1 tbsp. of soap,
1/4 cup of tea, and
1 tbsp. of Epsom salts**

in 1 gallon of water for up to 24 hours. This will revive the plants, and get them ready to grow.

If you have just set out strawberry plants, don't cultivate heavily near the roots. Use a rake, and just lightly stir the soil surface not more than a half inch deep.

Mulch as soon as you can, using pine needles, old newspapers, straw, etc. Dry ground covered with mulch will, guess what? Stay dry! So make sure that it's moist to begin with, and you won't have any problems.

SUMMER

Late spring/early summer is the time to prune and "pinch off" plants. Do this while the plants are still in their spring and summer growth mode, and not when the wood begins to ripen.

In early summer, rake the ground in your berry patch once a week. This will eliminate weeds, and help keep the ground moist.

Keep on mulching, making sure that you have an adequate amount around all plants. It, too, will keep heat and weeds out, and moisture in. Again, don't mulch dry ground; mulch will only make the ground drier. If need be, soak the ground first, then apply the mulch.

Grandma Putt's Words of Wisdom:

"A pinch in time saves nine."

Pick all fruit, if possible, in the cooler parts of the day when it is dry. And don't leave any just-picked fruit in the sun because it'll start to lose its freshness and nutrients. Take it to a cool, shady spot immediately.

A BERRY, BERRY GRAPEFUL GARDEN

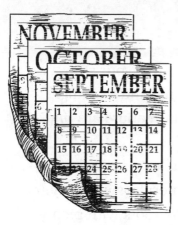

FALL

If you have a heavy spring gardening agenda, save some of that precious
time now by planting blackberries,
currants, gooseberries, and raspberries.
Check with your local nursery to
make sure the varieties you select
can be fall-planted.

Do as much soil preparation in the fall as you can—spread
compost, yard fodder, and other debris, and then till it under.
As you know, there never seems to be
enough time in the spring!

If your soil is heavy, and you
plan on planting in it the following
spring, plow it deeply now. Then go
back over the furrows to make them
even deeper. This exposes your
berry patch to what is called "win-
ter-heaving"...which will make it
more workable in the spring. It also
exposes insects and their larvae to
the killing winter cold.

Top-dress all small fruit with
good, rich compost mixed with bone
meal or any natural slow-release fertilizer. Spread it along
the rows, and work it in the soil just above the roots.

This is also the time to eliminate all weeds that may have
crept into your berry patch. Hand-pull the big ones, and cultivate the smaller ones out of existence. Be careful—don't disturb the berry roots because exposure to frost will kill them.

Fall Checklist

Fall clean up is a must.
This includes:
- ✔ Renew the mulch.
- ✔ Pick off remaining fruits,
  and destroy them.
- ✔ Clean up dropped
  berries.
- ✔ Cut out any weak, dam-
  aged or diseased canes.
- ✔ Destroy any and all
  diseased plants.

WINTER

Just as the ground is about to freeze, cover your strawberry plants with mulch to prevent freezing and thawing. Leaves, straw, hay, or light manure are fine for this job.

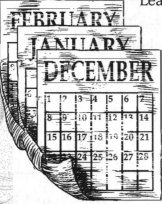

You can continue to plant bramble berries on mild winter days when there is no frost. Cover the roots with plenty of planting mix, but don't allow frozen earth to come into contact with them.

In the early winter, send away for new nursery catalogs, and get going on your spring fruit growing plan. When the fruit catalogs arrive, study them carefully. I always used to love going through the catalogs, and dream about how luscious the fresh fruit was going to taste. But don't let all those pretty pictures lure you into buying more work this winter than you can handle next spring and summer!

Late winter is the perfect time for pruning grapevines, but do it before the sap rises. Otherwise, your vines will bleed like crazy. Unfortunately, grapevines are like hemophiliacs—their sap doesn't clot! So be prepared, or you may end up visiting the ER!

Green Thumb Tip

As you're sitting by the fire, all cozy and comfy, don't forget your berries. That's right, the fire you're sitting by will be great for your berries—once it burns out. The wood ashes are a fantastic source of nutrients for your small fruit, so periodically sprinkle ashes around your plantings for powerful growth next spring.

6

AN APPLE A DAY...

A FRUITFUL FRIENDSHIP

Grandma Putt loved her fresh-from-the-tree fruit, and she had loads of different types of fruit trees on her property. Most of her trees were pretty well placed into her landscape, yet there was always plenty of apples, either on the trees, the ground, or in barrels and bushel baskets down in her root cellar.

None of the plants in your yard will pay you back for the care you give them as much as fruit trees will. Unfortunately, most homeowners tend to ignore these bountiful botanical buddies. I'm not going to suggest you plant an entire orchard; most people simply can't spare the land or the time, nor can they cope with the kind of harvest that twenty standard fruit trees will produce!

But every home gardener should have at least one fruit tree, if for no reason than to experience the joy of biting into a shiny red, delicious apple, knowing that you and Mother Nature worked together, against all odds, to produce this object of man's heritage. Remember, all gardening began in an orchard, and when you stop and think about it, the fruit tree, with just a little care, returns more for the time and effort expended than any other friend in the plant kingdom.

GOTTA LOVE LANDSCAPING!

Grandma Putt started my lifelong passion for growing fruit trees, which continues even up until this day. I don't know what it is, but there's something about growing my own fruit that never ceases to amaze me! As a result, I've picked up a fair amount of fruit-growing knowledge over the years that I'd like to share with you. While I'm no expert, I do know that if you use some common sense and a few of my tips, tricks, and tonics, you, too, can grow fruit that would do Grandma Putt proud.

Every time someone asks me for landscaping advice, I tell them to take a close look at the ornamental beauty and shade that fruit trees provide. The proper use of fruit trees can set the average home apart from an original one. Where else can you get so much for so little? Floral beauty and fragrance in the spring, shade from the foliage in the summer, and the payoff, well, the payoff in late summer and early fall is obvious!

AN APPLE A DAY...

REVOLUTIONARY FRUIT TREES

No, I'm not talking about George Washington and his famous cherry tree! The difference between fruit trees in Grandma Putt's era and today is that in the past forty years or so, there's been a revolution in their development with the introduction of semi-dwarf, dwarf, double-dwarf, and even columnar shaped trees. These trees make large fruit production possible for those of you who only have the smallest amount of land available.

A standard apple tree, like the ones Grandma Putt and her neighbor, Roy States, had in their yards, grew to be 25 to 30 feet tall, and 25 to 35 feet wide. The spur-type semi-dwarf tree grows only 10 to 20 feet high, and 10 to 15 feet wide.

Luck of the Iowish!

Believe it or not, the newer, dwarf-type trees are the result of a chance discovery. A dwarf crabapple tree was found growing in the wild in Iowa. Researchers at Iowa State University used twigs from this tree to turn a normal, standard type tree into a potential dwarf by grafting it. These trees, which only grew to be 8 feet tall, produced standard-sized fruit. The rest, as they say, is history. Talk about luck!

Factors affecting tree height include variety, pruning, soil conditions, climate, and rootstock.

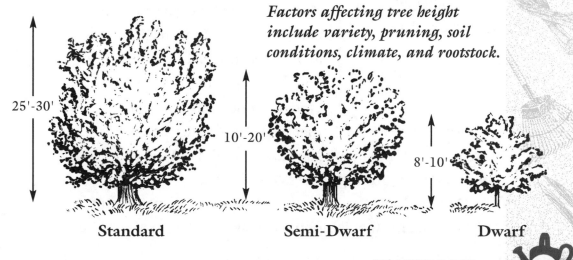

25'-30'   10'-20'   8'-10'

Standard   **Semi-Dwarf**   **Dwarf**

What this means is that you can now plant 200 semi-dwarf trees on the same acre that used to hold only 40 standard trees. And, you can get just about the same amount of fruit per tree because the semi-dwarfs set fruit throughout their foliage, while the standard trees set fruit only on the outside perimeter of the foliage.

Even more *amazing* are dwarf fruit trees which have been developed to produce larger fruit than standard trees. One of the best developments is a series of double-dwarf varieties that only grow 5 to 10 feet tall, yet set large fruit and bear very young. These trees are ideal for you folks with small yards or serious space problems.

GROWING
Requirements

To get the most out of your fruit trees, make sure they have most, if not all of the following:

- ✔ Good drainage.
- ✔ Soil pH of 6.0 to 7.0.
- ✔ Plenty of sunlight.
- ✔ Good air circulation.
- ✔ Higher elevation.
- ✔ No competition for food or water.

STANDARD PLANTING TIPS & TRICKS

LOCATION IS THE KEY

Unlike your vegetable garden, a home fruit-grower usually has little choice in the matter of where he's going to plant a fruit tree. This isn't all bad because, like Grandma Putt, you can scatter them about your yard. But one thing I've learned is that what constitutes a good planting site and a poor planting site can mean the difference between fruit growing success and failure.

The best site? Grandma Putt always tried to plant fruit trees in an area that is sloping and slightly raised above the

AN APPLE A DAY...

general grade of her yard. This provided two essential growing requirements—good air circulation and good drainage.

A site like this allows the foliage to dry rapidly after a rain, and helps to reduce the spread of many diseases that thrive on moisture on the leaves. If at all possible, you should avoid low spots, or frost pockets, where cold air may settle on still nights. These pockets are colder in winter, and more likely to experience late spring frosts, either of which can damage the trees and their fruit production.

Fruit trees also need lots of sunlight to bear a bountiful harvest. Inadequate sunlight delays the beginning of fruit bearing, and may reduce the amount of fruit the trees eventually produce. So avoid placing your trees where they will be shaded by other trees or by buildings.

Grandma Putt also paid plenty of attention to the soil surrounding the trees. Fruit trees grow more vigorously and bear better if they have an adequate amount of soil to develop their root systems. Don't plant them where the roots of other trees extend into the same soil. If they do, you'll have a battle on your hands for food and water. Finally, you must cultivate or mulch to reduce competition from weeds or grasses.

Remember that these fruitful poets like the kiss of the sun, room to develop, and not too much cramping of their style. They are convivial fellows, and do their best if they have someone to keep them company.

DON'T BE FOILED...BY BAD SOIL!

Fruit trees need well-drained soil where water does not puddle up after a rain. This type of soil encourages deep

> ## Soil Builder Mix
> To improve the soil around your fruit trees, make a batch of Grandma Putt's Soil Builder Mix:
> **3 bushels of compost,**
> **5 lbs. of bone meal,**
> **2-1/2 lbs. of gypsum, and**
> **1 lb. of Epsom salts**
> Work it thoroughly into every 100 sq. ft. of soil area.

root growth, and gives the trees a large amount of soil which they can draw their moisture and nutrients from.

Grandma Putt taught me that trees planted in poorly-drained soil grow poorly, will suffer more in a drought, and are usually short-lived. Soil texture, while important for your vegetable garden, is not that important for fruit trees. Medium-to-heavy clay loams are fine, but you can grow good fruit trees in both lighter- and heavier-textured soils if they are well-drained and contain sufficient organic matter. If at all possible, avoid very compact clays, coarse sands, and/or gravel.

If you're going to plant a few trees, make a row about 4 feet wide and as long as needed. If you're only going to plant a single tree, till and mulch the site (which should be at least four feet across) a year in advance to kill the sod. Before planting in the spring, remove the mulch to permit the soil to dry out before you dig the hole.

SPRING TIME IS THE RIGHT TIME

Grandma Putt always planted her trees in spring, as early as the ground could be prepared—why, she'd have it ready before she even got her trees! Follow her example—if you buy from a local nursery, get your trees in the ground as soon as you bring them home.

AN APPLE A DAY...

If you buy trees by mail, open and examine the stock as soon as you possibly can after you receive it. If you can't plant it at once, old-timers safely held their trees for a few days by covering the roots with some type of moist material, and storing them in a cool place away from sun and wind to prevent them from drying out. Leaves, compost, soil, or wet burlap will do the trick, but make sure you use enough so that you completely cover the roots.

If the tree stock must be held for more than two or three days, then you've got to heel it in to some out-of-the-way place. First, you need to dig a trench, and carefully set the trees in it. Then bury the roots in the ground. Pack soil firmly around the roots so that you don't have any air pockets, and keep it moist until you're ready to plant. Come planting time, carefully remove the trees from the trench, making sure you don't damage any of the roots.

In the milder areas of the country, you can plant fruit trees in the fall of the year from the time the leaves begin to drop until the ground freezes; but in colder regions, spring time is still the best. With fall planting, the trees are fresh out of the ground, and have not been wintered over in the nursery cellar. Also, they'll be in place and rarin' to grow as soon as the weather warms up in the spring.

OH, GO SOAK YOUR ROOTS!

When we were ready to plant fruit trees at Grandma Putt's place, she first had me soak the entire root system in a tub that contained her famous **Fruit Tree Rejuvenating Tonic.** We left them in the tonic overnight, which helped replace any of the natural moisture from both the roots and the branches that may have been lost during the dormant period.

Fruit Tree Rejuvenating Tonic

To perk up her fruit trees, Grandma Putt soaked them in her Rejuvenating Tonic before planting them:
1/2 cup of Fels-Naptha Soap Solution,
1/2 cup of Epsom salts, and
1/2 cup of tea
mixed together in 5 gallons of water.

When you're ready to take your trees to their permanent home, be sure to keep their roots covered at all times with wet burlap or other material to prevent even a momentary drying out from the sun or wind. If you have several trees to plant, let them soak in a bucketful of Grandma Putt's Rejuvenating Tonic until they're ready to go.

Grandma Putt always said to carefully examine the plant while you're preparing it for planting. You never know what you'll find, and it's a lot easier to fix things now, while the tree is still out of the ground, then later, after it's in its new home.

So, she trimmed all broken or damaged roots with a clean, slanting cut, using a sharp knife or a pair of shears. This helped the healing process, and spurred rapid growth of new feeder roots. She also top-pruned her trees before planting, but she didn't just chop off excess branches at random. Grandma Putt did it carefully with a sharp knife to avoid any damage to the bark.

AN APPLE A DAY...

Prune at a proper distance from a bud. Too close, and the bud will die. Too far, and the excess wood will rot back into the limb.

Correct

Too Far

Too Close

When trees are dug out of the ground at the nursery, a portion of the root system is unavoidably left behind. Grandma Putt said that you should not leave more top on a tree than the remaining root system can reasonably support. So she usually removed at least a third of the top by cutting the undesirable branches off and shortening the rest. All cuts were made just above a strong bud on the outside of the branch.

DIG IN!

One thing Grandma Putt made sure that I knew how to do was to dig a proper hole. She said that the hole should be deep enough to hold the roots without crowding them.

When you dig the hole, keep the topsoil in one pile, and the subsoil in another. Before refilling the hole, mix in some compost with the topsoil. When you place the tree in the hole, and the roots are spread out, shovel in this mixture first, and pack it around the roots. As you fill the hole with soil, jiggle the tree up and down a little so that this soil will work in and around the roots—which will keep

Grandma Putt's Words of Wisdom:

"Never plant a five dollar tree in a five cent hole."

AN APPLE A DAY...

air pockets from forming. Also, work the soil under the roots with your hands, and at intervals, tamp it down good and solid with your feet.

When your planting is complete, the soil should be firmly packed around the roots, with no air spaces in between them. *Don't* fertilize your fruit trees at planting time, and never allow the roots to dry out during the planting process.

Your newly-planted fruit tree should be set 2 or 3 inches deeper than it was in the nursery. Make sure the trunk is straight, and if you're planting several trees in a row, line them all up carefully. Water all trees thoroughly after planting, then add a light blanket of mulch with leaves, hay, or compost to help keep the soil surface from drying out too rapidly.

Planting procedures in the fall are the same as in the spring, but with one important extra step. After the ground is frozen, Grandma Putt always covered the soil around the tree with straw, hay, leaves, or other organic material to a depth of 6 inches. This prevented heaving, which is caused by alternate freezing and thawing of the ground.

WHO NEEDS WEEDS? NOT *YOU!*

Grandma Putt's Words of Wisdom:

"Mulch is a must, so you *must* mulch!"

Fruit trees *hate* competition for nutrients, so you must keep weeds down the first year by either cultivating or mulching. Grandma Putt preferred the latter method because a good mulch will decompose, and feed the surface roots of the young trees.

AN APPLE A DAY...

Mulch suppresses weeds, thus saving you a lot of work, and keeps the soil from getting too hot from the sunlight. It also prevents a loss of moisture from the soil by evaporation.

Mulching material around Grandmas Putt's place was usually dictated by whatever was available—grass clippings, sawdust, straw, and compost all were used as mulch. Grandma Putt was particularly fond of using hay which she bought cheaply, or had for the hauling from a nearby dairy farm. Wheat and other straws also make excellent mulch.

Grass clippings and compost add organic matter to the soil and supply food for earthworms, which are very valuable in aerating the soil. The organic matter helps to keep the soil crumbly and easy to work. Farmers call this good tilth. At the end of the growing season the mulch can then be worked into the soil to supply organic matter for the following year.

To properly mulch, simply spread a 3-to 6-inch layer of one of these organic materials on the soil surface around your trees. The material will break down during the growing season, so keep the layer deep enough to do the job all season long. This means that you'll have to add more mulch as the old layer decomposes.

Green Thumb Tip

Here's a neat trick Grandma Putt taught me to keep fruit trees weed- and insect-free. Before mulching around the tree trunk, she laid down several sheets of newspaper, and sprinkled some Diatomaceous earth and a few mothballs on top of it. This kept the "creepy crawlies" like bugs and slugs away. When you're done, add mulch on top of it.

Iron Out Chlorosis

You may be feeding your fruit trees properly, yet the leaves turn yellow and die, or their growth may be stunted. What's going on? Grandma Putt said that where the amount of iron in the soil isn't enough, plants suffer from a disease called iron chlorosis.

This disease is marked by yellowing leaves due to faulty chlorophyll development. The areas between leaf veins become light green, yellow, or white. The greater the iron deficiency, the paler these areas become. In severe cases, entire leaves turn brown, and the plants can die.

Iron chlorosis is often due to a high pH, and it occurs most often in soils that are high in lime. It may be caused by an actual iron deficiency, by excessive amounts of lime, over-irrigation, poor drainage, or high levels of certain heavy metals in the soil (manganese, copper, and zinc).

If over-irrigation or poor drainage is a possible cause, correct it. Otherwise, you can control the disease by giving your plants soluble iron in the form of liquid iron, either through the soil or the foliage.

GIMME A TONIC AND WATER!

Fruit trees expand a great deal of effort to bear fruit. So just as your appetite increases during periods of hard, physical labor, so it goes with fruit trees.

Grandma Putt didn't feed her fruit trees the first year, but after that, she fed her young trees in both the spring and fall. A dry 5-10-5 garden food is just fine—scatter 5 lbs. of this food mixed with 1/2 lb. of Epsom salts out at the weep line, and water it thoroughly.

As your trees reach middle age, their appetites increase according to the amount of fruit they produce. So, double the amount of your spring and fall feedings to 10 lbs. of food and 1 lb. of Epsom salts each time you feed them.

Then, when the faithful old fruit trees reach their "golden years," they need all the help they can get. So, give these grand old guys 15 lbs. of food and 1-1/2 lbs. of Epsom salts in the spring and in the fall.

After we fed the trees, it was time to water. Grandma Putt watered her fruit trees during the hottest, driest days of summer or during unseasonable droughts. Otherwise, they never saw the hose. This may sound cruel, but the proof is in the pudding— it worked!

When you do water your fruit trees, soak the ground thoroughly to a depth of at least 8 to 10 inches, all the way out to the weep line. Grandma said that sporadic or uneven watering is next to useless! It is better to water deeply once a week than to water lightly more often.

IT TAKES TWO TO TANGO!

Without getting into the specifics of the birds and bees, Grandma Putt explained to me that all fruit trees need to be pollinated to produce fruit. Unless adequate pollination takes place, trees may bloom a lot, yet not bear any fruit.

Some fruit trees have "perfect" flowers—both anthers that contain pollen, and the pistils, which develop into fruit, are in the same blossom. If they bear fruit as a result of pollination from their own blossoms, these trees are called "self-fruitful." Many fruits with perfect flowers, however, will not set fruit from their own pollen, but require pollen from another variety to set fruit. Such varieties are called "self-unfruitful."

Pollination Station

Here's a few tips to ensure that there's plenty of hanky-panky going on in your orchard:

Apples: except for Golden Delicious, most apple varieties are self-unfruitful, so plant at least two varieties. Plant poor pollen-producing apple varieties—like Winesap, Staymen, Gravenstein, Baldwin, and Rhode Island Greening—with at least two other varieties.

Sweet Cherries: Bing, Lambert, and Napoleon (Royal Anne) varieties do not pollinate each other, so plant a pollinating variety like Black Tartarian, Black Republican, or Governor Wood in the vicinity.

Pears: many pears are self-unfruitful, so plant at least two varieties together. Seckel and Bartlett pears will not pollinate each other.

Plums: most Japanese and American plums are self-unfruitful, so you'll need to plant two or more varieties together.

Most apples, sweet cherries, Japanese- and American-type plums, and pears are self-unfruitful. So, for adequate pollination, you must plant two or more varieties near each other.

Nearly all citrus trees are "self-fruitful." So are figs, sour cherries, quinces, peaches, apricots, and the European-type plums.

Occasionally, we ran into a situation where certain fruit trees, particularly apples, bore heavily one year and largely failed to bloom the following year. Grandma said this condition was called biennial bearing. Since the buds of most hardy fruits that open in spring are formed during the previous summer, a very heavy crop one year may prevent bud formation for the next year.

Biennial bearing is difficult to change or correct. You can try to induce a return to normal yearly fruit production by early, heavy thinning of the fruit during the year when the trees are producing a large yield. Only about one fruit per foot of branch should be left, and the thinning should be done within 30 days after blooming.

JUST BEAR WITH ME

A fruit tree normally begins bearing fruit after it becomes old enough to blossom freely, provided other conditions are favorable. Tree health and environment, adequate pollination, bearing habits, and your own cultural practices all directly influence the tree's ability to produce fruit.

If any of these conditions are not just right, your yields may be reduced or the tree may not bear at all. Remember that miracle of producing fruit I referred to on the first page of this chapter? Well, it's not quite that bad—a conscientious grower can exercise some control over most of them.

Bearly Fruiting?	
Variety	**Years to Fruit**
Apple	4 to 7
Apricot	4 to 5
Sour cherry	4 to 5
Sweet cherry	5 to 7
Citrus	3 to 5
Fig	2 to 3
Peach	3 to 4
Pear	4 to 6
Plum	4 to 6
Quince	5 to 6

Most nursery-produced fruit trees have tops that are one to two years old. The length of time required for them to bear fruit after planting varies with the variety. The "Bearly Fruiting?" chart indicates the ages (from planting time) at which fruit trees can be expected to bear.

PRACTICE MAKES PERFECT ... PRUNING!

I assume that if you're thinking of planting fruit trees, you're not just inviting these fellows to your home just to produce fruit. They will be expected to do a bit more, namely, to contribute a little beauty to your outdoor green scene.

How-to Hint

Homemade branch spreaders will help your fruit trees grow in the proper shape, and promote earlier fruit-bearing.

Grandma Putt made branch spreader sticks with notched ends cut into the desired lengths.

When positioning branch spreaders, she never placed them too near the crotch of the branch and trunk.

If you do, the branch will soon return to growing vertically beyond the spreader. Use longer spreaders farther away from the crotch. Be sure the spreaders are securely in place so that winds swaying the branch will not dislodge them. Begin when the trees are young because the sooner the branches are "set," the better.

Here's a crash course in pruning (or a pruning pruner as I like to call it) that was taught to me by Grandma Putt and Roy States many, many years ago.

For most homeowners, the appearance of the trees is more important than their fruit. Therefore, you will probably want to trim your trees high enough to allow you to walk under them, unlike the commercial orchardist who trims his branches low, sometimes barely above the ground. You may also prefer to sacrifice some of your fruit production by eliminating bearing branches and fruiting spurs to have an attractive, clean-limbed, open center.

THE INITIAL CUTS

Prune your fruit trees to keep them thin enough so that they won't break down under a heavy weight of the fruit. They should be high enough so that your budding "Isaac Newtons" can sit under them to think.

When your trees are young, prune them severely to form what is called a "head." This means that five or seven

AN APPLE A DAY...

branches are evenly distributed around the main stem; then cut this main stem back by at least a third. And don't allow two branches to grow directly opposite each other. This causes forking which creates a weak spot where the wood might split. If you thoroughly prune the first two seasons, you should need to do little in the way of pruning thereafter.

Before

After

TAKE ME TO YOUR LEADER

There are three basic systems of training fruit trees. The first is the **Central Leader System** which is most often used in training ornamental trees. In this system, all other growth is considered subservient to the one central or main trunk. This system is rarely used in orchards because of the difficulty in working with taller trees and the tendency to shade the lower branches. In home gardens, however, it is still useful because it generally produces an attractively shaped tree. The tree is also less subject to break under the weight of snow and ice.

MODIFIED LEADER SYSTEM

Central Leader

The **Modified Leader System** is more widely used by home gardeners. With this system, the main branches never change height. If you start them at 3 feet, that's where they'll stay. So the moral of the story is to start them out where you want them to stay!

Sweet cherry, pear, and some plum branches grow sharply upward at very close angles. Apple, plum, and peach branches are more likely to sprawl, so they must be started higher.

The method is the same as for the central leader system, but you must select a few other branches in addition to the central leader. These branches, usually the two lowest, are of almost equal importance. Remove all others, or head them back to become secondaries.

Modified Leader

OPEN-CENTER SYSTEM

The third system is the **Open-Center System**. With this system, all the scaffold branches are selected at the same time, and encouraged to branch out from the trunk at the same height. This produces a tree with a round shape.

An open-center tree is, however, more susceptible to damage from ice and snow, which may break the branches or cause pockets to form at the junctures of the limbs. (Water will collect in these pockets and cause rot to set in.) While this system is not recommended for the North, it is commonly used for peaches, nectarines, sour cherries, pecans, and almonds in areas where winters are not so severe.

If you want to use this method, try the "delayed" open center. Start out some branches early, as with the modified leader system, then let two or three grow out at a higher point by heading back the leader a little higher up. The branches will have better spacing than if you used the straight, open-center method.

Of course, the basic rules of pruning have not really changed over the years. You still must thin out, and let the sun ripen the fruit. Remove all branches that rub against or shade each other. All suckers and water sprouts should also be promptly removed, as well as all damaged, dying, or diseased wood. That about does it!

Open Center

RENOVATING OLD ORCHARDS

Not all of us buy or build a new home on a new site. Occasionally, an older home or a long-neglected farm may be exactly what you're looking for. If that's the case, then more often than not, you'll find older fruit trees which have borne little or nothing for years.

Grandma Putt's Words of Wisdom:

"There may be snow on the roof (of old orchards), but the fire still burns in the chimney."

Don't chop them down and start over! Lots of these "oldsters" have plenty of life left in them yet; they just need a helping hand, which is where you come in.

I remember going over to a neighbor of Grandma Putt's one time, and helping Roy States whip an old orchard back into shape. Restoring it required following all of the steps we just discussed.

The Whipping Post!

I'm the guy who tells folks to beat their fruit trees! This always gets a few folks laughing… not to mention some raised eyebrows.

Although they may laugh, lots of folks get the message, and sneak out in the dead of the night (when their neighbors are sleeping) to administer their tree whippings.

Whipping lazy old fruit trees with a "bearing" switch is something I learned from Grandma Putt. Sometimes, a tree suffers from "hardening of the arteries." Its sap vessels become constricted, and don't carry the vital fluid to the leaves, buds, and spurs. If this happens, the tree's "metabolism" slows down, and it is unable to bear fruit. That's when you really need to whip it into shape!

Use a three-to-four-foot sturdy willow switch or rolled-up newspaper, and give the trunk a thorough lacing as far up as you can reach. You will be amazed at the fruit that you will get old lazybones to produce!

Grandma said to whip your trees on moonlit nights in the early spring, and you'll have a good harvest when bearing season arrives. Let neighbors arch their brows all they want…this trick really works!

First, we fed the old trees (they had probably been starved for many years). Then we shoveled as many loads of compost as we could possibly find around the trees. We spread it liberally, right out to the drip line. Also, we worked some greensand and phosphate rock into the soil around the trunk; try it, it works wonders!

Then we began pruning. With apples and pears, you must remove all broken and diseased wood the first year, as well as water sprouts, and all upright and crowded branches. The surge of growth that will follow will separate the vigorous branches you want to keep from the tired old ones that should be removed the following winter.

If the trees have grown too tall, head back a few branches quite severely each year to reshape the tree, and get all of the growth within easy reach. Of course, you must consider each fellow as an individual, for no two neglected trees are alike.

Use your judgment, and above all else, *don't be afraid to perform any necessary surgery!* You're the doctor, and what you want to do is restore your patients to health and happiness! Encourage strong new growth, but thin it out whenever it becomes too thick.

These methods differ from those that were used many, many years ago in that they are less drastic and more gradual— we didn't want to give our grand old gentlemen heart failure! But if you follow my advice, the shock to the trees will not be so great, and the intervening loss of crops will be eliminated.

UGH! BUGS AND OTHER THUGS

Believe you me, you will not be the only admirer of the beauty and tastefulness of your home orchard! The bugs of the world have their eye on it, too! But don't despair—with a little knowledge and insight, you will be able to ward off most intruders.

In Grandma Putt's heyday, gardeners controlled the onslaught of bugs with the insects' natural enemies. For example, Grandma would plant nasturtiums underneath each of her fruit trees, and then mulch around them with shredded oak leaves. She knew that grubs didn't bother oak trees, so she would use the oak leaves against them.

From the Kitchen Cupboard

Some of the best old-time bug busters came right out of the kitchen cupboard. For instance:

Red spider mites— would run from sour milk on a table, so folks fought them with sour milk (use 2 cups of wheat flour and 1 cup of buttermilk to 5 gallons of water).

Codling moths— on pears could be controlled by growing spearmint underneath them.

Tent caterpillars— were controlled by wrapping the trees with aluminum foil, and painting a thin band of oil on the foil.

This was what we now call bio-dynamic gardening at its best, long before it was ever popular. The only chemical control these folks used was nicotine sulfate and Fels-Naptha Soap Solution, which is still in use to this day.

If you keep your trees well-pruned and clean, chances are the insects will pass them by. Insects attack the weak and the sick—they are most likely to attack trees where they find damaged wood. So see to it that you always remove this wood immediately after an injury.

Grandma Putt also made it a habit to dispose of all fruit tree leaves in the fall. This was almost like a religious ritual. She said these leaves attract disease-bearing insects, so we gathered them up, and burned them as soon as we could.

THE GOOD...

No insect is either all good or all bad; some are just more helpful than others, and some are just more destructive than others. Bumblebees and wasps, as well as other flying insects, act as pollinators, though usually to a lesser degree than honeybees. Other insects beneficial to fruit growers are aphid lions; praying mantis; carabidaes (a large family of predator beetles); soldier beetles; fireflies; dragonflies; damselflies; and even ants and spiders. Ladybugs are especially helpful where aphids are a problem.

THE BAD...

The fearsome foursome of the fruit tree crowd include:

Oriental Fruit Moth—The only stage of the oriental fruit moth that does any damage is the larvae, which tunnel into the tips of rapidly growing twigs, thus preventing normal growth. Releasing parasitic insects that prey on the larvae can control them. The most important of these parasitic insects are the egg parasite and the Trichogramma wasp. The natural control is an All Seasons Dormant Spray which smothers the insects. Apply it as soon as they appear.

Peach Tree Borer—This native American insect attacks plums, prunes, cherries, almonds, apricots, and nectarines, but is most destructive around peaches. It's found throughout the United States, wherever peaches are grown.

The larvae bore just beneath the bark near ground level, destroying the cadium layer, and often girdling the tree or surface roots.

There are a number of ways to combat these borers.

Painting Out Borers

Fruit tree borers are a nemesis to all of us who grow their own peaches, plums, apricots, and apples. Grandma Putt's method literally painted out borers with a solution made up of one gallon of cheap grade interior latex paint (exterior latex may damage some young trees), 3 gallons of water and (optional—latex alone is sufficient) one pound of BHC—benzine hexachloride, trade name Benzex. Less water is needed if the solution is to be applied by brush rather than sprayed. Apply the "paint" to the trunks of the trees around late July each year; it is very effective in protecting fruit trees from this destructive pest.

One of the oldest is to simply find them, and cut them out by hand. Another is to sprinkle a handful of mothballs around the base of each tree in spring and fall. A third calls for circling the tree with nutshells, with black walnuts being the most effective.

Tarnished Plant Bug—This bug commonly attacks the blossoms, buds, and developing fruits of apples, pears, peaches, plums, and quinces.

Peach trees also suffer a lot of twig injury. Adults are barely 1/4 inch long, and brown, tan, or green, with darker markings. Most have a rusty appearance that gives them their common name.

Control these pests by keeping the area around the fruit trees clean. Don't allow weeds and other leguminous plants to grow unchecked.

Curculio—A native North American insect found from Canada to Florida, and westward to the Mississippi River. It most commonly attacks apple, pear, crabapple, and hawthorn trees.

Nailing Up...*Bugs?*

One of Grandma Putt's favorite old-time orchardist's trick was nailing her fruit trees to get rid of caterpillars. That's right... nail your trees!

She used to take cast-iron nails, and hammer them into her trees about a foot from the base, spacing them every 4 or 5 inches, according to the size of the tree. She claimed that in a week or so, all the caterpillars packed up and left the nailed trees, never to be heard from again.

According to Grandma Putt, the iron in the nails oxidizes in the tree sap, and turns it into ammonia. The hint of ammonia evidently makes caterpillars gag. That's what this idea does to me, and if the trees could ever be interviewed on the subject, I'm sure their comment would be a resounding, "Ouch!"

AN APPLE A DAY...

A weak solution of salt water (1 tbsp. to 1 gallon of water) or Fels-Naptha Soap Solution sprayed on the trees provides good control against these thugs.

...AND SOME SIMPLE SOLUTIONS

Most of the "stuff" Grandma Putt needed to fight the battle of the bugs was found right in her home. Here's some of her best solutions:

Water—one of the simplest possible sprays for controlling or dislodging insects is good, old-fashioned H_2O. That's right—water! Apple growers should use a water spray in the spring for effective control of codling moths. Spraying loose bark will also dislodge harmful larvae.

Grandma Putt's Words of Wisdom:

"Simple solutions are the best solutions."

Calcium—several sources of calcium can be used to control insects around your fruit trees. Ground oyster shells, placed around apple, peach, and plum trees, has been found to reduce insect damage.

Bone Meal—steamed bone meal repels ants (which so often spread plant disease), and prevents them from spreading aphids. It also keeps leaf rollers away from strawberry plants.

Whitewash—this old-fashioned remedy is still useful today. It is simply a mixture of lime and water, and it combats the insects and disease that burrow into the bark of trees. It is particularly useful against peach tree bark beetles. It also helps prevent scald and heat injury in the bark tissues of very young trees in the hot, sunny regions of the South and Southwest.

Homemade Dormant Oil

Here's how Grandma Putt made her homemade dormant oil spray: First, she got a gallon of light-grade oil. Then she shaved two pounds of soap into it to use as an emulsifier. She mixed it as thoroughly as possible in a large container, and brought it to a boil, stirring to blend thoroughly. After letting it cool, she then diluted this mixture in 20 gallons of water.

Grandma Putt used the spray when the weather permitted in both spring and fall. When you spray, make sure you get the entire tree thoroughly to the point of run-off.

Dormant Spray—oil sprays, known as dormant sprays, are also very effective. They should be applied to your fruit trees in the late fall and early spring. Grandma said that in her day, she sprayed her fruit trees with nicotine sulfate mixed with two-and-a-half pounds of soap (like Fels-Naphtha Soap) to 50 gallons of water.

I've since learned that an All Seasons Dormant/Hort Oil sprayed in the late fall when the foliage has dropped, and again in the spring before the buds swell up, does the job just fine. This type of dormant spraying is especially effective if you give your fruit trees a good soapy water bath every two weeks. If a chemical control is necessary, use an all-purpose liquid fruit tree spray at the recommended rate. It's a good idea to check with your ag-extension service for spraying times and sprays best-suited to your local area. Make friends with these people; after all, you help pay their salaries with your taxes!

WINTER CARE

Winter was the time when Grandma Putt really kept her eye on her fruit trees. She knew that most hardy fruit trees

AN APPLE A DAY…

must be exposed to at least *some* cold winter weather in order to break their dormancy, and start their spring growth. Without sufficient cold weather, spring growth is delayed, and when the growth does start, it's irregular and slow. Hardy fruit trees growing in climates considerably warmer than their native ones usually bear poorly because of insufficient winter cold.

Extremely cold weather during the winter, however, can kill the fruit buds. Winter cold rarely threatens the hardy apples, pears, sour cherries, and plums, but peaches and sweet cherries are most sensitive to cold.

In the spring, as the fruit buds grow and open, they become more susceptible to frost injury. Also, keep in mind that injured blossoms may appear normal after a severe frost, but if the center parts (pistil) of all the blossoms are killed, the tree will not bear fruit.

THE ICE MAN COMETH...

We used to get hit with some real doozy ice storms that brought everything to a screeching halt. That included Grandma Putt's plant people. She used to say that there's nothing much you can do to keep tree branches—and some-times the whole tree if it's unusually slender—from bending down under the weight of an unexpected ice storm. Nine times out of ten, we simply had to wait until the sun melted enough snow so that it dropped off by itself.

As soon as the burden was dropped, we rushed out to push the bent parts carefully back to normal with a pole or our arms and hands. It was surprising how quick the branches took advantage of this timely assistance.

AN APPLE A DAY...

201

VARMINTS BEWARE

Like most folks, we used to have a problem with varmints damaging our young fruit trees. Grandma Putt's solution was good old-fashioned, poultry wire fencing. She made her fences wide enough to enclose the entire plant, not merely the trunk, and as tall as was necessary to protect it 18" above the deepest possible snow. This extra "margin of safety" prevented those darn hungry rabbits from hopping a lower barrier, and gobbling up all of the prunable wood in sight, right down to the ground!

Follow these few common-sense procedures, and your trees will be well-protected. Then they'll be able to concentrate on their job of providing you and your family with mouth-watering, taste-temptin' treats!

All-Purpose Varmint Repellent

Grandma Putt's dynamite varmint repellent was made by mixing:

2 eggs,
2 cloves of garlic,
2 tbsp. of hot chili pepper, and
2 tbsp. of ammonia,

in 2 cups of hot water. She let it set for several days, then painted it on the tree trunks.

DWARF VARIETIES

Dwarf fruit trees are the answer to the small property owners' prayers! They were specifically developed to meet the demand for trees that require less growing space than those of standard size.

AN APPLE A DAY...

Although they were considered a novelty in Grandma Putt's day, dwarf apple and pear trees are now widely available. For that reason, I want to give you a brief overview of how to take care of these mighty midgets.

Peach, plum, cherry, apricot, and nectarine trees have not, as yet, been produced extensively as dwarfs. Many of these trees, however, come in varieties that don't grow especially large anyway and, with careful selection, you will probably be able to find trees which will fit your yard without too much crowding.

DWARF PLANTING TIPS & TRICKS

You can usually buy dwarf fruit trees as one-year-old whips. They may be single stems, or they may have two or three branches along the main stem. Plant them early in the spring if you live in areas where the winters are severe; in late fall or early spring if you live in a warmer climate.

Plant full-dwarf apple trees 10 to 12 feet apart each way, or 6 to 8 feet apart in rows 15 feet apart. Plant semi-dwarf apple trees about 20 feet apart each way. Plant dwarf pear trees 15 to 18 feet apart.

Dwarf Advantages

For the average homeowner, dwarf fruit trees have many advantages over their larger, standard cousins. Here's a few:

1. They usually begin to bear 1 or 2 years earlier than their standard cousins.

2. Several varieties of fruit with different ripening seasons can be planted in the space required for one standard size tree.

3. All maintenance on the dwarfs can be done without the need for heavy-duty orchard machinery.

4. Dwarfs can be pruned and trained as ornamentals in your landscape—on wires or trellises, against walls, or along walks or driveways.

With these trees, it is very important to plant them 2 inches *higher* than they were grown in the nursery. Place fertile soil around the roots so that there are no air pockets. Fill the hole with soil for about two-thirds of the way, then fill the sides so there is a saucer-like depression near the trench to catch rain.

The graft or bud union should be just *above* the surface of the soil after planting. This is very important because if the union is below ground level, then the part of the graft below the union will take root, and you'll have lost the dwarfing characteristic. Mulch around your newly-planted tree, and water well at least once a week, unless there is a heavy rain.

Graft Union (bud) 30"

DON'T LET YOUR DWARFS GROW INTO TROLLS!

When you set out dwarf fruit trees, prune them back to keep the top in balance with the roots. A loss of roots *always* occurs in transplanting. If the trees have single stems 3 to 4 feet high, cut them back so that they stand about 30 inches tall. Then cut off about one-third of each side branch. Generally, you won't need to do any further pruning during the first year.

At the beginning of the second year of growth (the first winter), you should select three well-spaced branches on each tree, and remove the rest. Leave branches that point in different directions, spacing them 6 to 8 inches above each other. Don't

AN APPLE A DAY...

Water Sprout

Rootstock Sucker

prune the central leader. Trees that are to be grown as natural bushes need no further pruning except occasional thinning.

If you want to maximize your output, however, then you'll need to follow up. The second winter, shorten each branch by one-third, remove any shoots that are growing at narrow angles, and eliminate all water sprouts and suckers. Then cut back the central leader so that it's about 2-1/2 feet above the crotch of the uppermost side branch.

TOO MANY FRUITS SPOIL THE TREE!

You must thin out excess fruits on your dwarf trees, or you're asking for trouble! If the fruit is not thinned, dwarfs—who are just as eager to show off as their big brothers are—may set more fruit than they can carry and develop to good size and quality. If the trees bear excess fruit, they may not bloom the next year, *so you must restrain their exuberance!*

More than one fruit for each 6 to 8 inches of branch is usually too much. Thin the fruits within 20 days after the trees start to bloom.

UP AGAINST THE WALL, SUCKER!

An espaliered tree is trained so that both the trunk and branches lie in one plane. You can grow these trees against a wall or fence, in an open garden, or alongside a pathway. The best trees nowadays for this type of training are apples, pears, and figs.

AN APPLE A DAY...

Preparing a Fence Row

First, make sure there are no underground tiles, pipes, or electrical wires that will interfere with proper root growth. Then dig a 2 x 2 ft. trench, and take out all of the soil. Fill the bottom 3 inches with a generous quantity of bone meal or any other mild, slow-release garden food.

Mix in 25 pounds of peat moss and 25 pounds of compost, leaves, or leaf-mold for every 50 feet of "fence row." When these materials are thoroughly mixed together, shovel them back into the trench, and cover the top two inches with gypsum. Then walk away, and allow it to set during the winter.

Although they look very fancy, espaliered trees are not at all difficult to grow. Grandma Putt and Roy States were particularly proud of the espaliered apple trees Roy had growing out back of his garage. Because of their size, they are easy to reach for pruning, spraying, and harvesting. Best of all, under a watchful eye and skillful management, they will produce the highest quality fruit.

Spring planting is best, but you can plant container or balled-and-burlap trees for your living fence in the fall where winters begin early and are severe (temperatures should get down to at least 10°F). If winter in your area has alternate thaws and freezes, don't plant these trees in the fall, or they will get off to a bad start. A better way to do it is to locate your "fence-row" in the fall, and prepare the soil as one of your gardening projects.

Espalier designs range from simple four-arm designs used in grape trellising to a more complicated series of "U," "vegetable," or diamond shapes. If you are buying your trees by mail, send a copy of your design and a note along with your order. That way, the nurseryperson filling it can select trees with the proper limb placement to make your design work. If you can, and if there's a good nursery in your area,

AN APPLE A DAY...

it may be best to go and pick out your trees yourself.

If you have never grown espaliered trees, try to find a nursery which has trees that have already been shaped and formed. Remember also that espaliered fruit trees should always be on a dwarfing rootstock.

Triple U-Form Espalier

Support Your Local...

These trees *must* have support on a trellis or wall. The branches should be evenly spaced and securely fastened, but not fastened too closely to the bricks or wood. In an open garden, a trellis works great. A temporary support may have to be provided for the little tree, but you'll save a lot of time and trouble by erecting a sturdy, permanent trellis in the first place.

It's easy to train your trees. First, select only springy, healthy branches for training. Tie them to a secure and sturdy support with pieces of old nylon panty hose for at least two years. Never make such sharp bends in the branch so that the wood cracks or tears. If the bark does wrinkle up, bind it with a cloth bandage, and paint the area liberally with tree wound dressing.

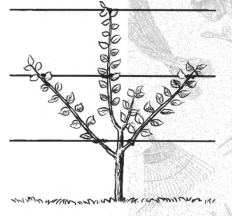

At Planting

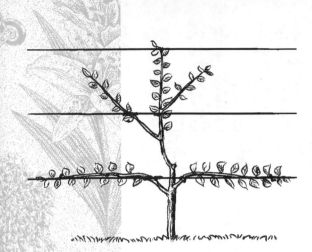

The Second Winter

PROPER PRUNING

As soon as the leaves fall, it's time to prune your espaliered trees. Each side or lateral shoot that has developed along the horizontal branches should be cut back to within two or three buds of the base. The leading shoot at the end of each branch should be tipped lightly if it's of moderate growth.

A very long leader shoot should be shortened by about a third of its length. The spurs along the main branches as a result of this pruning should be kept 6 inches from each other. If they become long and many branched, they should be cut back sharply, leaving at most four fruit buds on each one. As the trees grow older, pay special attention to shortening and regulating the old, gnarled spurs, or you'll end up with weak blossoms and a poor fruit crop.

Espaliered trees should also be pruned in summer. Around about July, each lateral or side shoot should be pinched back to within six leaves of the trunk. If the secondary growth follows this pruning, pinch it off as soon as it appears.

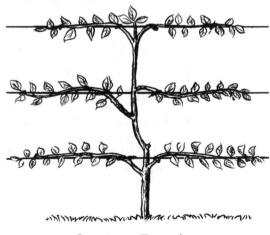

Summer Pruning

Root pruning is sometimes necessary with young trees if they grow too vigorously. This will help to check growth and encourage fruiting. To do this,

AN APPLE A DAY...

lift them up in October, shorten the coarse roots, and replant the tree in the same spot. It may not be practical to root prune older trees. If that's the case, then dig a trench around the tree, and use a flat backed spade to cut back the thick roots in the fall.

TAKE IT ALL OFF!

Don't feed your espaliered fruit trees in the first year! Transplanted trees grow entirely on water the first year in their new surroundings. In the years ahead, though, they'll enjoy all of that rich, fertile soil that you prepared in the planting area.

The first time the trees bear fruit, it's probably a good idea to pick all of it off because its weight may destroy all of your training efforts. That's right—**TAKE IT ALL OFF, BABY!** Cut off all suckers unless you need a particularly healthy sucker to replace a trained limb that has been damaged. Tie the sucker alongside the damaged limb until it begins to take shape, then cut the old unwanted limb off.

RUB-A-DUB-DUB... FRUIT TREES IN A TUB!

For most folks, this is the only way you'll home-grow citrus fruit like oranges, lemons, and limes. Although Grandma Putt didn't have any container-grown fruit trees, I've since learned that they can be loads of fun, and will thrill you every now and again with a baby-bumper harvest!

The best tubs to use for these trees are wooden, and the best wooden tubs are made of cedar, cypress, oak, and

Citrus trees will grow well in tubs provided they have good, rich soil. To get yours off to the right start, pass this mixture, through a half-inch screen before using it.

Super Citrus Potting Soil Mixture

Here's how to make a power-packed, super citrus soil mix:

1 part sand,
1 part leaf mold,
2 parts garden loam,
1 part cow manure, and
1 tbsp. of bone meal

per quart of the mixture.

redwood. With good drainage, you can reasonably expect a tub to last for ten years or more.

Be sure to place plenty of drainage material in the bottom of the tub before putting in the soil. The soil should be enriched with good humus material that is loose, porous, and well-balanced in plant nutrients. If you have any doubts about it, have this soil tested just as you would for an outdoor garden.

CARE AND FEEDING

Remember that fruit trees, like other potted plants, cannot reach out with their roots, so you must bring what they need to them. Manure tea, compost-water tea, and diluted fish fertilizer are all good to feed them. Used sparingly and periodically, they will keep the plants healthy and stimulate growth.

Next to soil, the other important factor is light. As I've repeatedly mentioned, fruiting plants need all of the light they can get. You will get some fruit in a fairly sunny location, but fruit trees will bear far more heavily in full sun.

Temperature is also important, and the best growing climate ranges from 65 to 75°F, with cooler temperatures at night—down to about 55 to 60°F. Trees, like other plants,

AN APPLE A DAY...

need to rest at night. This helps them to mature the growth they've made during the day.

A final reminder—water with care! No house plant should be allowed to suffer from lack of moisture, but overwatering can be just as bad as underwatering. Many a house plant has been killed with kindness.

When you water, water deeply, and then let the plant remain dry for a while until more water becomes necessary. Giving the trees a soap-and-water bath occasionally will keep the leaves clean and free from dust, and will also discourage insects. Try to do this in the morning, so that the leaves will dry out before nightfall. And always allow the foliage to dry off before placing the plants in direct sunlight.

House Plant Treat Tonic

Grandma Putt used to lightly mist spray her house plants with this tonic as a special treat. I've found that it works just as well for potted trees.

1 tbsp. of liquid soap,
1 tbsp. of Epsom salts, and
1/4 cup of tea

in 1 quart of warm water.

MOVIN' ON UP!

If you're going to grow dwarf trees in containers, you must keep increasing the size of the container every two years or so to give the roots room to spread out. In four years time, your tree should be in its permanent home. For dwarf trees, the final tub size can be limited to 2 x 2 feet. You can keep your tree in this size tub if you prune it severely to a height of no more than 4 feet.

When it becomes necessary to repot tub-grown plants, add generous amounts of organic material to the soil. As with other plants, you can sometimes delay repotting by removing the top layers of soil, and replacing them with new material, causing little disturbance to the roots below.

It's also important to trim the roots back whenever you repot. The final root ball should fit comfortably in the 2' x 2' tub. Place the tub on a platform with castors so that it can be wheeled indoors whenever chilly weather or frost threatens.

All-Purpose Bug Repellent Tonic

To make this tonic, mix:
1 cup of dish soap,
1 cup of antiseptic mouthwash, and
1 cup of chewing tobacco juice
per 20 gallons of warm water, and apply it to the point of run-off.

A BLIGHT PROSPECT

Blight is a common and destructive bacterial disease of apples, pears, and other ornamental fruit trees.

Blight usually appears first when fruit trees are in bloom, and stays active until rapid spring growth stops (about a month later). Don't prune or fertilize your fruit trees too heavily during this time because this may stimulate new growth, which is extremely susceptible to blight.

To control blight, inspect your trees in late summer, and cut out all blighted twigs. Make cuts at least 8 to 12 inches below the diseased part of the twig. Cut out the blighted tissue in the large limbs and trunk, taking the cuts well into healthy tissue.

To prevent infection in tree parts that you have pruned, treat wounds larger than 2 inches in diameter with tree wound dressing. After making each cut, dip your pruning tools in diluted household bleach (one cup of bleach to 9 cups of water). Since this solution corrodes metals, wash your tools at the end of each day's pruning with rubbing alcohol. Then dry and oil them to prevent rusting.

AN APPLE A DAY…

7

Nuts to You!

For some mysterious, yet wonderful reason, the least ecology-minded real-estate developer can usually be counted on to *not* cut down a stand of nut trees. These guys, who normally bulldoze everything in sight to squeeze out that last available square foot on a piece of property, seem to know that nut trees make land more valuable. And the average homeowner who buys a homestead that has a few nut trees on it seems to have some subconscious understanding that "nuts are nice." Of course, as Grandma Putt observed a long time ago, people have been eating nuts as long as the squirrels have!

All this is my way of suggesting that you should treasure the nut trees you find growing on your property. If you don't have any, well then, plant some so that you and your family can enjoy some good crackin', easy pickin', and tasty eatin' nuts! I can still remember those early fall days around Grandma Putt's place when we did just that. I tell you, nothing beats the taste of a fresh-baked pecan pie!

Grandma Putt had several large nut trees on her property, and I learned a thing or two about the care and feeding of these gentle giants under her watchful eye. She knew that no self-respecting homesteader could do without these taste-temptin' treats. Here's what she taught me to do:

A LITTLE ELBOW ROOM, PLEASE!

First and foremost, don't think that you'll be able to tuck a nut tree into some out-of-the-way corner of your home landscape. These babies grow big…very big! You'll want to consider these majestic giants as shade trees or large ornamentals on your property. The best example is the Black Walnut, which when mature, will scrape the sky at about 150 feet, with huge limbs that stretch outward and upward to 50 feet. So space is the single most important consideration whenever you're thinking of adding these beauties to your outdoor green scene.

Like fruit trees, these stalwart warriors of the tree world like well-drained soil on a sloping location. Their principle requirement is no competition from weeds, so you must eliminate them by cultivating or mulching. If the soil in which nut trees are to be planted is not fertile, work some compost into it around the tree *after* it has been planted.

Nut trees are too vigorous and grow too large to be grown in the same orchard with fruit trees—they will overpower their gentler brothers, and soon take up all the space! Also, the feeder roots of the two varieties of trees should not have to compete with one another. So grow them in separate places, or as specimen trees in your yard. Nut trees are normally well-shaped, and with just a little pruning assistance, they will look good almost anywhere!

SPRING INTO PLANTING!

Even though trees in general can be planted almost any time of the year, Grandma Putt preferred planting hers in either spring or fall. Her reason? Trees planted in spring have several months to get themselves settled into their new home before winter sets in. Fall is also good because the soil is usually soft and moist, which makes digging easier, and the weather is cool and comfortable for both you and the tree. Also, the roots will have enough time to make <u>some</u> progress before winter, which gives fall-planted trees a head start over those planted in spring.

Transplanting's A No-No!

Many nut trees have deep tap-roots, which make them rather difficult to transplant. I learned this the hard way at Grandma Putt's, when I inadvertently killed one of her young walnut trees. So, once you've found a suitable home for your nut tree, make sure you'll both be happy with it —*forever!*

MAKE 'EM HAPPY

Home Sweet Home

To your trees, soil is their home; if they're not comfortable in it, they'll *never* be happy!

So before you plant anything, find out if your soil is suitable for the type of tree you're going to plant.

Most nut trees do best in a slightly acidic soil that has a pH between 6 and 7. To determine the acidity of your soil, test it using Grandma Putt's methods I described in Chapter 1.

If the soil test results show that the pH is unsuitable for the trees you want to grow, raise the pH by adding limestone, or lower it by adding ground sulfur. Apply either material over a wide area to accommodate spreading roots, and work it into the soil to a depth of 18" or more.

Your soil may not be perfect—or even very good. It may have too much clay or too much sand. Remember—trees can literally drown in clay soils! Sandy soils, on the other hand, are often too dry because they drain so quickly. Trees planted in sandy soils can die of thirst. You can solve either of these problems by adding liberal amounts of organic matter to the soil. For nut trees, work this material into the soil over a wide area to a depth of 18" or more.

ROOM TO ROAM!

Probably the best advice I ever got from Grandma Putt, which you may have heard me say before, is that whenever you're planting a tree, you need to dig a $10.00 hole for a $5.00 tree. There is nothing worse for a young tree that's trying to establish itself than being crammed into a tight-fitting hole. Grandma Putt used to ask me, "How would you like it if a shoe salesman crammed your foot into a shoe that was two sizes too small? Not a pleasant experience, eh?"

Grandma Putt's Words of Wisdom:

"The planting hole should be twice as wide as the root ball is tall."

Well, the same is true for your nut trees, and the situation will get only worse when the tree starts to grow! The roots will have a hard time spreading out into the packed soil around the planting hole, and eventually, the tree may just give up and die!

To prevent this from happening, Grandma Putt had me dig my planting hole big enough so that the tree roots had plenty of room to roam. Once the hole was dug, she had me spread a layer of organic material in the bottom, and then work some of her special **Nut Tree Booster Mix** into the hole. I tamped the material down, and made sure the tree was sitting at the same depth as it was in the nursery. If it wasn't, then I adjusted the amount of the organic material in the hole.

THAT'S A WRAP!

Once we moved our nut trees into their new home, Grandma said that it was very important to protect them from the elements until they become firmly established members of your family. Young trees have a very delicate complexion, so it's up to you to keep them from getting sunburned! No, you don't have to go out and apply suntan lotion to the bark every day; just give your trees a "jacket" by wrapping the trunks from their "toes all the way up to their elbows" with burlap, cheesecloth, or tree wrap. The wrap should stay on the tree for 2 years or so to give the bark time to toughen up.

Wind is another problem that you need to be concerned about, so we always staked our trees to keep them standing straight and tall. On opposite sides of the trunk, we'd drive two long stakes about 2' into the ground, making sure that the stakes did not pierce the rootball. We used heavy-gauge wire, threading it through a short piece of old garden hose. Then we'd loop the wire around the tree, placing the garden hose around the trunk to keep the bark from being cut or bruised by the wire. Finally we'd attach the ends of the wire to the stakes, and then repeat the process on the opposite stake.

We usually left the stakes on for about 2 years—about the same length of time as the tree wrap. By this time, the trees will have planted their feet firmly in their new home, and should be able to withstand whatever Mother Nature throws at them on their own.

From the Garden Shed

In addition to a suit of armor, here are several other things Grandma Putt did to protect her nut trees from varmints:

✔ Put **human hair** in **cheesecloth "bags,"** and hang them on the lower branches.

✔ "Paint" a mix of pureed **garlic, hot peppers, and ammonia** on the trunks.

✔ Liberally apply **tobacco dust** or **Tabasco Sauce®** around the base of the trees.

A SUIT OF *ARMOR?*

Sun, wind, and the elements aren't the only problems that young trees face— varmints like rabbits and mice can seriously damage, or even kill young trees by gnawing their tender bark. And then there are the two-legged varmints, who can inflict a lot of damage with a lawn mower in high gear! *(Honestly, I didn't do it!)* Tree wrap will protect your trees from lawn mowers and rodents during its first 2 years, but what then? Grandma Putt used to make her nut trees a suit of armor.

To make the "suit," we cut a length of 2' wide hardware cloth, large enough to form a cylinder that would stand about 2" away from the tree trunk on all sides. We wrapped the cloth around the trees, and wired the ends together. If there was mulch around the tree, we pushed the cloth down into it. If the tree was not mulched, we left the "armor" loose so we could easily raise or lower it, depending on the weather.

THE FIRST YEAR

During your nut trees' first year in their new home, you must give them enough water until they establish themselves. During the growing season, water them once a week, unless there's enough rainfall. Always take the time to give your trees a long, thirst-quenching drink; don't just sprinkle the soil surface!

Other than an occasional watering, nut trees don't require much in the way of care. Just follow Grandma Putt's Nutty Checklist, and talk to them every now and again. Tell them what splendid progress they're making, and introduce them to the other plants in your yard. Soon, they'll feel right at home!

> ## Grandma Putt's Nutty Checklist:
> ✔ Water occasionally
> ✔ Mulch well to retain moisture in the soil
> ✔ Prune to a central leader
> ✔ Do *not* feed
> ✔ Snap off all suckers

CHOW TIME!

Even back in Grandma Putt's day, there was a great deal of discussion about when and how, not to mention whether, you should even feed nut trees. Well, Grandma didn't see much sense in not feeding her trees, particularly when she expected them to produce those delicious nuts.

WHEN TO FEED?

In Grandma Putt's mind, early spring was the only time to feed a nut tree! In the first place, they wake up ravenously hungry after their long winter naps. Second, if you give a tree a good, balanced dry meal in early spring, the nutrients will be available to it throughout the growing season. By early fall, the tree will have used up most, if not all, of the nutrients from its spring meal.

But this doesn't mean that you should fertilize again! At this point, another dose of nitrogen would encourage the tree to keep on growing, regardless of the season. The new growth wouldn't have a chance to fully develop before winter sets in, and as a result, it would be very susceptible to winter damage.

To supplement this, Grandma Putt believed in giving her trees a special tonic (see page 222) during the growing season. She started in mid-spring, so she had time to give her trees several feedings before late-summer. Then, about the middle of August, she stopped feeding them altogether. I know this sounds cruel, but she really had her trees' best interests at heart!

DRILL 'EM & FILL 'EM!

This old-time, tried-n-true method of tree feeding has been used by farmers for many years in their orchards. It involves drilling or punching holes in the soil, and filling them with a special mix of dry fertilizer, which dissolves very slowly over a long period of time. This was basically a once-a-year chore around Grandma Putt's place, and she said that an afternoon of hard work once a year wasn't so bad after all!

We used to do this type of feeding on an early spring day, when the weather was perfect for gardening. The soil was usually moist, which made drilling the holes easier, and helped keep the fertilizer from burning the roots. If we had a particularly dry spring that year, Grandma would water the ground thoroughly a few days beforehand. I learned a very messy lesson one spring—if you wait until feeding day to water, the soil will be too wet to work!

Now, Grandma Putt didn't just go out and start drilling holes in the ground willy-nilly. No siree, she was *organized!* First thing, she prepared a batch of her **Super Dry Food Mix**. After weighing and mixing the food, she marked off the root feeding zone of the trees; all of the feeding holes were in this area.

If you've never root-fed a tree before, you might want to mark the spots where the holes should be. Plan on making at least 10 holes for every inch of trunk diameter, and space the holes approximately every 2 feet or so.

Grandma Putt didn't want the grass in the feeding zone to look as

From the Garden Shed

To feed her <u>mature</u> nut trees, Grandma Putt first made up a batch of her Super Dry Food Mix, mixing and weighing it according to what she needed.

Super Dry Food Mix

Grandma Putt's recipe for her fabulous Super Dry Food Mix was:

1 part bone meal,
1 part gypsum,
1/2 part Epsom salts,
1 part garden soil, and
2 parts All-Purpose (dry) Garden Food,

all tossed together in an old wheelbarrow, and mixed thoroughly.

To determine the proper amount to apply, you need to measure the diameter of each of your tree trunks. If the diameter is less than 6", use 1 lb. of Food Mix for each inch of diameter. So, if the diameter of the trunk is 3", you'll need 3 lbs. of Food Mix. For trees with a diameter greater than 6", use 2 lbs. of Food Mix per inch of trunk diameter.

if it had the chicken pox, so she had me remove small patches of grass with a trowel before she made a feeding hole. Then she would drive a crowbar or soil auger into the ground. She poured about a cup of the food mix into it. When I did it, she was quite clear—*I'd better not spill any of it on the lawn*, or we'd end up with tall patches of bright-green grass. Finally, we put the patches of grass back in place, and stepped on them to establish good contact between the roots and soil.

We repeated this process until we covered the entire feeding area evenly. Then we stood back, and wished the tree "bon appetit!"

Timely Tree Tonic

Grandma Putt sprayed her super Tree Tonic on all of her trees several times during the growing season:

1 bottle of beer,
1 cup of ammonia,
1/2 cup of tea, and
1/2 cup of Fels-Naptha Soap Solution,

mixed in 20 gallons of water in a sprayer.

LIGHT FEEDING

As I mentioned, Grandma Putt gave her trees a special tonic several times during the growing season. This method is now called foliar feeding, and it involves spraying a liquid solution on the leaves to the point of run-off. It produces the fastest and most dramatic results because the leaves have almost immediate access to the nutrients.

Grandma Putt didn't recommend this type of feeding exclusively; although it was the easiest way to feed her trees, the results were not long lasting. So she gave her trees an occasional beauty treatment with her **Timely Tree Tonic**—a week or so before a special barbecue or family outing, and to supplement her once-a-year root feeding.

NUTS TO YOU!

THE PAUSE THAT REFRESHES...

Grandma Putt's words of wisdom are especially applicable to watering trees. She said that whenever you water a tree, do a good, thorough job, or don't do it at all! The reason for this is because the water must be allowed to soak deep into the ground, so that it is accessible to the feeder roots. If you haphazardly sprinkle the ground for a few minutes, the water will only soak down a few inches. Repeated shallow waterings will cause the trees to develop shallow root systems, which will do a poor job of supplying them with moisture and nutrients.

Grandma Putt's Words of Wisdom:

"If a job's worth doing, it's a job worth doing well."

On the other hand, overwatering can eventually cause tree roots to drown and rot. Nowadays, folks with the best of intentions often accidently overwater their trees, especially if they have an automatic sprinkler system. So, if you water your lawn regularly, check the drainage around your trees. If they're standing with their feet in puddles of water, *you'd better cut back on your watering!*

THE BACKYARD NUT FARM

Nut trees generally don't need a lot of care, except when they start to bear—then you've got to pick up all the nuts, fallen debris, and leaves you find under the tree. Store the nuts, and burn or dispose of the leaves and debris.

In most cases, it'll take several years before your nut crops amount to much of anything. This is just Mother Nature's way of getting you accustomed to her pace and schedule, but it's no reason for you not to grow, *and go* nuts!

When it comes to selecting nut trees, you have a wide variety of native nuts and foreign imports to choose from. All will add beauty and bounty to your outdoor green scene. Here's a brief tour around the backyard nut farm.

Home Grown
Acorns
Beechnuts
Black Walnuts
Butternuts
Coconuts
Hazelnuts
Macadamias
Pignut Hickories
Shellbark Hickories
Peanuts
Pecans
Pine nuts

Foreign Imports
Almonds
Carpathian Walnuts
Cashews
Chinese Chestnuts
English Walnuts
Filberts
Ginkgos
Heartnuts
Litchis (leechee)
Pistachios

BUTTERNUTS AND WALNUTS

Both of these nuts are members of the walnut family, but the butternut is hardier than the native black walnut. Butternuts grow 60 to 90 feet tall, and have a more northerly range, growing from New Brunswick to Arkansas. It's a good choice for the northern home garden. The oblong nuts are oily, but have a rich, delicate flavor, and many folks prefer it to the stronger-flavored Black Walnut.

Black Walnut trees are very valuable for their wood as well as their nuts. They grow well over the eastern half of the United States, and will grow as tall as, or taller than, the English type, sometimes reaching 100 feet or more in the rich soil of the Mississippi basin.

If you're thinking about growing black walnuts, they can be easily raised from seed—simply layer the seeds in moist sand during the winter months to prevent them from drying out, then sow them in the spring in well-drained, light loamy soil. Sow the seeds in their permanent home because transplanted trees sometimes suffer root injury which can seriously retard its growth and production.

The Persian Walnut, commonly known as the English Walnut, is mostly grown along the Pacific Coast, but can be grown over a wider area. Certain varieties are very hardy, and can survive sub-zero temperatures. The problem is that late spring frosts can injure nut production.

CHESTNUTS

American Chestnut trees were magnificent, with enormous, low-spreading limbs, and gray-brown bark. This great native tree was once the living centerpiece of many American town squares. In the early 1900s, however, it was wiped out by a fungal blight.

Until the appearance of a killing blight, the American Chestnut was one of the most valuable trees in the world. If you ever saw one of these magnificent trees, or know where a survivor still stands, savor the memory, and count it as one of our lost treasures.

As a substitute, you can now plant the smaller, disease-resistant Chinese Chestnut. These trees can grow to be

Walnut Harvesting Tips

Black walnuts give off a sticky, black juice that can be quite hard to remove from your hands, skin, and clothing. So to keep it clean, spread cheap, plastic dropcloths on the ground around the trees before you start beating the branches. When you're done, simply gather up the dropcloths (and the crop) without getting your hands (or clothes) dirty!

To remove the husks, Grandpa Putt used to drive over the nuts on the driveway with his '37 Chevy. Grandma and I used to shovel the nuts under the wheels to make the job go faster. Then we'd wash and let them dry for several weeks before storing them away.

Those were the days...

One late autumn evening, the fire was crackling in the fireplace, and we were all gathered around it "cracking" and "picking" away. We were having a grand old time when Grandma Putt said the noise of the burning logs reminded her of when she was a girl, and Grandpa Putt was courting her. She said no wood spit and crackled like chestnut. Folks used to say the burning wood crackled and spit so much because it was complaining about roasting its nuts. I could understand that.

about 60 feet tall, and will generally bear a year or two after planting. They're not recommended for those areas where the temperature falls below 15°F in the winter, but may be safely planted elsewhere.

Chestnuts are best propagated by budding or grafting, although you can plant seeds (nuts), which should be sown outdoors in the fall as soon as they are ripe. Set them in beds, an inch or so deep, and cover with a soil/compost mix. They should sprout the following spring.

FILBERTS OR HAZELNUTS

This is one of the best nut growing plants, since they will grow on any good, well-drained soil. A northern facing slope, the north side of a building, or any other site protected from the cold, drying winds is best. They may be grown either as trees or bushes, but trees are most productive.

As a large shrub, a filbert will grow to a height of 12 to 15 feet. These trees are hardy wherever peaches can be grown, but two different varieties are needed for pollination. Pruning should be less severe than for peaches to prevent the possibility of winter injury.

NUTS TO YOU!

HICKORIES

Hickories are stately, fast-growing trees that grow wild in eastern North America and Mexico. The Shagbark Hickory can grow to be 100 feet tall or more, so plan on giving this big fellow <u>LOTS</u> of elbow room. The large leaves turn yellow in autumn before they fall, and the gray bark of the trees is very attractive, even in winter. They are excellent for the backyard nut farm, providing shade that is not too dense in summer, and allowing the winter sun to shed its light and warmth upon your home.

Several different kinds of hickory nuts are edible, but the pecan is by far and away the most well-known and popular.

Pecans

This type of hickory grows naturally from Indiana to Mexico. They thrive best in rich, deep, well-drained soil that contains a fair amount of organic matter, and has a pH between 5.5 to 6.0.

Many varieties of pecans are to some degree self-sterile, so it's best to plant more than one variety; make sure the flowers of the various kinds mature at the same time. Wild pecan trees usually bear smaller nuts, which are tasty and flavorful. Most people, however, prefer the larger, named species.

When pecans are grown in an orchard, it is best to plant them 60 to 70 feet apart. If you live in the South, plan on giving them even more room because they can grow to be upwards of 150 feet tall or more.

"Old Hickory"

Hickory trees have had a long-standing tradition in the history of our country. Andrew Jackson, known for his toughness, was nicknamed "Old Hickory." Abe Lincoln split many a hickory rail, which were very abundant on the Indiana frontier. And hickory trees literally united the country— many of the railroad ties that were used in the nineteenth century were made from hickory trees.

NUTS TO YOU! 227

NUT-PEAS?

I'd be remiss if I didn't at least mention America's number one favorite nut that's not really a nut at all! Peanuts are actually leguminous vegetables that should more properly be called "nut-peas." But who in the world would want a nut-pea butter and jelly sandwich? Not me!

Peanuts grow well in the southern part of the country, from the Atlantic as far west as Texas. But by-far-and-away, they do best in the Southeast. A "friend" of mine, and I use that term loosely, once fed me some green, Georgia boiled peanuts. I quickly found out how the rebels separated the good-ol'-boys from the carpetbaggers— talk about "the Green-Apple Quick-Step"— those green peanuts were a real pace-setter!

Peanuts are classified as "bunchers" or "runners." You can plant any shelled, unroasted kind you get at a health-food store. Grow them in a vegetable garden like you would peas or bush beans.

Peanuts take about 3-1/2 months to mature, but specific varieties may take longer. Grandma Putt's advice about growing peanuts? Grow them alongside of popcorn, so you could have a real ball game in the fall!

Peanut Particulars

To do well, peanuts need the following care and consideration:

✔ Well-drained soil.

✔ Very warm days and warm nights.

✔ Plant after the soil warms up or the threat of frost is past.

✔ Remove the seeds from the shells, leaving the skins intact.

✔ Space plants 1 ft. apart, and hill up soil around the plants when they're 1 ft. tall.

✔ Pull up the plants to harvest the nuts.

✔ Harvest the nuts when the shells are hard, and the skins are pinkish-red.

TOP TEN NUT TREES

Name	Recommended Varieties	Size and Hardiness	Description and Culture
Almond	Mission, Nonpareil, Peerless	Size of peach trees; grown into Ontario	Can't stand heavy, wet soil; likes deep mulch. Space 20 feet apart. Barnyard manure is the best fertilizer. Begins to bear in 3 to 4 years.
Black Walnut	Cornell, Snyder, Stambaugh, Thomas, Wiard	To 100 feet and more in New England and Minnesota	Stately, splendid lawn tree. Grafted varieties bear in 5 years. Heaviest bearer of all nut trees. Leaves and hulls make very rich fertilizer. Do not plant near apple trees, azaleas, rhododendrons—has damaging effect on them.
Butternut	Buckley, Craxezy, Sherwood, Weschcke	To 70 feet or so into Canada	Lofty, spreading lawn tree. Nuts are large, oily, and delectable; often used in maple sugar candy. Sometimes begins to bear in 4 years. Craxezy is thin-shelled variety.
Chinese Chestnut	Hemming, Hobson, Meiling, Nanking	Size of apple trees. To New England and Great Lakes	Decorative lawn tree that is fast grower, but needs plenty of water. Often bears only 3 years after transplanting. Leave unpruned to make bushy. Mulch heavily.
English Walnut	Colby, McKinster, Metcalfe	To 50 feet or more; grown in Canada	Beautiful ornamental; fast grower, heavy producer. Plant only on deep, rich soil, 60 feet apart. Begins to bear in about 6 years.
Filbert	Barcelona, Bixby, Buchanan, Italian Red, Long, Rush, Winkler	10 to 30 feet, or as a bushy shrub. To upper New England	One of the best nut-bearing plants for home gardeners. Needs good, rich soil; don't fertilize the first year. Trim to 3 stems for lawn tree; let suckers grow for bush. Begins to bear in 5 years.
Heartnut	Bates, Gellatly, Faust, Fodermaier, Marvel, Walters, Wright,	Size of apple tree. To lower Canada	Fine ornamental, and fast grower—often reaches height of 6 feet in 1 year. Large, spreading foliage. Richly-flavored nuts, 10 or more to cluster; meats crack out easily. May bear 3 years after transplanting.
Hickory	Bauer, Fairbanks, Stratford, Wilcox	Up to 120 feet. To Ontario	Majestic shade tree, but may be 15 years old before crop is produced. Kernels difficult to extract, but big with wonderful flavor. Will stand even in clay soil if rich.
Pecan	Busseron, Duvall, Greenriver	50 to 120 feet. Some varieties to Ontario	Fine lawn tree with plump, juicy nuts. Mature trees yield up to 600 pounds of nuts a year. Duvall and Sweeney are extra-thin-shelled nuts.
Pistachio	Damgham, Kerman, Lassen	12 to 60 feet. Southern Florida and the West	Resembles spreading apple tree. Prefers sandy, deep loam; very drought-resistant. Plant 1 male tree to 12 females. Produces at 4 or 5 years; fruits heavily one year, little the next.

JUST *WILD* ABOUT NUTS!

Ever since Americans left their farms and rural towns to create what is now known as urban sprawl, lots and lots of nuts have gone ungathered. In my book, that's a crime against our natural godmothers, Mother Earth and Mother Nature.

Going nutting was another one of those glorious adventures for me when I lived at Grandma Putt's. Fancy nut gatherers would take a picnic basket, but boys like me traveled relatively unencumbered, with three or four old gunnysacks slung over our shoulders.

It's best to locate your Black Walnut, Butternut, and Shagbark (shell bark) Hickory trees well in advance, before you actually go nutting. That way, you won't waste any time when the nuts are ready to go, unless you and your gal have other things on your minds like Grandpa and Grandma Putt.

Black Walnuts are the easiest to spot because they lose their leaves before any other tree in the woods. Butternuts grow wild all over the North, and silhouetted against an autumn sky, they stand out like a big letter Y.

Shagbark Hickories are easily recognizable because their bark curls up in two-foot gray patches to make an obstacle course for over-eager squirrels trying to harvest the tree's tasty nuts. This tree is a loner, but a standout! The nuts stay on the tree well into winter, so there's no hurry to harvest them.

Those were the days...

Grandma Putt told me when she was a young lady, one of the most anticipated fall activities was for a young man to take his "gal" chestnutting. Grandma said sometimes she and Grandpa would spend the greater part of the day strolling arm in arm all over the woods and meadows, looking for a likely tree. Since chestnut trees were enormous, and rather easy to spot, they must have been concentrating on something other than tree-hunting! Hmmm, I wonder what it was?

NUTS TO YOU!

SNAP, CRACKLE, AND POP THEM...
INTO YOUR MOUTH!

Even today, I'm wild about nuts! Black walnuts are my favorite because they are the tastiest nuts around. To get the meat, we used to jam the shells with the heel of our shoe. Be careful when you take the nuts out of the husks because they will stain your hands brown. As I write this, I can almost smell them; their fragrance is one of the great American smells, and black walnut fudge is simply superb!

Butternuts are close relatives to black walnuts; in fact, they are often called white walnuts. The husks are sticky to the touch, so Grandma Putt sometimes pickled them without drying them.

After we de-husked them, we used to soak a bag of them in a bucket of warm water, then hang the bag outside on a clothesline to dry. (I wonder if anyone still has a clothesline? If not, then hang your bag on a nail somewhere.) This will make it easy to crack the thin shells without smashing the meat.

Another great-tasting nut is the beechnut, which is easy to pry out of their shells with your thumbnail. They are small-kerneled, but sweet to the taste. Good-bearing beechnut trees are becoming harder and harder to find. So if you have an extra handful to spare, send 'em my way!

Grandma Putt's Candied Walnuts

We'd go nuts whenever Grandma made a batch of her candied walnuts. Here's how she did it:

1 lb. of shelled walnuts,
3 egg whites (not beaten),
1 cup of sugar,
2 tsp. of cinnamon, and
1/4 tsp. of nutmeg

Combine all of the ingredients in a bowl, mixing with a spoon until the nuts are covered. Spread them evenly on a greased cookie sheet, and bake at 300°F for 30 minutes. They will harden when cool. Then enjoy!

Those were the days...

Grandma Putt kept her nuts stored up in the attic, where it was cool and dry during the winter. On wet, snowy days, when it wasn't fit for man nor beast to go outside and tramp about, I'd climb up there with one of Grandma's big clay mixing bowls, and fill it full of black walnuts, hickory nuts, hazelnuts, and butternuts that were spread out on the floor to dry.

Then I'd go down, and sit in the big leather chair by the side bay window to crack and pick nuts for hours, watching the snow fall and listening to the wind howl. Boy, I tell you, it didn't get any better than that!

STORING YOUR HOARD

Deer and blue jays eat nuts, but as most folks know, the real nut experts are squirrels. These playful, but pesky varmints know just how to store the nuts they can't eat right away. So take a page from their book, and store your nuts in a cool, dry place like the squirrels do (in the crotch of a protected tree limb, or in some sandy soil).

After you've done enough nutting, you'll soon discover that too much

moisture makes nuts lose their flavor or become rancid. Black walnuts, in particular, are not too good fresh-gathered, but taste superb after being stored away for a while! So, bon appétit!

NUTS TO YOU!

PUTTIN' BY AND STORIN' AWAY

During World War II, over 60 million Americans were involved in raising home-grown fruits and vegetables as part of the Victory Garden Program. Food was rationed, and many of the most common kitchen staples, which had been available year 'round before the war, were diverted to feed our Army, Navy, and those of our allies. As a result, it was necessary for folks to take up the age-old practices of their forefathers in order to store and preserve the foods they raised in their home gardens.

For Grandma Putt, this was nothing new. Storing food, canning, and preserving it were all just a part of the annual fall routine. These were things that people close to the earth, like her, had done for many years. She was just continuing the time-honored traditions that were handed down from mother to daughter, generation after generation.

Nowadays, these puttin' by methods are just pleasant memories for most folks my age, and the younger generation, well, to them, "cannin'" and "freezin'" might just as well be two new, very cool, hip-hop terms. Nevertheless, I spent many a pleasant summer/fall afternoon in Grandma's kitchen, helping her store away our bountiful harvest for the year. Here's how we would do it:

WASTE NO SPACE!

Back in the old days, all vegetables were stored in some way, shape, or form, whether it was in a basement, cellar, outbuilding, or storage pit. Grandma Putt and her neighbors used many of these areas to put their crops by.

BASEMENTS

Although a basement under a house with central heating can be used for ripening tomatoes and short-term storage of sweet potatoes, onions, pumpkins, and winter squashes, if you really want to get serious about it, you've got to have a separate room for long-term storage of most vegetables. Grandma Putt's neighbor, Roy States, built such a room onto his basement.

His room was located in the northeast corner of his basement. The inner walls and ceiling were insulated to prevent heat from entering or chilling the floor above the room.

The room's only window allowed outside air in through a cold air intake that had a ventilating flue extending to the floor. Another part of the window, near the ceiling, served as a warm air outlet. He covered it with a screen to keep mice out. He shaded the window and vent so the room was kept cool and dark for potato storage.

Green Thumb Tip

Speaking of basements, Grandma Putt used her basement window wells as handy winter/spring cold frames. In late fall, she covered the wells with clear plastic (so the light could get through), and sealed around the edges with masking tape. That way, she could water and care for her seedlings from inside the basement without losing any heat.

THE COLD CELLAR

Grandma Putt's cold cellar, as she called it, was divided into two rooms. The first room was really not under the house at all, but used one side of the foundation as a wall. This was where Grandma kept her potatoes, pumpkins, squash, cabbage-family members, and cold-packed jars of canned goods. Apples were stored here too—barrels and barrels of them! Their fragrance hung in the dark, cool air like perfume. Cabbages were wrapped in several thick layers of newspaper to prevent their "perfume" from escaping, and "flavoring" the apples.

Concrete walls and a dirt floor kept this part of the cold cellar fairly moist. It stayed cool here even in the summer, and going down to get a pickle was one of my favorite cooling-off tricks on a hot August afternoon. Grandma Putt insisted I keep the doors shut tight to keep out the hungry field mice!

The second part of the cold cellar was another storage room which was located entirely under her house. It had a concrete floor, two wooden walls, and was somewhat drier—

Those were the days...

One of the most vivid memories I have of Grandma's big old house is the cellar. There were two ways to get to it. The first, and least interesting, was through a kitchen door next to the pantry. This led down to the furnace, and the big old washing machine.

The best way to get into the cellar, however, was through a stairway located outside of the house that was covered by slanted double doors just like Auntie Em's in *The Wizard of Oz*. When the double doors were closed, it was fun to slide down the outside of them. The closed cellar stairway was also a good place to hide during our evening games of hide-and-seek.

but just as cool. Here, Grandma stored dried beans, peas, and onions. The onions were up off the floor where the air could get at them. On the other side of a connecting door, in the furnace room, were two big double bins for sweet potatoes. This vegetable, in particular, needs warm, dry air for proper long-term storage.

How-to Hint

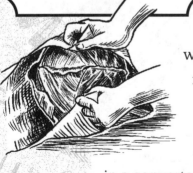

Grandma Putt said that storing cabbages is always a problem. Her solution was to store them in trenches. Grandma took off any bad outside leaves, wrapped the heads in newspaper, and placed them in the trench with the heads down. Then she covered them up with straw and chicken wire until they were ready to be eaten.

THE ROOT CELLAR

Grandma's root cellar, as the name implies, was where she kept her roots—beets, radishes, parsnips, carrots, rutabagas, and turnips. It really wasn't a cellar at all, but an old converted cistern. During the winter, the temperature in this area was just above freezing, and very, very moist.

If you don't happen to have a basement, you can use part of your garage for storing most crops. Celery and members of the carrot and turnip family can be stored outside, in the ground.

One good idea Grandma Putt had was to store several types of vegetables together (except those in the cabbage family). That way, when she opened a trench, she had all she needed without disturbing any of the other buried vegetables.

Cabbage was wrapped in newspaper, and celery was covered with straw, and stored outside in a converted sandbox or cold frame we kept. We kept the sand moist, and the sandbox was covered with leaves and boards. The flavor of the cabbage actually improved this way.

STORAGE CONDITIONS

Temperature's Tops

Grandma Putt knew that accurate temperature control is a must for long-term storage of vegetables. She used two thermometers—one placed in the coldest part of the storage area, and the other one set outdoors. Early in fall, she opened the window whenever the outside temperature was lower than the inside temperature, and closed it when the outside temperature was higher. When the weather got cold, only a small opening was needed.

For most vegetables, the ideal storage temperature is between 32-40°F. A lower temperature could result in injury, and vegetables stored at higher than 40°F could rot. Be careful your produce doesn't freeze during extremely cold weather.

Keep It Humid

I saw plenty of Grandma Putt's neighbors' stored vegetables quickly shrivel and lose quality; Grandma said that their cellars didn't have the proper moisture. A good storage area must have 90-95 percent relative humidity in order to maintain most vegetables. A simple humidity gauge is the best way to measure the relative humidity.

Wax Works!

In Grandma Putt's day, wax was used to improve vegetable storage because it reduced moisture loss, and thus, retarded shriveling. On some vegetables, waxing simply improved appearance.

This process was extremely difficult because the wax thickness is critical. Coatings that were too thin gave little, if any, protection against water loss; while a thick coat increased the risk of decay and breakdown. But don't fret, storing vegetables in perforated plastic bags today accomplishes the same thing with less effort.

Grandma's secret was to sprinkle the floor with water or cover it with wet straw. Nowadays, the easiest and most effective way to control moisture loss and prevent shrinkage is to put vegetables in polyethylene bags, or to line their storage boxes with polyethylene. Make several 1/4-inch holes in the sides of the bags and liners to permit ventilation. Three holes per pound of vegetables will give you enough high humidity.

When moisture collects on the inside of the bag, you'll know that the relative humidity is 95-100 percent, and you should punch a few more holes in the bag to reduce it slightly. (Grandma Putt didn't have Ziploc® bags, which are covered with hundreds of tiny holes that let the excess moisture escape.)

If you notice your stored vegetables shrinking and shriveling, you must raise the humidity *immediately*! Excessive spoilage or decay indicates the humidity is too high or that the vegetables have been stored too long.

Those were the days...

When the double doors of Grandma's cold cellar were opened, the root cellar was bright, fragrant, and very inviting. Grandma kept it very clean. She said it was foolish to store clean food in a dirty cellar. So she made sure it was *really, really clean!*

Cleaning the cellar was an annual spring chore. One year, Grandma gave me a large paint brush, several gallons of whitewash, and told me to go to it! I had to paint the entire area. Unfortunately, I wasn't as lucky as Tom Sawyer...no one happened by to rescue me!

Cleanliness Counts!

Whatever storage facility you decide to use, Grandma was very adamant—it must be kept clean, or your vegetables will rapidly deteriorate! You must watch vegetables carefully to avoid losing any to decay, growth, or excessive shriveling. Then remove decaying vegetables immediately to prevent the rot from spreading.

Then, at least once a year, remove everything (shelves, tables, etc) from your storeroom, clean them with a disinfectant, and let them air-dry in the sun. Thoroughly wash the walls, ceiling, and floor before putting anything back into storage. That way, you'll be sure that you haven't overlooked anything.

TEMPORARY PITS

One fall, when Grandma's garden had been particularly good that year, we ran out of storage space! We had potatoes coming out of our ears, and no place to put them!

So Grandma said that we were going to dig a pit, and let good old Mother Nature help us out that winter. After all, she got us into the fix we were in! The pits worked well for storing potatoes, root vegetables, and cabbage through most of the winter.

Grandma Putt's Words of Wisdom:

"If you've got potatoes coming out of your ears, then clean them—the potatoes, that is!"

We dug a hole 24-36 inches deep, and several feet in diameter in a sandy part of Grandma's yard where water run off was not going to be a problem. We also placed the pit where it would receive plenty of winter sunlight to prevent freezing of the vegetables.

We added a layer of straw to the bottom of the pit, and stacked the vegetables on the straw in a cone-shaped pile. Grandma said never to store fruits and vegetables in the same pit. We placed a thick layer of straw over the vegetables, and then added a good thick layer of soil on top of the entire pile.

We used an additional layer of straw and soil for storage through the winter. We packed the outer layer of soil with the back of a shovel to make sure the pit was waterproof. Then we finished by digging a shallow drainage ditch around the pit to allow water to drain away from the stored vegetables.

There was only one other consideration—ventilation. With small pits, ventilation can be provided by extending the straw layer to the top of the pile. Cover the opening with a piece of screen and a stone to prevent varmint damage. In late fall, when the soil starts to freeze, cover the vent with a layer of soil or a piece of board.

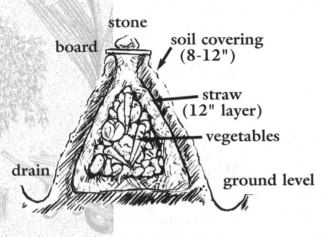

In large pits, place 2-3 boards or stakes up through the center to act as a flue. Cap the flue with two small pieces of board nailed together at right angles.

I remember that the pit was rather difficult to open in cold weather. Once it was opened, we had to remove all of the vegetables to prevent the remaining ones from freezing. So if you're going to try this method, make several small pits, each containing a mixture of vegetables. This makes it easy to open only one pit at a time to get a variety of vegetables.

TILE STORAGE

Another more permanent method Grandma Putt used to store her vegetables from time to time was in a buried drain tile. She stored root crops, potatoes, and other vegetables that require cool, moist storage in them.

The tile size varied, depending upon what was available at the time. She generally used ones that were about 30 inches wide by 3 feet long. Grandma said that clay tiles work best because they are more durable than wood, and conduct less heat than steel.

If you're going to try this, place the tile in a convenient, well-drained area, away from possible overflow water and downspouts.

Dig a hole just large enough in to let the tile fit snugly. The hole should be 6 inches deeper than the length of the tile. Place three or four bricks on end, flat side to the wall, for a base. This will leave some of the exposed soil below the tile to supply moisture to the vegetables. Lower the tile into the hole, and mound the soil up to the top edge of the tile. Add some coarse gravel or sand to the bottom for drainage.

Chill the ground around the tile by removing the lid in the evening, and replacing it every morning for a week. Then water the tile and drainage material in the bottom, and cover for several days to raise the humidity. The vegetables must be thoroughly cooled in a refrigerator or outside air before being packed for storage. Adding warm vegetables to the tile will only raise the temperature in the storage area.

Place the vegetables in bushel baskets, mesh bags, or other ventilated containers. Vegetables kept in containers will store better, and be easier to remove than if they are packed solid in the tile.

Cover the tile with a wire screen to prevent rodent damage and provide ventilation. Spread a thick layer of straw, chopped cornstalks, or other course mulch over the screen, and then cover the entire pile with a waterproof cover.

I remember we pulled vegetables out of the tiles all winter long, right up until the following spring! We opened the tile at any time, and picked out the vegetables we needed with a long handled hook made from an old coat hanger.

earth fill

tile

brick

drainage material

STORAGE TEMPERATURES, RELATIVE HUMIDITIES AND STORAGE LIFE FOR FRESH VEGETABLES

Vegetable	Temperature (°F)	Relative Humidity (%)	Length of Storage Period	How To Preserve
Asparagus	32-36	95	2-3 wk.	Freeze or can
Beans				
green or snap	40-45	90-95	7-10 days	Freeze or can
lima or broad	32	90	10-14 days	Freeze or can
Beets	32	90-95	1-3 mo.	Freeze, can, or pickle
Broccoli	32	90-95	10-14 days	Freeze or can
Brussels sprouts	32	90-95	3-5 wk.	Freeze or can
Cabbage	32	90-95	3-4 mo.	Sauerkraut
Carrots	32	90-95	4-5 mo.	Freeze, can, or pickle
Cauliflower	32	90-95	2-4 wk.	Freeze or can
Celery	32	90-95	2-3 mo.	
Chard, Swiss	32	90-95	7-14 days	Freeze or can
Cucumbers	45-50	90-95	10-14 days	Pickle
Eggplants	45-50	90	7 days	Can
Garlic	32	65-70	6-7 mo.	
Kohlrabi	32	90-95	1-3 mo.	Freeze
Leek, green	32	90-95	1-3 mo.	

Vegetable	Temperature (°F)	Relative Humidity (%)	Length of Storage Period	How To Preserve
Lettuce	32	95	2-3 wk.	
Melons				
muskmelon	32-35	85-90	15 days	Freeze
watermelon	40-50	80-85	2-3 wk.	Freeze
Okra	45-50	90-95	7-10 days	Freeze, can, or pickle
Onion				
green	32	90-95	3-5 days	
dry	32	65-70	1-8 mo.	
Parsnips	32	90-95	2-6 mo.	Freeze or can
Peas, green	32	90-95	1-3 wk.	Freeze or can
Pepper, sweet	45-50	90-95	2-3 wk.	Freeze
Potatoes	40-45	90	2-9 mo.	Can
Radishes	32	90-95	3-4 wk.	
Rhubarb	32	95	2-4 wk.	Freeze
Spinach	32	90-95	10-14 days	Freeze or can
Squash				
summer	32-50	90	5-14 days	Freeze or can
winter	50-55	50-75	2-6 mo.	Freeze or can
Sweet corn	32	90-95	4-8 days	Freeze or can
Sweet potatoes	55-60	85-90	4-6 mo.	Freeze or can
Tomatoes				
ripe	45-50	85-90	4-10 days	Freeze or can
mature green	55-70	85-90	1-5 wk.	Pickle

THE GARDEN GROCERY STORE

The most important harvest lesson Grandma Putt taught me was that a ripe crop should be picked and eaten, or "put by" as she called it, as soon as possible. To ensure high-quality, nutritious vegetables from your home garden, and to prevent waste, proper harvesting at the right time is essential. Here's a handy how-to harvest guide I've compiled over the years that'll help you harvest your vegetables at the proper time.

Asparagus—When the spears are 6 to 8 inches tall, before the tips start to open. Cut or break off stems at the soil line.

Beans, Snap—When the pods are almost full size, but before the seeds begin to bulge. Usually when the seeds are about the size of the head of a pin.

Beans, Lima—When pods and seeds reach full size, but are still fresh and juicy. Only use the seeds because the pods are tough, fibrous, and not very good.

Beets—As greens, when leaves are 4 to 6 inches long; as greens and small beets, when beets are 1 to 1-1/2 inches in diameter; as beets only, when they are 1-1/2 to 3 inches in diameter.

Those were the days...

We would let the shell beans, limas, and peas dry on the vine. Then Grandma and Aunt Jane would sit around the kitchen after supper, shelling them for hours on end.

The shelled seeds were dried in cloth bags until they became quite hard. Then the bag was pounded to break off the hard coating or hulls. Finally, they were cleaned in big basins of water. When all of the hull-chaff was removed, the beans or split peas were stored in the dry part of the cold cellar with a packet of bug-repellent herbs in each tin, bag, or keg.

Broccoli—When the flower heads are fully developed, but before individual flower buds start to open. Cut off 6 to 7 inches below the flower heads, but do not discard small, tender leaves because they are very nutritious.

Brussels sprouts—When sprouts (buds) at the base of the plant become solid. Remove buds higher on the plant as they become firm, but do not strip the leaves from the plants since they are necessary for further growth.

Cabbage—When heads become solid and firm. Excessive water uptake by the plant's roots causes splitting. To prevent splitting of mature heads, twist plants just enough to break several roots.

Carrots—When small and succulent, about 3/4 to 1 inch in diameter. During cool, dry periods, carrots may be left in the ground for later harvest.

Cauliflower—When curds (aborted flower heads) are full size (6 to 8 inches), but still compact, white, and smooth. Curds exposed to sunlight become cream-colored, rough in appearance, and coarse in texture.

Celery—When plants are 12 to 15 inches tall. While young and tender, the lowest leaves (8 to 10 inches long) may be removed from a few plants for use in salads, soups, and cooked dishes.

Chard—When 6 to 8 inches tall, to thin out plants. After that, remove only outer, older leaves as they become 8 to 10 inches long. New leaves will continue to grow for a continuous harvest of young, tender chard.

Chives—As new leaves appear in early spring, break off at the ground level. Use young, tender leaves throughout the season.

Grandma Putt's Words of Wisdom:

"Overripe, second-best produce makes for a third rate harvest."

Here's a trick old-timers used to tell if their corn was ready for picking. They used to pop'em, then pick-'em. They started testing their corn about 15 days after the silk appeared. Peeling back the husk a couple of inches, they pressed on a kernel with their fingernail until it burst open. If the juice was milky—the corn was perfect for picking. If it was watery, then they gave it a couple of more days. If it was pasty, then they knew they were too late—so they got to pickin' in a hurry!

Collards—When outer leaves become 8 to 10 inches long. New growth will provide a continuous harvest of young, tender leaves.

Corn, Sweet—When it is filled out well in the milk stage. There are only 72 hours from the beginning of prime eating quality until corn becomes over-ripe. Avoid high temperatures when gathering; the cool of the morning is best.

Cucumbers—For sweet pickles, when fruits are 1-1/2 to 2-1/2 inches long; for dills, when fruits are 3 to 4 inches long; for slicing, when fruits are near full size (generally 6 to 9 inches), but are still bright green and firm. Older fruits will be dull in color, less crisp, fleshy with a lot of seeds, and result in lower yields.

Eggplants—When fruits are near full size (approximately 4 to 6 inches in diameter), but still firm and bright in color. Older fruits become dull in color, soft, and seedy.

Endive—When the plant is fully developed, and the center leaves are blanched. Cool, moist growing conditions produce the best quality plants.

Garlic—When foliage loses its color, and the tops fall over.

Gourds—Edible varieties—when fruits are 8 to 10 inches long, and are young and tender; ornamental varieties—when fruits are mature and full-colored, but before first fall frost.

Horseradish—When the roots reach maximum size in late fall or early spring.

Kale—As the outer leaves become 8 to 10 inches long. New leaves will continue to grow from the center of each plant for a continuous harvest.

Leeks—When 1 to 1-1/3 inches in diameter, but before the first fall frost.

Lettuce—Leaf varieties, when outer, older leaves are 4 to 6 inches long; heading varieties, when heads are moderately firm. Outer, older leaves may be taken from plants of either leaf or head lettuce as soon as the leaves are 4 to 6 inches long. New leaves will provide a continuous harvest of tender, tasty lettuce until hot weather brings on bitter flavor and seed stalks start.

Muskmelons—When the base of the fruit stem starts to separate from the fruit. Fruit will be nearly ripe when separation starts, and fully ripe when a crack appears completely around the base of the fruit stem.

Mustard—Outer leaves, when 6 to 8 inches long. New leaves will provide continuous

---

From the Medicine Cabinet

Grandma Putt knew that the time of day you harvest vegetables can influence their quality. Her rule was to harvest all leafy vegetables early in the morning, while they were still glistening with dew.

To keep her veggies lasting longer, she washed them in warm water and a 3% hydrogen peroxide solution, which killed any bacteria that might have been lingering on the outside skin.

She also handled her fresh vegetables carefully to avoid cutting, breaking, or bruising them. We only stored healthy, fresh produce that was free from disease, insects, and other damage; if, in our haste or carelessness, we damaged some of the vegetables, then we used them immediately.

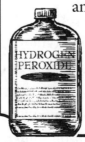

harvest until flavor becomes strong and leaves become tough in texture from hot weather. Seed again in late summer for milder flavor and tender texture.

Okra—Before pods reach the hollow and puffy stage, and while easy to cut from stalk. Continue harvesting, or they will quit producing.

Onions—For green onions, harvest when 6 to 8 inches tall. Harvest any with round, hollow seed stalks as soon as these stalks appear. For bulbs, harvest when the tops fall over, and begin to dry. Pull out with the tops on, and dry them in a protected place, cutting the tops one inch above the bulb for further drying.

Parsley—When older leaves are 3 to 5 inches long. Continue to take outer leaves for fresh, tender parsley until heavy frosts of winter.

Peas—When pods are fully developed, but still bright green. Harvest edible-podded varieties (snow, Chinese) when pods reach near full size (about 3 inches) and before seeds show appreciable enlargement. If only seeds are to be eaten, harvest when seeds are fully developed, but pods are still fresh and bright green.

Peas, Southern—When the seeds are near full size, but still bright green; as mature or dry seeds, when the seeds are full size and dry. Dry seeds may be cooked baked, or used in soups.

Peppers—When fruits are firm. In two to three weeks, ripe peppers will be fully colored.

Potatoes—When they are full size, and the skin is firm. New potatoes may be harvested at any size, but generally, they are not dug before they are 1-1/4 to 1-1/2 inches in diameter.

Pumpkins—When the fruits are full size, the rind is firm and glossy, and the bottom of the fruit is cream to orange color.

Rutabagas—When roots reach full size, but before heavy fall frosts. Thin early to ensure rapid, uniform growth and highest quality.

Spinach—When large leaves are 4 to 6 inches long. Pull larger, whole plants or harvest older leaves and allow new growth to develop.

Squash—When seeds and fruit are small. Continue harvesting, or flowering ceases. Winter squash is harvested when fruits are full sized, the rind is firm and glossy, and the bottom of the fruit is cream to orange color.

Sweet Potatoes—Late in the fall, but before the first early frost. Lift to avoid cuts, bruises, and broken roots. Cure in a warm, well-ventilated place for two to three weeks.

Tomatoes—When fruits are fully colored. Pick only fully ripe tomatoes for juice or canning to ensure full flavor, good color, and maximum sugar content.

Turnips—When the roots are 2 to 2-1/2 inches in diameter, but before heavy fall frosts. For greens, harvest leaves 4 to 6 inches in length.

Watermelons—When the fruits are full size, dull in color, and the bottoms turn from greenish-white to cream color.

Tasty Tomatoes

Have you ever wondered what to do with all of those tomatoes that ripen at once at the end of the season? We used to freeze them. That's right, we placed whole tomatoes on baking sheets, froze them, and then stored them in plastic bags. The skins cracked during the process, making them easy to peel when they thawed out.

PRESERVING FOOD

How-to Hints

To get the most out of your harvest:

Hint #1—Plan ahead so that you have the right kind of equipment ready to go before you start. Make sure you have enough jars and lids for canning, and bags or containers for freezing.

Hint #2—Label your preserved foods with the name, date, and variety. This is important because you should always eat food within one year of processing. And unless you've got x-ray vision, or can see through the container, *specify the contents!* Nothing is more frustrating than having to look through dozens of containers to find the right one. Labeling the variety will also help next year; if you've got dozens of jars of uneaten squash, a light bulb will go on, and you'll realize that it's *not* a family favorite any more!

Hint #3—Make a note of the recipe the food is used in so you can repeat your growing successes next year.

Now let's suppose you don't have a cellar like Grandma Putt did, and you don't have room (or it's impractical) for a pit. What do you do?

As any young person who has taken Home Ec 101 will tell you, the basic methods of preserving food includes **freezing, canning, salting, pickling, and dehydrating or drying.** Your garden bounty can be kept for months by using one or more of these methods, and following a few common sense rules.

CANNING

Back in Grandma Putt's day, every good gardener worth her salt canned fruits and vegetables. Nowadays, home canning has lost its popularity because of the time and effort involved, and danger of contamination. This is not to say that it's not still a viable and safe way to store your harvest. But nearly all modern refrigerators are equipped with a very efficient freezer, so home freezing along with drying (a/k/a dehydrating) have more than come into their own.

With the exception of cabbage, you can can (like the French do!) anything from apricots to zucchini. Whether fruits and vegetables taste better canned or frozen is a matter of personal taste; try both, then decide for yourself.

Here's a list that Grandma Putt used to determine roughly how many quarts of food she could expect from an average bushel of fruits and vegetables from her garden.

DEHYDRATING

Dehydrating is practical and easy, and can be done as each crop comes in. It's the process by which water is removed from vegetables to prevent decay. This can be accomplished by forcing heated air over them slow and fast enough in such a way to keep any change in cell structure from occurring.

HARVEST YIELDS

FRUITS	Fresh	Canned
Apples	1 bu. (48 lb.)	16 to 20 qt.
Apricots	1 bu. (50 lb.)	20 to 24 qt.
Berries	24-qt. Crate	12 to 18 qt.
Cherries	1 bu. (56 lb.)	22 to 32 qt.
Peaches	1 bu. (48 lb.)	18 to 24 qt.
Pears	1 bu. (50 lb.)	20 to 25 qt.
Plums	1 bu (56 lb.)	24 to 30 qt.

VEGETABLES	Fresh	Canned
Asparagus	1 bu. (45 lb.)	11 qt.
Beans, lima	1 bu. (32 lb.)	6 to 8 qt.
Beans, snap	1 bu. (30 lb.)	15 to 20 qt.
Beets	1 bu. (52 lb.)	17 to 20 qt.
Carrots	1 bu. (50 lb.)	16 to 20 qt.
Corn	1 bu. (35 lb.)	8 to 9 qt.
Okra	1 bu. (26 lb.)	17 qt.
Peas	1 bu. (30 lb.)	12 to 15 qt.
Pumpkin	50 lb.	15 qt.
Spinach	1 bu. (18 lb.)	6 to 9 qt.
Squash, summer	1 bu. (40 lb.)	16 to 20 qt.
Sweet potatoes	1 bu. (55 lb.)	18 to 22 qt.
Tomatoes	1 bu. (53 lb.)	15 to 20 qt.

*CAUTION: Certain bacteria can grow in a sealed jar if it is not destroyed by heat. Be careful whenever you process food; take every possible precaution, know exactly what you're doing, and follow directions to the letter.

To become an accomplished food dryer, you must practice, practice, and practice some more. There are many different sizes, shapes, and prices of food dehydrators, but over the years, after trying many different types, I've found the round style to be the best.

FREEZING

Freezing fresh vegetables is just about as easy as drying them, and twice as quick!

Pre-preparations for freezing means blanching a great number of vegetables to lock in the full flavor, nutritive, and vitamin value. To properly blanch, you must bring the water to a bubbling boil, and keep it there. Change the water for each new vegetable variety.

To properly blanch, simply submerge the produce into boiling water for the recommended amount of time. Remove the vegetables as soon as the time is up, chill quickly in ice water, then drain, and freeze!

To Freeze...

Artichokes	Kale
Corn	Squash
Peppers	Brussels
Asparagus	sprouts
Endive	Okra
Potatoes	Tomatoes
Beans	Cabbage
Greens (all)	Onions
Pumpkins	Turnips
Beets	Carrots
Herbs	Parsnips
Rutabagas	Cauliflower
Broccoli	Peas

Or Not To Freeze
(but dehydrate)...

Asparagus	Greens
Beans	Mushrooms
Beets	Okra
Broccoli	Onions
Brussels	Parsley
sprouts	Parsley
Cabbage	Peas
Carrots	Peppers
Cauliflower	Potatoes
Celery	Pumpkin
Corn	Squash
Cucumber	Tomatoes
Eggplant	Zucchini

DON'T EAT THE DAISIES, AND DON'T FORGET YOUR FLOWERS!

With the growing season winding down, vegetables weren't the only things that were harvested. Grandma Putt also brought in a lot of her herbs, bulbs, and flowers for storing until the following year. At the end of September or early part of October, before the first frost, Grandma would carefully cut around her geraniums, herbs, and other plants she intended to take inside the house for winter. Tender bulbs like dahlias and glads were brought into the cold cellar, where they were dusted with medicated foot powder and a little sulfur to prepare them for winter storage.

SAVING GERANIUMS

To "take in and overwinter" geraniums, Grandma used to jerk them up out of the soil when they turned brown after the first frost. She laid each geranium kitty-corner on a double spread of newspaper, and wrapped them up. She put the wrapped-up roots in her cold cellar, where she left them until March.

Sometime after the middle of March, she unwrapped her geraniums and cut off a third of the roots and two-thirds of the tops. She repotted them in clay pots filled with a mixture of half sand and half soil. She gave them a light feeding, and gradually started to bring them back to life.

How-to Hint

Grandma Putt would use her trowel or a knife to cut a circle around the plants she planned to put in pots for the winter. The circle was as big and as deep as the pot each plant was eventually going to go in.

Instead of digging them out right away, she would leave them cut out like that in the ground. This gave her plants a chance to absorb the initial shock of being cut up and moved. She watered them thoroughly, and then left them in the ground long enough for new rootlets to form within the ball.

After about three and a half weeks, she lifted the new root ball carefully out of the ground, and placed it in its new pot home, where it was as happy and contented as if it had always lived there!

FALLING INTO WINTER?

Toward the end of the year, asparagus beds, bramble berries, roses, cherry, and peach trees were all heavily mulched with leaves and corn husks to prevent frost damage. All except the winter-hardy grapevines were loosened from the trellis, pruned, laid down on the ground, and covered with a heavy mulch of leaves.

Apple picking was one of my favorite fall chores, although I remember eating a lot more apples than I picked. We'd go out to the orchard, and pick apples to our hearts' content. Afterwards, Grandma used to make the most delicious **cider**.

School in the country started later than in town because the boys were needed to work until the harvests were complete. But before long, we were back in school, and except for after-school and weekend chores, the garden was allowed to sleep.

Winter pruning of fruit and nut trees helped create a ready supply of kindling and firewood. Afterwards, we painted the tender young trunks with Grandma Putt's homemade varmint repellent to keep the critters away.

Winter was a time for sledding, skating, tramping in the snow, and then sitting by the fire drinking hot cocoa. The only gardening tasks were reading seed catalogs, and

Grandma Putt's Super Cider

Grandma Putt's not-so-secret cider recipe called for:
- 3 qts. of cider,
- 1 tsp. of cloves,
- 1 whole nutmeg,
- 1 cinnamon stick,
- and 1/2 cup of sugar.

She simmered the mix for 5 minutes, then strained, and served while still warm.

making sure Mother Nature didn't do to much damage in the form of heavy snow or ice storms.

Then, in late winter, it was time to tap the sugar maple trees!!!

MMM, MMM, MAPLE SYRUP!

The dark, dreary days of winter were spent dreaming of spring. The one special treat that I always looked forward to was making maple syrup. Here's how we used to do it:

You can use any kind of maple trees to tap for maple syrup, but Grandma Putt's sugar maples made the very best syrup. Each tree gave us about 20 gallons of sap, which boiled down to about 6 pounds of sugar.

On a nice winter morning (after a frost the previous night) in late February or very early March, we'd use a 1-inch auger bit to drill our first tap two inches into a maple tree. Grandma Putt said two taps per tree were plenty.

We inserted a hollow wooden trough that was cut in half to collect the sap. Grandma Putt used elder to make her troughs because the twigs and branches are hollow, and the pitch is easily removed to make a nice channel. Plus it's strong enough to hold a hanging bucket. After a week to ten days, we removed the tap, and bore two inches deeper.

From the Garden Shed

Grandma Putt believed in using homemade repellents whenever possible, and it seems that she had a million of them. To protect her trees, she made an effective varmint repellent by dissolving **7 pounds of tree rosin in 1 gallon of denatured alcohol**. She let the mixture stand in a warm place for 24 hours, stirring occasionally to dissolve the rosin. Then we painted it on the dry tree trunks in the fall, 2 feet higher than the expected snowfall drift line.

Ah, Sugar…

To make pure white sugar, Grandma Putt used to take the brown "salts" that came from the boiling down of the sap, and dissolve them in alcohol. Then she made several large cones out of galvanized sheet metal with an opening at the small end.

She put her brown sugar into the cones, and stopped up the hole in the bottom until it was completely cool. Then she removed the stopper, and poured rum or whiskey into the base of the cone. She allowed this to filter through the opening until the sugar was white.

Next, she put the white sugar back in the cone to harden. Finally, she took the white loaf of sugar from the cone, dissolve it in water to boil off the alcohol, and allow it to dry. That's all there was to it!

We used to empty our sap buckets into a large container, and carry it home. My Uncle Art, who was fondly known as "Mr. Lazy Bones," used to build a fire in an open spot in the woods so he wouldn't have to walk that far. (Nowadays, it is a good idea to check with the local fire department first, to make sure that's okay). He said the fire kept him warm while he was "working."

Check your buckets every day for more sap. It took many, many hours to boil away the water to make maple syrup that's not terribly runny. And many, many, many more hours to boil the syrup down into sugar! But believe you me, it was worth every minute of it!

9

SHARE YOUR LOVE ...WITH FLOWERS

I'm sure that many of us could live quite contentedly with far less than our share of Mother Nature's bounty. I, for one, wish that there were no more mosquitoes. Some folks in the South grow bored with all the nice weather, and head for snow country. In the North, a lot of folks get fed up with the slush and blizzards, and become "snowbirds" who head down South.

I suppose there are even some folks who would like to live far away from the flower fields that surround their homes. A world of plants without flowers might be a pleasant place for hay-fever sufferers, but the fact remains that plenty of plants live, prosper, and die without ever bearing a single bloom. It's perfectly clear that God didn't need to make flowers. But, stop and think for a moment, where would we be without them?

I was taught that it takes someone with the spirit of an artist to see the truth and beauty reflected in the face of a flower. Grandma Putt summed it up quite nicely…"We should all thank the Lord not only for creating the millions of flower varieties that cover the earth, but for letting so many of us feel the need to grow some of them in our gardens." 'Nuf said!

Those were the days...

When I first went to live with Grandma Putt, I didn't give a hoot about flowers. They were kind of sissy things, best meant for little old ladies who had too much time on their hands. Boy, it didn't take long for Grandma Putt to set me straight! I learned more about flowers in a couple of years than most folks do in a lifetime!

She was way ahead of the flower children of the 1960's with her message of love. Grandma Putt said that to grow flowers successfully, you have to love them, and communicate your feelings to them. She spoke to them affectionately whenever she worked or walked in her garden. Judging by the results, they obviously responded positively to her tender loving talk and tender loving care.

Grandma Putt believed that if you spent enough time in the company of flowers, you can't help but lose your ornery nature. I think she was right—after a while, whenever I weeded a flower bed, I lost my grouchiness and started to smile. The best part was that the smiles usually lasted all day!

MAKE IT EASY ON YOURSELF

Grandma Putt was never one to waste space or make an easy job too hard. Her motto when it came to flower gardening? "Praise large gardens, but plant small ones!" She said that since no one will ever force you to plant a flower garden, you shouldn't plant one that's so large, you'll have a hard time keeping it up.

All of Grandma Putt's flower beds were no more than 3 feet wide and 10 feet long. The reason for this was because a hoe reaches 5-1/2 feet out. Pretty practical, eh? If you make your beds any wider than this, you'll end up stooping too much, which is a pain-in-the-you-know-what!

On the other side of the coin, wider flower beds give you a better flow of continuous color than narrow beds. So if that's what you want, then you should put 8-to-10-foot wide beds out in the open, where you can work them

SHARE YOUR LOVE...WITH FLOWERS

from either side. Or, if you want even bigger beds and have the room, incorporate a garden path into the design to help you get at the weeds more easily.

Grandma Putt also thought ahead—she avoided sharp corners on her beds, and made sure that the flowers along the lawn areas were set back far enough so the lawn mower could trim the edge of the turf without snipping or trampling her flowers. I tell you, she had all of the bases covered!

DESIGNING YOUR FLOWER GARDEN

HOW FORMAL DO YOU WANT TO BE?

Grandma Putt approached building a new flower bed like an artist who was going to paint a picture—she made a few preliminary sketches until she got the shape of the bed, its colors, and the flower placement just right. She had both natural-looking plantings, and more traditional flower gardens.

When you're designing a flower garden, let your natural landscape, the setting of your home, and type of flowers you want to grow guide you in making your decisions. For instance, if you live near a woods and want local wildflowers in your garden, it might be best to go "natural" and informal.

For the Birds...

Grandma Putt used an old clothesline, electrical extension cord, or old garden hose to lay out her informal flower beds. That way, she could get the curves just right *before* she began to turn over any soil.

Another way to do this is to outline the shape of your flower bed with small pieces of stale bread. They're easy to rearrange, and when you're done, the birds will feast on the outline!

Those were the days...

Like a lot of flowers that fell out of fashion, hollyhocks are making a comeback today. When I was a boy, I remember the girls in the neighborhood would make dolls out of them. They would turn the face of the flower upside down to make the skirt, stick a wire or toothpick through the center to make the body, use a second kind of flower to make a face, and a third to make the bonnet. Why, in no time at all, they'd have a doll that was cute as a button! I guess I'm kind of dating myself with that one, eh?

Wildflowers have subtle colors that are shown off better by soft, curving lines than by abrupt, straight borders. Also, wildflowers in a formal garden are about as comfortable as Jethro, Ellie Mae, and the rest of the Clampetts were in Beverly Hills!

On the other hand, Grandma Putt put her formal beds against walls, fences, and hedges. She arranged her plants in decreasing height, with the tallest flowers like hollyhocks, hardy asters, gladioli, lupines, phlox, peonies, snapdragons, and dahlias in the background, so they wouldn't block their shorter cousins from view or from the sunshine.

In front of the "tall gals," Grandma put chrysanthemums, heleniums, delphiniums, and daffodils. Closer to the foreground were baby's breath, columbines, shasta daisies, tulips, phlox, veronica, salvia, poppies, and zinnias.

Finally, the front was filled with the low-growers like candytuft, crocus, sedum, sundrops,

SHARE YOUR LOVE...WITH FLOWERS

lavender, verbena, dwarf tulips, and marigolds.

Now, for the trouble spots—the ends. She'd plant the "tough guy," stronger flowers, like iris, at the ends of her beds. The neighborhood kids and dogs were always running about in her yard, and never quite seemed to make the corners. Grandma Putt knew that iris will stand up and continue to bounce back after more than a little close corner-cutting in a frenzied game of hide-and-seek!

> ## Floral Considerations
>
> When designing a flower garden of your own, make sure you consider all of the following:
> - ✔ Bloom time
> - ✔ Bloom color
> - ✔ Flower shape and size
> - ✔ Foliage shape and size
> - ✔ Flower and foliage texture
> - ✔ Progression of blooms

INTEGRATE OR SEGREGATE?

Don't get me wrong, Grandma Putt had some flowers, like her tulips and daffodils, that looked better and did exceptionally well in large, massed plantings. Daffodils, in particular, have been popular for many, many years because they grow so well in almost every area of this country. A word to the wise, however—a mass planted bed will look best if you limit the planting to one color or a blending of several complementary colors.

Grandma Putt also had some flower beds that were all mixed together—bulbs, biennials, annuals, and perennials. For those special beds, she kept a list of where everything was and when it was due to come up, so that none of her flower friends ever got lost or in each other's way. As far as she was concerned, it never hurt to mix up your flower friends. Getting them gossiping and growing together was more eye-pleasing and delightful than you might imagine!

PLEASE PASS THE PAINT BRUSH!

Speaking of colors, Grandma Putt always planned her colors so they blended together in a harmonious way that appealed to her and her setting. One pet peeve of hers was flower foliage; most folks never even gave it a second thought! They'd plant flowers with rough or drab foliage in a conspicuous place in their garden, and it would destroy the whole effect of the beautiful blooms.

When it came time to plant my first flower garden, Grandma Putt had me get out my crayons to color in my drawing of the flower bed. This helped me see if I was mixing the right colors. I went through many different designs—if the effect on paper wasn't pleasing enough, Grandma Putt had me put aside the sketch, and start studying the catalogs again.

CONSIDER YOUR CLIMATE

Our climate played a very important role in what kinds of flowers Grandma Putt grew. Before you plant your flowers, be sure to consider your local climate and weather conditions.

Don't assume that flowers growing in the East will grow

Altitude Counts!

Grandma Putt experimented with all types of different plants in her garden because she knew that there were certain plants which, at first glance, might seem to be suited to a tropical climate, only to do very well elsewhere. A good example of this was one of her favorites—tuberous begonias. Although they originated in Bolivia, they grow very well in Michigan, where we lived. This is because Bolivia is extremely mountainous, with elevations up to 15,000 feet. The higher plants grow, the more cold-hardy they will be.

SHARE YOUR LOVE...WITH FLOWERS

in the West, or that northern-temperate-zone varieties will thrive in the humid or tropical South. Check with your neighbors, or a local nurseryman to see what they recommend; who knows, you may even get lucky—your neighbor may have some extra cuttings or divisions to share with you.

I know Grandma Putt *always* gave plenty of her perennials away to anyone who stopped by to visit.

SOIL AND LOCATION

No matter how dry, moist, or poor the soil conditions of your future flower bed may be, I'm willing to bet you a buck that you can talk some of the flower varieties listed at right to grow there. Most flowers flourish in good sandy loam...so prepare it as you would for a vegetable or herb garden, with plenty of TLC added, and then watch them smile!

Flowers, Flowers Everywhere

For Dry Soil

Annuals	Perennials
cleome	baby's breath
cornflower	catchfly
four-o'clock	coneflower
portulaca	evening primrose
sunflower	hardy aster
zinnia	yucca

For Moist Soil

Annuals	Perennials
begonia	columbine
forget-me-not	forget-me-not
impatiens	geum
nicotiana	iris
phlox	trollius

For Poor Soil

Annuals	Perennials
cleome	bearded iris
marigold	coneflower
nasturtium	dianthus
zinnia	snowball

A PLAN FOR ALL SEASONS

From the first days of spring to the last days of fall, Grandma Putt had five major waves of color. How did she do it? By planning ahead! She made sure she had **early spring bloomers; mid-spring bloomers; early summer bloomers; mid-summer bloomers; and fall to early winter bloomers**. Over the years, I've found that with only a few exceptions (primarily in the South and Southwest), most flowers can be classified into one of these easy-to-remember categories. Of course, you can move your blooming times up or back by forcing flower and using succession planting.

Grandma Putt's Words of Wisdom:

"Plan before you plant."

To keep a constant flow of color in your yard, and to take full advantage of each of the five blooming periods, you have to get acquainted (as I did) with annuals, biennials, bulbs, and perennials. Here's a Grandma Putt primer on each of them:

BEAUTIFUL BULBS

Tubers, corms, and true bulbs make up what we gardeners commonly call the "bulb family." You don't need to spend too much time worrying about the differences at this stage because they are generally planted and cared for in the same way.

This lovable part of the flower family will make your garden bloom for all except the coldest months

SHARE YOUR LOVE...WITH FLOWERS

of the year. And the best part is that they require very little in the way of care.

Luckily for us, Mother Nature and bulb growers have combined to sort out bulb stock so that it's relatively easy to pick and choose a fool-proof garden. The result of this sorting gives you three main groups:

Group 1—Hardy spring and summer flowering bulbs;

Group 2—Half-hardy summer flowering bulbs;

Group 3—Tender summer and fall flowering bulbs.

HARDY SPRING AND SUMMER FLOWERING BULBS

These bulbs are sold in the late summer for planting in the fall. Bulbs

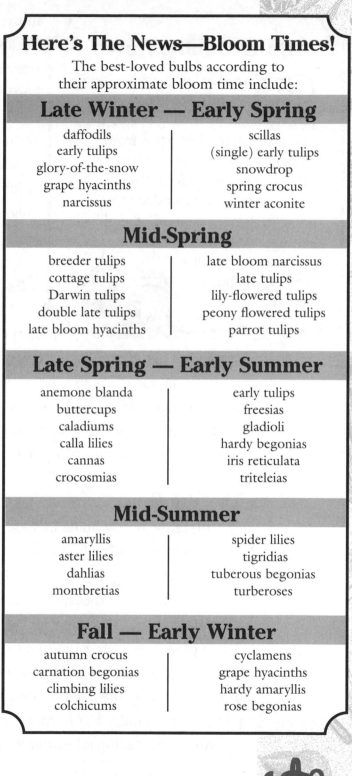

Here's The News—Bloom Times!

The best-loved bulbs according to their approximate bloom time include:

Late Winter — Early Spring

daffodils	scillas
early tulips	(single) early tulips
glory-of-the-snow	snowdrop
grape hyacinths	spring crocus
narcissus	winter aconite

Mid-Spring

breeder tulips	late bloom narcissus
cottage tulips	late tulips
Darwin tulips	lily-flowered tulips
double late tulips	peony flowered tulips
late bloom hyacinths	parrot tulips

Late Spring — Early Summer

anemone blanda	early tulips
buttercups	freesias
caladiums	gladioli
calla lilies	hardy begonias
cannas	iris reticulata
crocosmias	triteleias

Mid-Summer

amaryllis	spider lilies
aster lilies	tigridias
dahlias	tuberous begonias
montbretias	turberoses

Fall — Early Winter

autumn crocus	cyclamens
carnation begonias	grape hyacinths
climbing lilies	hardy amaryllis
colchicums	rose begonias

Doin' Double Duty!

Grandma Putt used dried blood-meal to do double duty in her garden. First, by mixing it into the soil, it protected her bulbs from chipmunks and other varmints. Then she sprinkled it on the soil after planting, and its odor repelled the little critters. Second, it supplied a much needed dose of nitrogen that made the bulbs very happy the next year.

in this group are hardy enough to stay in the ground over the freezing winter months. The hardy bulb varieties include small bulbs which put in the earliest appearance of any flowers, and the famous Dutch bulbs. They can be further divided into spring bloomers and summer bloomers.

The Little Fellers

The smallest hardy bulbs bloom before Old Man Winter has ended his annual visit. They are the telltale sign that he is just about ready to start packing up and moving on. Like the tulips, these "little fellers" are best planted in the late fall and on into the winter. They include crocus, glory-of-the-snow, snowdrop, winter aconite, and the scillas.

The Big Guys

The large, hardy bulbs include lilies, Dutch iris, hyacinths, daffodils (narcissus family), and tulips. Lilies and hyacinths should be planted in early fall. Tulips, irises, and daffodils can be planted later (at the same time as the little fellers); if you plant them after the first frost, add in a professional planting mix, and mulch well with compost or leaves to keep the soil temperature as constant as possible. Freezing won't harm these bulbs, but alternate thawing and freezing all winter long will.

SHARE YOUR LOVE...WITH FLOWERS

THE HALF-HARDY, SUMMER FLOWERING BULBS

The bulbs included in this group are calla lilies, montbretias, spider lilies, and hardy begonias. In many parts of the country, these can be left in the ground through the winter. If you live north of the Ohio River, however, I wouldn't advise you to do this.

THE TENDER SUMMER AND FALL FLOWERING BULBS

These bulbs really make bulb growing worthwhile. Don't be misled into believing that these tender darlings are too much trouble, and have to be coddled. If you do, you'll miss out on growing some of the finest flowers, including dahlias, cannas, tuberous begonias, gladioli, tuberoses, anemones, and caladiums in your own backyard.

PLANTING TIPS

Tip #1—Start growing bulbs like tulips, hyacinths, daffodils, etc., indoors, or in pots wrapped with newspaper, and buried under the ground for eight to ten weeks. This will give you winter beauty and fragrance, as well as an early start for middle and late spring blooming bulbs.

Green Thumb Tip

One of Grandma Putt's gardening rules for her tulip beds was to redo them every three years. She knew that planting tulips in the same soil year after year was an open invitation for diseases such as fire blight to come a callin'. So every three years, she changed the location of her bulb beds, or replaced the soil. If she didn't feel like changing the soil, then she let the area rest for two years, and applied plenty of lime to it in the interim.

Tip #2—Plant the earliest bloomers like winter aconite, crocus, snowdrop, scilla, and Siberian squill in clumps as soon as they are available in snow country, and in early December in the South and West. Plant these little fellers about 3 inches deep. They'll unfold their tender little blossoms from February through March.

Tip #3—Snowdrops and crocuses need a sunny exposure if you want them to open at the earliest possible date. Other early bloomers can take partial shade and damp soil; mulch them until they bloom, then remove the mulch, but make sure you keep the soil moist.

How-to Hint

Grandma Putt taught me how to properly plant bulbs. She said to make sure that the bottom of the bulb was in firm contact with the bottom of its planting hole. If not, then there will be an air pocket between the two, which will not let the bulb root properly, and cause it to rot.

Tip #4—Plant tender bulbs like tuberous begonias, cannas, dahlias, gladioli, and tuberoses as soon as the ground warms up in spring. Prepare the bed the same way as you would for tulips. Tuberous begonias like a northern exposure; half-sun and half-shade. They need lots of moisture and slightly acidic soil so, mulch with pine needles.

Tip #5—Dahlias like almost any type of soil; start them indoors in pots, and then move them outside as soon as the ground warms up. Plant the bulbs 4 inches deep. Nip off extra buds, and only grow one flower per plant.

Tip #6—Succession plant gladioli for summer-long blooms. Plant your initial ones a half foot deep, and then every two weeks thereafter until the Fourth of July, plant some more.

Tip #7—Lilies should be set out early in the fall; the earlier the better. Plant them around 8-10 inches deep,

 SHARE YOUR LOVE...WITH FLOWERS
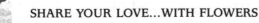

and 15-20 inches apart. Lilies look best when they're planted in groups. The planting bed should have plenty of well-drained soil.

Tip #8—Most of the true bulbs, like tulips, develop deep roots. Plant them as soon as the weather cools in mid-fall, after the first hard frost, right on up until the ground freezes. Plant daffodils and tulips 6 inches deep, and 6 inches apart.

MAKE THAT BED UP RIGHT!

For mass large plantings of several different types of bulbs, Grandma Putt would dig up the entire bed to 8 inches deep, remove the soil, and mix in her **Breakfast of Champions** with about 10 pounds of peat moss for each bushel of garden soil she removed. She then refilled the bed with this planting mixture.

Then she taught me a neat trick—how to layer the bulbs like we were making lasagna. We'd plant the biggest bulbs (tulips) on the bottom, with the top of the bulb (their nose) facing up. We'd cover them with soil, and then put in the second layer.

Make sure you don't plant this second layer right on top of the first. Plant small bulbs and daffodils in clusters

From the Garden Shed

Whenever Grandma Putt planted spring flowering bulbs, she fed them an organic Breakfast of Champions that would see them through the long, hard winter. Then over the winter, she'd add fireplace ashes (up to 5 lbs. per 100 sq. ft.) to her bulb beds. The ashes supplied potassium which helped the bulbs develop strong stems and fat, firm bodies.

Breakfast of Champions

This "breakfast" was made by mixing:
10 lbs. of compost,
5 lbs. of bone meal,
2 lbs. of blood meal, and
1 lb. of Epsom salts
in a wheelbarrow, and then working it into every 100 sq. ft. (10' x 10') of soil.

Dem Bones, Dem Bones...

Bones have been used as fertilizer for many years because they contain many vital plant nutrients and last a long time in the soil. Bone meal is the form we use today, but years ago, Grandma Putt used both ground and crushed bones in and around her garden, particularly around her bulbs.

She reduced the bones to a useable form by mixing them with ashes. She put the bones and ashes in alternate layers in an old barrel, moistened the whole thing with water, and set it in her shed for several months. During this time, she kept the contents continually moist.

Grandma Putt's rule of thumb for using this homemade "bone meal" was to add one part bone meal to fifty parts of soil for a potting mix, or one pound of bone meal worked into twenty feet of row. She would use this mixture on all plants, except her acid-loving plants like azaleas and rhododendrons.

because they look best growing in clumps. Don't plant bulbs too shallow.

As we completed each layer, we'd continue on to the next one, until we were finished. Careful planning like this should give you two months of flowers.

To finish off the planting, we mulched the top of the bed with leaves, shredded bark, pine needles, or wood chips. This protected the bulbs from temperature fluctuations during the winter.

As a final measure, we'd lay a piece of chicken wire over the bed, and tack it down in the mulch. Then Grandma Putt would sprinkle some moth balls over the top; this kept squirrels, chipmunks, and other varmints from digging up her prized possessions.

As soon as we saw signs that our bulbs were trying to pop their little heads out of the ground in spring, Grandma Putt removed the mulch, and fed them a handful of 5-10-5 garden food. This helped them become stronger, and bloom longer in the spring.

SHARE YOUR LOVE...WITH FLOWERS

After that, Grandma Putt would give her bulb beds a soap-and-water shampoo, which would be a real body-building booster for the tender, young emerging bulbs. This shampoo would keep the local insect population in check; if we found any damage, Grandma Putt would reach for the nicotine sulfate and Fels-Naptha Soap Solution, which would nail 'em dead in their tracks!

HOW DO YOU SET A WATER TABLE?

I used to wonder why bulbs did so well in Holland. Grandma Putt said it was because they got plenty of water. The water table there is constant, and not far below the surface—which is just a fancy way of saying that you can dig down a few feet, and hit water just about anywhere in the Netherlands!

You don't have to pack up your bulbs and move to the Netherlands, though. Just make sure they get enough water when they need it most. There's usually enough rain in the spring to provide bulbs with the water they need to produce blooms. If, however, Mother Nature is stingy with the April showers, or she's feeling sulky and cooks up a prolonged dry spell, then you'll have to give your bulbs a helping hand.

Even after the spring flowering bulbs have stopped blooming, they're still producing foliage. If it dries out and dies before it matures properly, your bulbs will put on a poor show the next spring. So don't be a fair-weather friend, and neglect your bulbs after they've stopped blooming for you.

Grandma Putt used a soaker hose for watering her bulbs. You can use a sprinkler, but you run the risk of burning the

Grandma Putt's Words of Wisdom:

"Shallow watering causes a shallow root system."

foliage if you water on a sunny day. Sprinkling is especially hazardous for tuberous begonias and tulips.

Be sure you water deep. Shallow watering does more harm than good. As Grandma Putt used to say…"When you're watering your bulbs, get to the root of the matter, don't just sprinkle their uniforms."

Green Thumb Tip

There's a real simple solution to the ugly dying foliage problem, and that's to camouflage it. That's right—plant your bulbs in among some bushy biennials or perennials. That way, their emerging leaves will help hide the dying bulb foliage, and no one will be the wiser!

AFTER THE LAUGHTER…

As soon as the blooms faded on her spring flowering bulbs, Grandma Putt picked off the seed pods, and waited as long as she could (letting them turn brown) before she cut off the stems. Although they didn't look very good, hyacinths, daffodils, and tulips need healthy stems to help fatten up the bulb for next year's flower.

When the foliage finally turned brown, she bent it down, and fastened it in a tight ball around the stem with a piece of string. Once the foliage completely dried up in late spring, she cut it off just above ground level.

If you decide to dig up your hardy bulbs in order to divide or move them, you should do this just when the foliage dies. But in that case, don't cut the foliage off. Try to break them apart, and replant them right away. Then you can cold-store them like onions.

THE POPULATION EXPLOSION

Bulbs will multiply as surely as chickens come home to roost. After a few years, take a good, hard look at your daffodils. You'll probably notice that their blooms aren't as large and pretty as they used to be. Chances are, the bulbs are overcrowded, and need dividing. The longer you wait to divide the bulbs, the harder the job will be, and the smaller your bulbs will be. As Grandma Putt used to say…"Bulbs can't grow if there's no place to go."

It's best to dig up your bulbs for dividing at the beginning of the dormant period just after the leaves die back. As soon as the leaves are dried up, go to work moving them.

The best tool for dividing bulbs is a spading fork. Grandma Putt liked ones with large tines so that she could get the fork under a clump of bulbs, and not in the middle of it. She didn't want to lie down at night with bulb shish-ka-bob on her conscience.

Try to lift out the whole clump at once. Then find a cool, dark place for separating the bulbs. You're going to replant them immediately, but you still don't want them to dry out any more than necessary. Working in the sun will dry both you and the bulbs out, so find a shady spot for you and your uprooted friends.

Once you've divided the bulbs, immediately replant them. Put the larger, parent bulbs in the most conspicuous place, with their smaller offspring behind them. If you prefer, you can put the babies in a nursery bed until they reach adulthood, and begin to blossom heavily. Then they can be moved into the limelight with Mama and Papa.

HARDY PERENNIALS

Perennial All-Stars

Here's a list of popular perennial pals to help you paint a permanent flower garden picture:

Low Growing

alyssum	hosta
chrysanthemum	lobelia
dianthus	pulmonaria
dicentra	violas
English daisy	yarrow

Medium Growing

bleeding heart	evening primrose
butterfly	hardy aster
coneflower	shasta daisy
coral bells	phlox
coreopsis	veronica
daylily	weed campanula

Tall Growing

centaurea	lupine
delphinium	lythrum
helenium	monk's hood
hibiscus	peony
hollyhock	phlox

These flowers live on, year after year, and are among the easiest flowers you can grow. Grandma Putt used hardy perennials as the faithful old family anchors of her flower garden, and you'll want to do the same. They provide your garden with color, design, and endurance. You just plant them and keep them mulched, watered, and trimmed. They'll do the rest!

Add to your perennial plantings each year, but don't overplant! Just like people, these flowers don't like to spend too much time in a crowded place. So give them room to spread out.

FALL INTO PLANTING

In Grandma Putt's day, spring was the busiest time of the year for folks who lived in the country. The farmers and vegetable gardeners had so much work getting in their spring crops that they put in incredibly long, hard days. Any part of the work load that could be moved from this time of the year to a less hectic one was greatly appreciated.

  SHARE YOUR LOVE...WITH FLOWERS

As a result, hardy perennials were put in the ground in the fall, when things slowed down, after the autumn harvest was completed. Then, vegetables like asparagus, artichokes, and rhubarb were planted. Peonies, chrysanthemums, iris, bulbs, and some biennials were also planted at that time.

If you are gardening for the first time, limit your fall plantings the first couple of years to see how well a few individual perennials survive the winter. If all goes well, plant root divisions (not seedlings) more heavily the following year, but keep in mind that Old Man Winter is like Nolan Ryan—he mixes up his repertoire of pitches every time you come to bat. Be prepared to have him throw you a few slow, warm curves as a change of pace following a good, hard winter that was icy and fast.

Grandma Putt's Words of Wisdom:

"Think big, but plant small."

The best fall-planting conditions are a long, warm fall, followed by a hard, freezing winter. What you don't want is too many alternate freezes and thawings. So after the first frost, make sure that your perennials are well mulched to keep winter temperatures constant. If you want to play it safe, spring-plant so your perennials develop strong, healthy roots over the long, growing season.

SPRING PLANTING

Grandma Putt used to start her perennials for spring planting indoors in peat pots. These were set outside as soon as the days become sunny. Then, after the last frost, when the ground began to warm up, she placed her perennials in their permanent homes. If everything went according to plan, they stayed there 'til the cows came home.

From the Kitchen Cupboard

Whenever Grandma Putt brought a new perennial to her garden, she gave it a little extra-special TLC. First, she'd fill the hole with plenty of organic matter, and then follow that up with a dose of her Perennial Planting Tonic. That got them up and growing on the right root! After planting, she'd feed them once a month with this tonic for super results all season long.

Grandma Putt fed them with a good garden food (5-10-5 or 4-12-4 mixed with compost) as soon as they were in place, and threw half a handful on the surrounding soil several times during the spring and summer. After that, she followed her good cultural maintenance practices to keep them healthy and insect- and disease-free.

Perennial Planting Tonic

To make this power-packed perennial punch, mix:

1/2 bottle of beer,
1 tbsp. of Fels-Naptha Soap Solution,
1/2 cup of barnyard tea, and
2 tbsp. of hydrogen peroxide,

in 2 gallons of warm water, and sprinkle it over your blooming beauties.

SHAMPOO TIME!

As Grandma Putt told me many, many times, bugs don't like soap in their mouths any more than kids do…so she would shampoo the foliage of her perennials every other week with her Fels-Naptha Soap Solution. If insects became a problem, she'd mix a little nicotine sulfate into the solution. Nowadays, I use antiseptic mouthwash and chewing tobacco juice. You can also mix a teaspoon or two of a pyrethrin-based insecticide into the solution to get rid of the bugs.

SHARE YOUR LOVE…WITH FLOWERS

DEADHEADING

This process sounds gruesome, but what we did was remove the faded flowers after they have bloomed. If you don't use many of your perennials for cuttings, then you *must* do this procedure. It prevents the plant from overworking. It also revives the worthless flowering parts of the plant, and stimulates it into further blooming action. So if you want more blooms, deadhead, man!

WATERING

Except for shampooing and insect control, Grandma Putt always warned me to direct my hose toward the feet of her perennials. She said that watering the leaves was a waste of time. Perennials root deeply, so you must soak the ground thoroughly, especially in hot, dry weather.

DIVIDING PERENNIALS

Over the years, I've learned that many perennials prefer to be left alone once they've taken root and become accustomed to their new home. But that's not always possible. Many perennials can be divided in the fall if they get too crowded. If you live in the North, do this in the spring because fall-divided roots may not have a chance to develop properly before winter sets in.

Green Thumb Tip

Grandma Putt had a surefire, no muss, no fuss way of separating perennials like daylilies. First, she'd dig them up, and thoroughly wash all of the soil off of the roots. Then she'd gently roll the plants back and forth on the ground with her foot until they separated by themselves. She found that by doing it this way, the plants weren't damaged, and she had happier, healthier transplants!

The simple process of digging up and dividing crowded perennials will rejuvenate old plants, and give you new flowers for planting elsewhere. We tried to do this about every 3 to 4 years, depending on how they were growing. Here's how to do it:

Step #1—Dig up the whole plant carefully, and wash off the roots. Check for insects, disease, or other damage.

Step #2—Clip off any damaged roots or stems.

Step #3—Divide thick-rooted plants (like iris and peony) with a knife. Cut the roots into bud-bearing segments.

Step #4—Divide fibrous-rooted plants with your hands. Simply tear the root clump into segments.

Step #5—Divide creeping perennials by cutting away new shoots.

Biennial Buddies

Here are some old-time favorites:

canterbury bells
English daisy
foxgloves
hollyhocks
mullein
pansies
sweet William
wallflowers

BLOOMING BIENNIALS

Most folks only see their biennials bloom one time. As you may know, these plants complete their entire life cycle in two short years. They produce leaves the first year; the second year after they are planted, they flower only once, set seed, and then die.

Some biennials are self-sowers during the first year. So, you may be happily surprised to see a year-old second-stringer sprouting up just as your two-year-old begins to fade.

But according to Grandma Putt, it was easy to get biennials to flower during the first year, even in the North. First off, she started her biennials indoors in peat fiber pots. This gave them a jump on the weather. She planted them in full sun once the ground warmed up to growing temperature. Then don't look now, but hers would be blooming that first year!

NO-NONSENSE ANNUALS

Although they are relatively short-lived, Grandma Putt always said that annuals packed a dazzling display of color into a small package. Annuals have been around forever—the ones you can invite into your garden will become new friends with old familiar names. Petunia, morning glory, and marigold—those names are known so well to most of us that it's hard to believe they belong to flowers that grow, flower, set seed, and die all in a few short months.

From the Medicine Cabinet

To relieve the pain of sore, burning feet after a long, hard day in the garden, Grandma Putt rubbed a bit of her magic Marigold Salve on her feet. It provided fast, soothing relief. One thing to remember— put on a pair of soft socks to prevent the grease from staining your sheets if you use this salve.

Marigold Salve

To make this magical salve, Grandma Putt mixed together:

**1 cup of marigold petals and
1/2 cup of Vaseline®**

in a pan, and cooked it on low heat for about 30 minutes. She strained the mixture through cheesecloth until it was clear, and stored it in a jar until her tired, old dogs were a barkin'.

Grandma Putt referred to annuals as her "no-nonsense flowers" because they don't fool around. Their sole purpose in life is to make seeds. In order to do this, they also make attractive and colorful flowers that provide beauty and fragrance from the last frost in the spring to the first one in the fall.

Annuals are very easy to grow. In general, they are disease-, drought-, and heat-resistant. They come in all colors and sizes. They are inexpensive, whether you grow them from seed, or buy them as seedlings from your local nursery. With all that in mind, what more could you ask for?

Your Annual Growing Needs

For Borders

Ageratum	Larkspur
Alyssum	Marigold
Balsam	Nicotiana
Bells of Ireland	Petunia
Centaurea	Salvia farinacea
Cleome	Snapdragon
Cosmos	Zinnia

For Window Boxes

Begonia semperflorens	Coleus
Cascade petunias	Lobelia

For Foliage

Amaranthus	Coleus
Canna	Dusty miller
Castor bean	Perilla

For Partial Shade

Balsam	Lobelia
Begonia	Nicotiana
Calendula	Pansy
Coleus	Salvia
Impatiens	Torenia

Ground Covers

Cobaea	Nierembergia
Creeping zinnia	Portulaca
Lobelia	Sweet alyssum
Mesembryanthemum	Sweet pea
Morning glory	Thunbergia
Myosotis	Verbena
Nasturtium	Vinca

GROUPING ANNUALS

Annuals can be put into three convenient groups that make it easy for you to choose which ones will do best in your garden:

- Hardy annuals
- Half-hardy annuals
- Tender annuals

Hardy

Hardy annuals include sweet peas, pansies, poppies, and love-in-a-mist. They can be sown as seed late in the fall, and they'll bloom early the following spring.

Half-Hardy

The half-hardy annuals include marigolds, petunias, lupines, and zinnias. We usually planted cold-resistant types from flats in the spring, right after the last frost. Grandma Putt's advice was to not risk an entire planting on the whims of Old Man Winter.

Your Annual Growing Needs

For Edging

Ageratum 6-12"	Impatiens 6-8"
Alyssum 4-6"	Lobelia 8"
Begonia 4-12"	Pansy 6-8"
Calendula 12"	Petunia 12-15"
Candytuft 8"	Phlox 7-15"
Celosia 4-12"	Portulaca 4-6"
Centaurea 10-12"	Snapdragon 6-8"
Coleus 12-15"	Verbena 8-12"
Dianthus 12"	Vinca 10"
Dusty miller 6-10"	Zinnia, dwarf 6-12"
Heliotrope 12-15"	

Medium Growers

Balsam 15"	Impatiens 15-18"
Basil 15"	Knee high 12-15"
Bells of Ireland 24"	Nicotiana 12-24"
Carnation 15-20"	Petunias 12-15"
Celosia 20-24"	Rudbeckia 16-18"
Cynoglossum 18"	Salpiglossis 20-30"
Dahlia 20-24"	Salvia 18-30"
Dusty miller 12-24"	Snapdragon 15-24"
Gaillardia 24-30"	Verbena 12-24"
Gomphrena 18"	Zinnia 18-30"
Helichrysum 24-30"	

Tall Growers

Amaranthus 3-4'	Larkspur 2-3'
Asters 36"	Marigold 30-36"
Celosia 30-48"	Ricinus 8-10'
Centaurea 30"	Scabiosa 2-3'
Cleome 3-4'	Statice 30"
Cosmos 3'	Snapdragon 30-36"
Dahlia 30-48"	Zinnia 30-36"
Hollyhock 4-5'	

If you must plant in the fall, plant only half of your flowers. Cover them with a very loose mulch like straw, pine needles, or shredded shrubbery prunings. Then you can hedge your over-wintering bed with another half crop in the spring. Seeds are cheap, but believe you me, there's something really depressing about losing an entire planting before you're halfway into spring! You're listening to someone who's been there, done that!

Tender Annuals

The tender annuals like begonias, China asters, dahlias, gourds, morning glories, and stocks make up the bulk of the annual flowers. Most of these are native to areas that have long, warm growing seasons. It's almost always best to let your nurseryman start these plants for you, and you just buy the seedlings. Then all you've got to do is plant them from flats when the ground is warm enough in your area to permit them to grow.

BACK TO THE FUTURE... PLAN BEFORE YOU BUY!

Before you rush out and buy whatever annuals strike your fancy, you need to ask yourself if the annuals you are thinking about will fit in with the bulbs, biennials, and perennials already there. Review the checklist on pages 280-281. Will they blend in as far as size, shape, and

Green Thumb Tips

Grandma Putt reminded me that:

Tip #1—Before buying annuals, plan your beds on paper, close to scale, so that you eliminate waste.

Tip #2—Don't plant annuals that grow wildly in the same bed with perennials because they'll end up crowding each other out.

Tip #3—Don't wait until frost-free weather to start your flower garden. Lots of bedding plants, like sweet alyssum and calendulas, actually enjoy the cooler weather.

color of your other flowers? Will they bloom quickly enough to provide early garden color, or take up the slack when your bulbs or early blooming perennials begin to fade? Does your garden have any special soil or shade problems?

Once you've answered these questions, you can go ahead and buy what you need. If you're buying seed, remember that a little bit will go a long way. Don't oversow. It's usually best to buy both seeds and seedlings by name. Seed mixtures, especially, are often not very reliable in producing the size, shapes, color, and varieties you want most. Check the age of the seed, and the germination percentages on each packet.

ANNUAL PLANTING AND CARE

Grandma Putt prepared her annual flower beds the same as she did for tulips or perennials. Although these flowers are less choosy than most, she still liked to give them a treat. She figured that the less work they have to do

Bed Energizing Mix

To get her flower beds ready to grow, Grandma Putt would make up a batch of her Bed Energizing Mix:

50 lbs. of peat moss,
25 lbs. of gypsum,
10 lbs. of garden food, and
4 bushels of compost

and work it well into the soil.

in rooting and feeding themselves, the more time they'll have to produce fabulous flowers.

For a tip-top annual bed, Grandma Putt mixed up her **Bed Energizing Mix**, and worked it into the soil. Afterwards, she would rake and level the entire area. Then she let it set for a week to ten days.

After sowing the seed, she'd mulch the ground with several sheets of newspapers to protect the seedlings. She'd remove the papers as soon as the seeds begin to sprout.

After sprouting, Grandma Putt would spread a mulch of grass clippings around the seedlings. This would keep the ground moist, and prevent weeds from taking over.

Annuals have amazing appetites; the more you feed them, the more they'll like it! They need lots of energy and growth power, so Grandma Putt fed her flowers monthly with a handful of garden food, followed by a dose of her **Fabulous Flower Tonic**.

These beauties prefer to wash their own foliage in the rain. But when it's dry, we watered them with a watering can or old-fashioned soaker-hose. Be careful—water their toes, not their nose; they can't stand wet foliage!

Fabulous Flower Tonic

Grandma Putt gave this special treat to her flowers every month or so during the growing season:

1 cup of barnyard tea,
1/2 bottle of beer,
1/4 cup of ammonia, and
1/2 cup of Fels-Naptha Soap Solution

mixed in 20 gallons of water, and sprayed over all of her beds.

Thin, Snip, & Pinch

Grandma Putt taught me that thinning is a very important part of growing annuals successfully. She said to be strong-minded; otherwise, they will crowd each other out, and prevent those around them from growing. So, pull out all but the hardiest seedlings. You'll be glad you did when you see the survivors bloom big, strong, and proud!

Another important job Grandma Putt showed me how to do was to cut back her flowers, which was actually good for

SHARE YOUR LOVE...WITH FLOWERS

them. She would allow them to bloom once, then the second blooms were cut. She did this to encourage more and bigger blooms later on in the season.

Finally, there was the deadheading job. I found that if I pinched off faded blooms, the flowers would repay me with new and vigorous growth for many, many more weeks.

A VERY CUT AND DRIED SUBJECT

Over the years, I've learned that every home garden should include an area set aside for growing cut flowers. The size will depend upon your need for flowers, and the amount of space available. Enjoyable as flowers are in the garden, most of us want some in the house for a table centerpiece, to brighten a room for guests, or just to have around for our own enjoyment.

Locate your cutting garden in a fairly out-of-the-way place, but don't get it too far away from the house. Choose a sunny spot

Petunia Power!

Grandma Putt loved her petunias, and she always seemed to have the best-looking ones in town. Her secret? Well, let's just say she knew that a "pinch in time saved nine."

Grandma would plant her petunias when it was cool, and then pinch off all of the flowers before they bloomed. This first pinching directed the new growth efforts into producing leaves and branching. Planting before the temperatures got real warm also encouraged the petunias to branch naturally, and got the plants off to a healthy start.

By the second week in July, they are ready to be pinched again. Grandma would snip each stem about 4" above ground level. She didn't mourn those lost blooms because about 2 weeks later, she had another full display to enjoy.

Grandma made the third pinch late in the season, with the fourth at the end of September if there hadn't been a heavy frost. Since petunias like the cooler temperatures, she had a rather massive bed of perfect petunias until the first killing frost!

Easy-to-Grow Cutting Flowers

For Beauty

Baby's breath	Petunia
Chrysanthemum	Plume
Coneflower	Poppy
Dahlia	Salvia
Foxglove	Stock
Marigold	Sweet pea
Pansy	Yarrow
Peony	Wallflower

For Fragrance

Artemesia	Lavender
Bee balm	Peony
Columbine	Rose nepeta
Dianthus	Southernwood
Gardenia	Sweet violet
Heliotrope	Wallflower

where the soil is well-drained and fertile—or make it so before you plant.

Grandma Putt kept her cut-flower plantings tucked away in various nooks and crannies, and in a fairly large bed out near the vegetable garden where it wouldn't be so noticeable after a recent harvest. She cut some flowers for beauty, others for their fragrance, and still others for thinnings.

There are several advantages to having a special garden set aside just for taking cuttings. First, you won't have to detract from your display beds by cutting from them; second, you can grow flowers especially for cutting in orderly rows, just like vegetables, and they'll be much easier to care for. Weeding, watering, and other minor maintenance can be performed much more conveniently.

To get the longest season of bloom possible, you should sow your annuals more than once. That way, new flowers will be coming into bloom as the older ones fade. Of course, you shouldn't sow any more annuals than you can reasonably use. It's better to make small, successive sowings of those you are particularly fond of—then you can invite the pretty maids, elves, and dwarfs into your house all spring, summer, and possibly even up to frost in the fall, and enjoy each in turn!

Longer-Lasting Cut Flowers

There are a number of tricks Grandma Putt showed me to keep her cut flowers lasting for days beyond what they should have. First, she'd cut them either early in the morning, or late in the evening. A cool, cloudy day was even better. Then, as soon as she cut them, she'd cut an inch off of the stem, and put them in a pail of water in a cool place.

To revive fading flowers, Grandma Putt would use three drops of mentholated rub mixed with three drops of rubbing alcohol. She'd take her fading flowers out of their vase, throw out the old water, and add new water and her old-fashioned elixir. Then, before she put her flowers back into the vase, she stuck the base of the stems in boiling water (to open up their constricted passageways), and made a fresh, slanting cut.

Cut Flower Extenders

Here are several of Grandma Putt's secrets for extending the life of your cut flowers:

Secret #1—Put a few drops of camphorated oil and rubbing alcohol in the water with cut flowers.

Secret #2—Add 2 tbsp. of clear corn syrup per quart of very warm water; then add it to the vase.

Secret #3—A cube of sugar per pint of water and a copper penny in the vase can extend their life.

Secret #4—A solution of 2 tsp. of antiseptic mouthwash in 1 quart of water will perk them up.

Secret #5—A tea made of 15 foxglove leaves in 1/2 cup of boiling water; let it cool before adding to the vase.

Secret #6—Add an aspirin or small amount of bleach to the vase water.

Dry Them Out!

There are a number of attractive annuals that can be included in a cutting garden especially for use in winter bouquets. This, of course, is not the only way that dried flowers can be used. Grandma Putt made some very beautiful dried arrangements framed for hanging on a wall. Others were beautifully preserved under a glass bell.

Strawflowers are excellent for this purpose. The large, double flowers start readily from seed, and are easy to grow. They have much to recommend them—they are showy in beds, free blooming, and will grow in any good garden soil!

Grandma Putt harvested strawflowers when they were about half open so they would be fully opened when dry. She stripped the stems, and hung the flowers up to dry. She grouped three to four stems together, and tied them securely. Stems lose their moisture and shrink as they dry, so tie them tight enough to keep them from slipping out.

She hung the bunched stalks upside down to keep the flower heads upright, and the stems straight. Make sure that there is good air circulation over all surfaces. You can hang them on a line as you would clothes, or you can attach three or four bunches to a wire coat hanger with old-fashioned clothespins.

Best Drying Annuals

baby's breath
bells of Ireland
celosia
cornflower
everlasting
gaillardia
marigold
petunia
phlox
stock
sunflower
sweet alyssum
sweet pea
verbena
zinnia

SHARE YOUR LOVE...WITH FLOWERS

Grandma Putt hung her flowers in her attic or shed. Don't cover or shut them up in a closet—free circulation of air is an absolute must! Most plants will dry in eight to twelve days, but if the air is humid, it might take a bit longer.

When your flowers are dry, handle with care. They will be stiff to the touch, and the stems will snap easily. Store them in a covered box until you're ready to use them. Experiment a little with one or two flowers to see how they handle.

It's A Frame-up!

Here's another method Grandma Putt used for making beautiful pictures with dried flowers—a bit more elaborate than the first, but well worth trying.

For these pictures, you'll need thinner and lighter types of flowers like cosmos, columbine, larkspur, pansies, and petunias. If Queen Anne's lace grows somewhere nearby, try drying that, too.

Grandma Putt used to gather all her plant materials around noon on a sunny day—when they were still fresh and fully opened, but had the least amount of moisture. She chose the most perfect specimens in her garden; plant stems were no longer than 4 to 6 inches, and she removed thick stems entirely.

She placed her flowers, nicely smoothed out and apart from each other, on paper towels. She then placed a second paper towel on top of them. She laid them carefully between the pages of a telephone book, and placed a weight (like bricks from the barnyard) on top of the book.

Grandma Putt found that the color set better and the moisture would be removed more quickly if she replaced the paper towels with fresh, dry ones the following day, and again the day after that. She also replaced the weights.

The best advice I can give you is to be patient when assembling your design. With this method, you don't use any glue; glass presses against the design, and holds the completed picture in place. Use tweezers to move tiny or fragile pieces about. You can create an illusion of depth by placing one piece on another, but be sure to first clip away any bulky areas.

Most of your flowers and leaves, when dried, will not be quite as bright as they were when they bloomed in your garden, so keep your background colors soft and neutral. Remember you are working with natural materials and colors.

When your design is complete, place the glass upon it, and fit a frame molding around it. Turn the whole composition over with a quick, firm movement. Then, just as with any other picture, tack the back in place.

If you prefer, you can leave the glass in the frame, and make the design of pressed materials on it in reverse instead of right-side-up on the background. After completing the pattern, place a background material on it, and tack the backboard in the frame.

SHARE YOUR LOVE...WITH FLOWERS

RING ME UP, ROSEY!

The first roses may well have been growing in that First Garden. If so, then Eve should have been more like many ladies who, I find, take much more interest in a bouquet of roses than in a basket of fruit!

In Grandma's Putt's day, folks had lots of room, even in the city, so most homes had at least a modest rose garden. I remember June as being the month when roses seemed to be everywhere!

Rose Hips Tonic

When the flowers fade as fast as the setting sun, try making Grandma Putt's Rose Hips Tonic before they're all gone:

**2 tbsp. of rose hips, and
2 cups of boiling water**

Steep, covered, for 20 minutes. Strain and sweeten. Use this tonic as is, or add it to your favorite tea. It's great for colds (lots of extra Vitamin C), and it will shorten your recovery period.

Almost all roses have a delightful fragrance and flavor, in addition to blooms beyond compare (unless compared with other roses). Grandma Putt took advantage of these qualities by using rose petals in sachets, potpourris, salads, and teas. In addition, she made rose wine and rose hips jelly. Rose hips, by the way, are the fruit of the rose plant, and are very rich in nutrients, especially Vitamin C.

Even if you can't promise yourself a rose garden, you can grow roses and get more for your money. Modern roses often bloom for a second season in the fall. So, why not learn a few of Grandma Putt's tips and tricks that will help you grow your own beautiful roses?

WHICH ROSE IS WHICH?

Roses are identified by the way they grow, and by their structure. There are four basic types: **bushes, climbers, shrubs, and trees.** The bush-type plants are the most commonly grown, with hybrid teas, grandifloras, floribundas, polyantha, hybrid polyantha, hybrid perpetual, and miniature roses included in this group.

❧*Hybrid Tea Roses* are the most popular backyard rose, grown for their long stems and giant blooms. They are fast growers, easily reaching a height of 3 feet and a width of 4 feet in one season. If the lady of your house is a student of flower arranging, or a lover of cut flowers, then this is the variety for you. The Peace Rose, which is the world's most popular rose, is a hybrid tea rose.

❧*Grandifloras* are produced from crosses of floribunda and hybrid tea roses. If you like big blooms, then these are your cup of tea. They grow tall and make a good background for any garden. They are also the easiest roses to grow and care for.

❧*Floribunda* is just what the name "flowering abundance" implies. They come from crossing tea roses and polyantha roses. This rose has numerous flowers arranged in large clusters. They're good for planting along hedges, or in front of hybrid teas.

❧*Polyantha Roses* are baby ramblers used for edgings. The flowers are small, but appear in dense clusters.

Rose Perfume

Grandma Putt made a delicate rose perfume by putting 6 cups of fresh rose petals in one gallon of water in a large aluminum pot. She simmered it for 2 to 3 hours, and then strained the mixture several times through cheesecloth. She discarded the pulp, and the water that remained was her rose water. She stored it in a clean, stoppered bottle.

SHARE YOUR LOVE...WITH FLOWERS

Hybrid Perpetuals are the roses that Grandma Putt grew, with her favorite being General Jacks. The famous American Beauty Rose was one of these (still is, for that matter). These June roses brightened the summer days of the early settlers. Nowadays, they're not very common because of their one flowering season.

Miniature Roses always seem to be in bloom from spring to fall. They grow from 12 to 18 inches tall, and can be used in borders, or as single specimens.

Climbing Roses mostly bloom in June, including the pillars, ramblers, and even some new, ever-blooming varieties. They make excellent boundary plants, and serve as perfect cover for an ugly wall or fence. Climbers have heavy canes that need staking or some other support. Ramblers have thinner, more flexible canes, which are great for walls. Pillars don't grow as high as climbers, so they can be trained on poles, pillars, and posts.

The Sweet Smell of . . .

Grandma Putt used fragrant rose petals along with other ingredients to make a potpourri that could perfume an entire room. She had all sorts of recipes for potpourris; as a matter of fact, anything that smelled good was a likely candidate—flowers, sweet herbs, fragrant grasses, vanilla, lemon and orange rind, and even walnut leaves.

She air-dried the petals on paper towels until they were crisp; about three days usually did the trick. She sprinkled the other ingredients over the petals, stirring them gently, and then put the lid on the jar. She used to open it whenever she wanted the wonderful fragrance to escape, especially in the winter.

Perfect Potpourri

To make her favorite potpourri, Grandma Putt took a pint-sized glass jar with a lid, and put these ingredients in it:
4 lightly packed cups of fresh rose petals,
3 tbsp. of mixed spices like ground cloves and allspice, and
1 tbsp. of powdered orris root
That's all there was to it!

❧ *Trailing Roses* are an offshoot of the climbers. Often called ground-cover roses, these trailing types can form huge mats and mounds.

❧ *Tree Roses* are an exception to the rule that "Only God can make a tree." Any bush-type rose (and even some climbers) can be grafted onto tree stock. The trunks are commonly 4 feet tall, and the flowering top part bushes out about the same distance.

❧ *Shrub Roses* are descendants of the original wild rose. They are very hardy, and well worth growing in your garden.

ROSE GROWING SECRETS

Grandma Putt taught me that roses are not only beautiful, but they are also among the easiest plants to grow. She said that if you give these Royal Mistresses lots of **fresh air, sunshine, food, and water**, you should have no problem. Her good cultural practices were so important to rose growing success. If you follow these practices in a sound, common-sense way, then you too will have beautiful roses.

Grandma Putt's Words of Wisdom:

"You get what you pay for, so always buy the best."

The All-Important Selection

You can buy canned, potted, or bare-root varieties of roses. Grandma Putt was always kind of partial to the bare-root roses, which are usually two-year-old budded stock that is dormant. These plants are graded, and Grandma's rule was to always buy the best.

SHARE YOUR LOVE...WITH FLOWERS

Perfect Planting

Grandma Putt's roses had been growing in the same place for many years by the time I lived there, but I have planted thousands of roses since then. So here's a few words of advice.

The best time to plant roses is in the fall or spring, whenever you can get a spade in the ground. Plant them the same day you bring them home. That's important, so I'll repeat it...*plant them the same day you bring them home!* Don't let them languish in the car trunk, the garage, or against a wall, or you're asking for trouble!

Work the soil deeply; it should be fertile, loose, and well-drained. Roses need 8 to 12 hours of sun a day, so make sure they get it! If your soil doesn't quite stack up for a large rose bed, then you'll need to renovate the bed. To do so, add **5 pounds of Rose/Flower Food** to the soil surface. Then, mix in **50 pounds of peat moss, 25 pounds of gypsum, and 3 bushels of 60-40 gravel.** All of this goes in a hundred-square-foot area. Mix this planting soil well.

Plant potted roses in a hole that's wide enough and deep enough to allow their roots to spread out, and be comfortable. Fill the hole to the top with water, and let it drain off before putting Miss Rose in her new home.

From the Medicine Cabinet

Grandma Putt told her gardening friends to sprinkle a half cup of Epsom salts on the surface of the soil (not touching the plants) around newly-planted roses. This is still good advice, because the Epsom salts gives them deeper color, thicker petals, and stronger roots. Then, talk to your rose... welcome her to her new home!

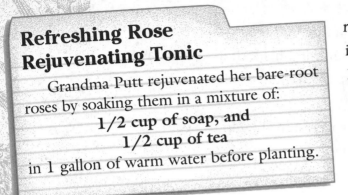

Refreshing Rose Rejuvenating Tonic

Grandma Putt rejuvenated her bare-root roses by soaking them in a mixture of:
1/2 cup of soap, and
1/2 cup of tea
in 1 gallon of warm water before planting.

In the case of bare-root roses, soak the roots in Grandma Putt's **Refreshing Rose Rejuvenating Tonic** before planting them. Cut off any dead or damaged parts. Don't bury your rose; the hole only needs to be wide and deep enough to give the roots plenty of growing space.

Grandma Putt always placed a mound of soil in the bottom of the hole, and spread the roots out. When you begin to refill the hole, push the soil down firmly. When your hole is half full of soil, fill the remainder with water, and allow it to drain. Then fill the remainder of the hole with soil. Be sure that the bulge or graft union ends up two inches *below* the surface of the soil. This is important if you want to raise grafted stock instead of first-root stock.

Once your rose is planted, build a small wall of soil around the outside perimeter of the hole to hold water. Water deeply. If it's spring, cut the canes back to 6 inches. Make sure that the cuts are above the outside bud. If it's fall, leave the canes alone. Cover the entire plant with a light soil mixture, and allow it to set for ten days.

Feeding and Weeding

Grandma Putt used to feed and water her roses at the same time. She did this by planting a large coffee can that was open at both ends between each rose. She filled these

SHARE YOUR LOVE...WITH FLOWERS

cans halfway to the top with pebbles, and from time to time, added a small amount of food to the can. Then when she watered deeply, the food would soak down to root level, where it's needed most.

Put down a thick mulch of shredded bark between your roses to keep their feet moist, and the weeds down. You can use any one of the preemerge weed killers to keep <u>you</u> off your knees. Also, plant some garlic and parsley nearby to repel insects, and make the flowers more fragrant.

Don't Let Them Wither!

When you pick or cut roses, be sure to leave at least one healthy five-leaf cluster on the stem. Leaving these good leaves will permit future growth from the same cane.

Grandma talked to and cared for her roses…they were her pride and joy. She made a regular practice of pinching off side buds of her hybrid teas to promote big, healthy blooms from the leading buds. Also, she never let faded flowers hang on for dear life; I suggest you pick these off as soon as you see them like she did.

Green Thumb Tip

Grandma Putt used to give her roses a midsummer pick-me-up by sprinkling any leftover tea leaves on the soil underneath each bush. The tannic acid in the tea made the soil slightly acidic, which roses just love! You can also mulch with pine needles which will give you the same result.

Grandma Putt washed her roses once a month, and grew chives at their feet to ward off aphids and other pests. At the first sign of trouble, she'd make up a batch of her **Black Spot Remover Tonic** to keep them healthy.

Black Spot Remover Tonic

To control black spot on her roses, Grandma Putt used to mix:

1 tbsp. of baking soda,
1 tbsp. of vegetable oil, and
1 tbsp. of Fels-Naptha Soap Solution

in 1 gallon of water. She lightly sprayed this mixture on her bushes once a week, or at the first sign of trouble.

If anything escaped her attention and got out of control (which rarely happened), then she removed the diseased parts of the plants, and sprayed them to prevent future damage from the same source. Every now and again, she'd get her hands on some tobacco powder, which she spread in and among her roses to keep future problems at bay.

That's about it for a beginner's overview of growing roses. I hope growing roses is easy, fun, and as worthwhile for you as it was for Grandma Putt, and still is for me. As Grandma Putt used to say:

"May the first rose you see each spring bring you joy, and the last rose of autumn bring you peace."

SHARE YOUR LOVE...WITH FLOWERS

10

GRANDMA'S ALL-AMERICAN LAWN

Grandma Putt was fond of saying that her beautiful green grass was *"predominantly* made up of Kentucky bluegrass." But, she was always quick to add, "It has a little bit of this, and a little bit of that mixed in for good measure." She claimed that her lawn was a typical, good old-fashioned "All-American Lawn."

After working on thousands of lawns over the years, I tend to agree with her. Most lawns that I've seen do contain "…a little bit of this, and a little bit of that."

Bluegrass is the grass that made Kentucky famous, and it is the granddaddy of all the really good-looking lawn grasses in the United States. It's easy to rhapsodize about this grass because of its beautiful dark-green color which shows best in the spring and fall, and its tendency to grow very dense and erect.

Unfortunately, this grass doesn't do very well in the heat of the summer months without a lot of water. During this time, it goes dormant, so it is usually mixed with other grasses that thrive in the sun and heat. Some "pals" of

Fact of the matter is, a little research revealed that Kentucky bluegrass is not a single strain of grass, nor is it even native to the "Bluegrass State." It's as old as Ancient Greece, and migrated to Western Europe and England during the Middle Ages, where it became known as "English grass."

Bluegrass is made up of thousands of variations of the original strain that was imported from England in colonial times. No one knows exactly how, but it beat Daniel Boone and the other settlers to Kentucky and the Ohio Valley. But despite this misnomer, for more than 200 years, it has been the basic seed or sod for most of the northern lawns in this country!

Kentucky bluegrass who take up the summer slack include the fine-leaf fescues, Meyer's zoysia in the South, or, in the North, one of the modern adaptations of Kentucky bluegrass that include merion, arboretum, Canada, delta, Newport, park, and Troy.

THE SUMMER SAVIOR

The traditional companion for Kentucky bluegrass back in Grandma Putt's day was white Dutch clover. Grandma Putt's lawn was planted before the development of the new variations of Kentucky bluegrass and the other good summer grasses, so clover was the "summer savior" of most green lawns. By July, when Kentucky bluegrass would begin to give in to diseases like mildew or to weeds like crabgrass, the white Dutch clover would take over, and keep the lawn green throughout the hot, dry summer months.

Nowadays, clover is almost completely unknown in most grass seed mixtures. When it does turn up in a lawn, it's usually treated like a villain—a dreaded weed!

Clover lost its appeal because it stains clothing and becomes very slippery when wet. These two problems made it very unpopular with mothers, football coaches, and playground superintendents everywhere.

Grandma Putt, however, never wanted to get rid of the clover in her lawn. To her, it was both beautiful and essential. She complained whenever winter lasted well into April saying that it will kill all of this year's clover. She also liked clover because it would fight off chinch bugs better than anything else in the lawn.

If you don't want to "leave clover where it's at," you can eliminate it quickly and easily. Simply spray it with soapy water, then follow up with a good broadleaf weed killer, following the directions carefully!

MAINTAINING YOUR ALL-AMERICAN LAWN

Grandma Putt used to say that taking care of your lawn is like looking after the health of a close friend or relative. She said that we should take care of our lawns the way the ancient Chinese practiced medicine. They believed that you hired a doctor to keep you well. Then, if you got sick, you fired the doctor, and got a new one.

Obviously, your lawn isn't going to fire you if it gets sick. But if you follow Grandma Putt's good cultural practices outlined below, and a good, common-sense lawn care program, then you won't spend a lot of time, money, and effort tearing up your lawn, and starting all over. Lawn care really should be fast, fun, and easy to do. Here's how we did it:

Rollin' in the Clover

Although clover is no longer a favorite grass buddy, it still has many uses around the yard. For example:

- Rabbits love clover, so plant some around your vegetable garden to keep them occupied.
- Butterflies find clover to be irresistible, and are instantly drawn to it.
- As a cover crop or green manure, clover adds much needed nitrogen to the soil.
- Certain parasitic wasps count clover among their favorite nectar sauces.
- In those out of the way or heavily trafficked areas, clover makes a very resilient ground cover.

MOW, MOW, MOW*
YOUR LAWN, GENTLY...

PREPARING TO MOW

That's right; back in the good old days, we actually prepared to mow the lawn. It *didn't* include revving up the riding
lawn mower, or running the weed wacker at the highest RPMs.

What we did was in the late afternoon on the day
before I was supposed to do my duty with the lawn mower,
Grandma would hand me a big bowl, table knife, and an old
pair of scissors. Then, together we would go out and prepare
the lawn for mowing. In those days, nothing went to waste,
and that included things that were growing in the grass.

Grandma Putt and I would sit or
kneel in the grass, and start to work digging out dandelion greens and weeds.
Grandma would save the dandelion
greens for stewing, or for use in soups
and salads. If there was plenty of fresh
dandelion flowers, she'd have me pick
enough of them so she could have a
nosegay or two—and for her yearly batch of Dandelion
Wine (See pages 86-87).

Grandma Putt's Words of Wisdom:

"Weeds are just plants that happen to be living in the wrong place."

Grandma would also pick as many chamomile flowers as
we could find. Later, after they dried, they were suitable for
making the chamomile tea which she set great store by. She
believed that chamomile was one of the most useful herbal
medicines with its tea being the best remedy for stomach
cramps and intestinal flu.

*Sung to the tune of Row, Row, Row Your Boat...

Steady and Slow— Weeding, That is!

Digging out weeds with a table knife is a terribly tedious job. But Grandma Putt believed there was great value in "getting *close* to the earth" and "touching" it; so, guess who got *real* close to the earth that summer? She said that was really the most important reason for having a garden.

Usually, we would use the time to give each other accounts of what happened during the day. Or, if I was lucky, Grandma would tell me an Indian story or a slightly exaggerated tale about how silly Grandpa Putt had been when he was courtin' her.

In case you're wondering, Grandma Putt also had plenty of crabgrass, plantain, chickweed, and horsegrass in her yard. I had to dig them out with the table knife, especially in those months before the crabgrass went to seed (July and August).

Those were the days...

Grandma Putt had a considerable amount of knowledge about Indian herbal medicines, and she would find a good many of these medicinal "herbs" (a/k/a weeds) growing right in her own yard.

I was always willing to try Grandma's "Indian medicine" so I could show off to my pals about it. She brewed plantain into a wicked-tasting medicine that was supposed to be good for headaches. I thought it earned that reputation because it made you feel so sick to your stomach, you tended to forget about your headache! Applied to the skin, plantain could also heal cuts and bruises. Grandma Putt said that the Kiowa used plantain leaves in their corn salads. I don't recall if she ever did, but if so, then I'm sure I ate it with relish!

In those days, I had a small boy's curious appetite. I remember one time I ate some grass. I figured that if the cows, horses, and sheep liked it so much, it must be pretty good. Needless to say, I was a pretty sick fellow! Grandma simply laughed when I told her about it. She said I should have skipped the grass, and tried the clover. Indians were very partial to clover, especially when it was young and tender. After my experience with grass, I decided to skip the clover!

Wash That Dirt Right Out...

Grandma Putt used a regular lawn-washing program as a basic part of her good cultural practices.

Grandma Putt's favorite soap was Fels-Naptha, which is still around (but hard-to-find) today. The soap stretched her gardening dollars—it was a great spreader, catching the nitrogen in the fertilizer before it was washed out of its regular carrier (the bulk material the manufacturer uses to carry the nitrogen). It also made weed killers and other garden controls more effective by helping them stick to the grass where they could do the most good. And yes, it's true; bugs don't like the taste of soap any better than you do!

These techniques have been around a long time; why, I bet you remember *your* grandmother throwing the sudsy dish or bathwater out over the roses and kitchen garden.

As you probably know, crabgrass grows low enough to escape the lawn mower blades, so hand digging was really the only way to remove it. It's not all that bad if you have a couple of youngsters; why, you can even make a game out of it!

While mowing isn't the most effective method of fighting off crabgrass, it will limit its ability to go to seed. Crabgrass needs lots of sunlight to flourish; if it doesn't get it, it can be "shaded" out of existence. So let the good grass around the crabgrass grow slightly taller than normal to keep the crabgrass in shade.

Grandma Putt used time-tested methods for ridding her lawn of pesky weeds—what she called "good cultural practices." These practices consisted of regularly dethatching, washing, aerating, and feeding her lawn, as well as mowing as often as necessary.

She said a good, healthy lawn was the first line of defense in the battle against weeds. Then, if that fails, you may have to resort to more "modern" methods of removing weeds.

Bring Out The Artillery!

Often, a so-called "new" scientific method is really an "old-fashioned" idea that has been forgotten, and then is suddenly "rediscovered." A good example of this is the application of these "new" preemergent weed killers which are based on one of the oldest techniques ever used in the lawn grower's war against crabgrass.

The idea is to apply a chemical treatment just prior to seed germination, so it will attack the weed seed just as it germinates. In the early days of their use, these preemergent controls were dangerous to earthworms and, therefore, to birds. Nowdays, manufacturers have eliminated the arsenate compounds that were previously used, and the new preemergent weed killers are pretty much nontoxic to animals.

Grandma Putt's Words of Wisdom:

"One year's weed is many years' seed."

But remember, the most important rule for using any weed killer, fungicide, or pest control lawn treatment is to be careful, and follow the directions on the package to the letter. If you do this with the preemergent weed killers, you should be able to get rid of crabgrass once and for all.

Then if you don't want to eat and/or use broadleaf weeds, the best way to get rid of chickweed, clover, plantain, and dandelion is to give them a good soapy water bath followed by an application of 2-4 D, a growth stimulator hormone that literally makes the plants grow themselves to an early grave. The hormone is usually combined with a herbicide that'll really knock the socks off of these weeds once and for all!

You may be thinking—what would Grandma Putt have to say about all of these new-fangled concoctions? Well, she would have been one of the first to use modern controls like the preemergent weed killers and growth stimulators if her cultural practices couldn't get the job done. She believed in using every practical means available to get the gardening results she desired. But she also believed in using an extra dose of good common sense whenever she set out to kill a troublesome pest, lest she cause herself and Mother Earth some harm.

With all the shouting about the dangers of weed killers today, not enough people on either side are paying heed to Grandma Putt's prescription for common sense. Weed killers are fine if you just pay attention to the directions on the package and use them properly. Remember, you wouldn't drink a gallon of Aureomycin to get rid of a common cold. The same idea holds true for weed killers. Use your head, and *follow all directions!*

Reasons to Mow

Besides looking nice, there are many other good reasons to mow your lawn, including:
- Stimulate branching
- Promote root growth
- Keep the blades standing straight and tall
- Maintain green color
- Crowd out weeds

HOW AND WHEN TO MOW

Although I didn't initially realize it, there is a right way and a wrong way to mow a lawn. I sure learned how to do it right in a hurry!

Grandma Putt taught me that I shouldn't take cutting the grass for granted. It's very important to cut it at just the right time, and in the right way.

If you don't know how and when to cut, you'll defeat the whole purpose, which I hope is to have the greenest grass on *your* side of the fence.

One reason to mow the lawn is to stimulate branching of the grass blades and root growth. Another is to keep the blades standing straight and tall. You also want to maintain good green color, and the best way to do it is by…guess what? Mowing! When grass blades are cut off at the top, the chlorophyll rushes back up the blade to seal off the cut!

Nighttime Is The Right Time

Actually, that's a correct statement if you've got head-lights on your lawn mower. But if you don't, then start a little bit earlier in the evening. Never cut your grass in the middle of the day. Why? Well, Grandma Putt used to ask me

Grass Variety	Mowing Height	Mow When
Fine fescue	2"	3"
Kentucky bluegrass	2"	3"
Perennial ryegrass	2"	3"
Tall turf-type fescue	2"	3"
Zoysia	1 to 2"	1½ to 3"

how I would like it if the dentist pulled a tooth without giving me gas or a shot of novocaine? This is *exactly* what happens to your lawn when you cut your grass during the heat of the day.

When grass is cut, the tunnels to the roots are suddenly exposed to heat and surface winds. If you mow in the evening, the winds will have subsided, and the sun will have settled low, which will make it more comfortable for both you <u>and</u> your grass.

Grandma Putt also taught me that grass should be cut when it is dry. She also recommended cutting it in the evening, and then watering the next morning. Mowing your lawn when it is too wet causes grass to build up on

Those were the days...

Grandma Putt said I was a throwback to her Indian ancestors because of the way I objected to mowing the lawn. She said that the Indians weren't able to grow grass because the native grasses weren't suitable for pasture lands.

The first lawns were an imitation of the open meadows that were brought inside the medieval walled gardens. Back in those days, it was customary to sprinkle wildflowers here and there over the lawn. You couldn't cut the grass for fear of disturbing the flowers. I must admit, at age ten, I thought that was a splendid custom—a tradition, I believed, that should have been carried down to modern times!

But, some wiseguy came up with the mowing idea, and like sheep, millions of us have followed his lead ever since. And speaking of sheep, Louis XVI of France was a great believer in the beauty of a close-cropped lawn. In fact, he imported hundreds of sheep to graze on the grass at his fabulous palace at Versailles. The grass may have been great to look at, but the smell was enough to choke a horse! In fact, many of his courtiers complained about the odor emanating from the palace lawn. Grandma Putt said it's better to have a boy cut your grass than a sheep. I guess we boys don't smell so bad after all!

the undercarriage of the mower, which will then have a tendency to tear the grass blades instead of cutting them cleanly. Pulling and tearing weakens the grass blades, and may actually damage the roots. The result? A dead or dying lawn!

Keeping your grass at the proper height will also improve the quality and density of your lawn. Each variety has a recommended cutting height that will make it vigorous and healthy. Check the chart to determine when to cut your grass (See page 307).

HOW OFTEN?

Folks have been arguing about this question folks for many, many years. As a not-so-ambitious ten-year-old, once a month seemed just about right to me.

But Grandma Putt set me straight in a hurry! She had me cut her "All-American Lawn" every four to five days when it was growing vigorously, and every week to ten days when it was not.

Of course, how often you mow should really be determined by how fast your grass is growing. During the spring, when the grass is growing rapidly, cut it often. As the season progresses, and you and the grass grow more tired, cut it less often. Believe it or not, if you have a true bluegrass lawn, you should cut it every two to three days. That's right—it needs to be cut that often to maintain its vigor!

Other grasses require different frequencies; rye grasses and fescues should be cut twice a week, while Bentgrass every other day. And although I'm in the minority, I've found that dichondra thrives when it is cut once a week.

One very important lesson Grandma Putt taught me was that once you start cutting your grass short, don't let it get real long before you mow it again. The smaller the portion of leaf surface you remove each time you mow, the less of a shock it will be to your turf.

No Close Shaves!

I had a bright idea one time I was mowing Grandma's lawn. I lowered the mower blade, and cut the lawn extra short, hoping to stretch out the time between cuttings. Brother, did I ever get an earful over that one!

Grandma Putt said that most grass doesn't do well with a brush cut, so don't think I could skip cutting "next time" by cutting the lawn extra short this time. All I was doing was hurting the grass's ability to maintain itself. Too many close shaves like that she said, and pretty soon, we'd begin to see her fine-quality lawn thin out. It simply wouldn't have the

Exceptions to the Rule

Of course there are exceptions to every rule. The exceptions to the No-Close-Shave Rule are Bermuda grass, carpet grass, and centipede grass. These warm-season grasses can be cut at half an inch or even slightly shorter to maintain their vigor. The trade off? All of these grasses should be cut with a reel-type mower.

strength to adjust to the every-day problems like overwatering, compaction, insects, and disease.

The final thing to remember about mowing frequency is to adjust the height on your lawn mower a couple of times during the growing season. Too many people set it once, and then forget about it for the rest of the season. Remember, during the heavy growing season, you can cut closer and more often; but in the middle of summer, raise the height of the cut to the maximum noted on the grass-growing charts (See page 307). Come late fall, drop the height one notch, and mow one last time to give your lawn its final clean-up cut before winter.

THE COMFORT ZONE

First of all, you need a lawn mower that you're absolutely comfortable with. Grandma Putt had an old riding reel mower that was fairly fast, but she preferred a self-propelled, hand mower. She said she wanted to be able to smell the grass after it was cut, and by golly, smell it she did—she pushed her old mower even when she was well up into her seventies! I have to admit, the smell of fresh-cut grass is still one of my little pleasures in life; it can transport me, almost instantly, back to those wonderful days of my childhood.

GRANDMA'S ALL-AMERICAN LAWN

Once you've got your mower, you need to set it for the desired height. Remember, you want to <u>cut</u> the grass, not <u>rip</u> it out by its roots!

See to it that the blades are *and* remain sharp. A dull blade will rip, tear, and beat the poor blades to death! If you have an old mower, make sure that the blades are sharpened near the beginning of each growing season. Other times, you can take a flat sharpening stone to the mower's blades.

There's a lot of discussion over which kind of mower is best. It's only fair to warn you that eighty percent of all lawn mower accidents involve rotary mowers. So be careful! Make sure it's completely turned off before you touch the blade. I know it sounds pretty basic, but obviously, lots of folks need to be reminded just like I did when Grandma told me to be careful, and not cut off my toes with the scythe!

Don't Rub Them The Wrong Way!

Grandma Putt said that grass blades are like people in that they don't like to be constantly rubbed the wrong way. Her philosophy was once you run your mower around the outside of your property, you can go ahead and be as creative as you want to be.

From the Kitchen Cupboard

What should you do about grass clippings? There are two schools of thought that go way back, even to Grandma Putt's day. One says that the debris and clippings that build up at soil level should be removed because they tend to shed water and encourage disease. The other says that they act as a mulch, and are good for the soil.

Since the experts themselves disagreed, Grandma Putt played the middle ground. She had me catch as many grass clippings as I could, then we used them for mulch in the garden. We let the rest fall where they may. That was it, although twice a year, she sprayed her lawn with her Clipping Remover Tonic to help her lawn "breathe," as she put it.

Clipping Remover Tonic

To help her lawn, Grandma Putt sprayed her Clipping Remover Tonic on it twice a year:

1 bottle of beer,
1 bottle of soda pop,
1 cup of ammonia, and
1 cup of Fels-Naptha Soap Solution,
mixed in 20 to 25 gallons of water

At age ten, I was fond of curved lines and diagonals, but sometimes I'd make straight rows lengthwise or widthwise just to vary the mowing pattern. Unbeknownst to me, that was Grandma Putt's real secret to proper mowing—vary the pattern each time you mow!

Grass should be mowed from several directions, especially during the growing season. This ensures that the grass blades are never allowed to grow in just one direction.

Start in one direction, then when you come back from the opposite direction of a previous cut, make sure your mower overlaps at least half-way. This will ensure that you don't miss grass that was rolled flat by the mower wheels.

You should begin mowing in the spring when the grass reaches 2 inches tall. Keep mowing into the fall...as long as you can continue unhampered by snow or a soggy lawn.

CHOW TIME!

I soon learned that lawn feeding is one of the most important steps to a great looking, healthy lawn. Unfortunately, it is also the most confusing.

Homemade Lawn Food

Grandma Putt would feed her lawn twice a year with the following mix.

3 lbs. of bone meal, and
3 lbs. of Epsom salts
mixed in with **50 lbs. of dry lawn food**
She applied this mix at half of the recommended rate, 2 weeks apart.

Grandma said that grass plants, just like people and animals, can only take in and digest so much food at any one time. They like a decent, well-balanced diet, in adequate quantities, on a regular basis. Excess food causes upset stomachs and discomfort.

At the start of each growing season, she fed her lawn with her own special blend of dry fertilizer. The fertilizer you use makes a difference, but what is more important is how, when, and how often you apply it.

In both spring and fall, Grandma Putt would add 3 lbs. of bone meal and 3 lbs. of Epsom salts to a large bag of the cheapest lawn food she could find. She'd then apply that mix at half the recommended rate with a spreader. Almost immediately after that feeding, she'd give her lawn a snack, which she said helped it digest the dry lawn food. This snack consisted of equal parts of beer, soap, and ammonia mixed in her tank sprayer, and sprayed evenly over the turf.

Then about once a month, she'd spray this same mix on her lawn, adding either barnyard tea or homemade fish fertilizer to it to maintain the deep, dark green color.

WATERING

You can't live very long without water, and your lawn is no different. If you let your grass go too long without a good fresh drink, it will dehydrate. On the other hand, if you soak it with too much water, the grass will get fat, soft, and tender. In this condition, it is susceptible to disease and injury. You can't turn off a thundercloud, but you can control the sprinkler. So give your lawn at least 1 inch of water per week to keep it tough, and in tip-top fighting shape.

Dollars & $ense

To translate 20-10-10, 10-5-5, 5-5-5, or any other hyphenated fertilizer nutrients into dollars and cents: remember that 20-5-5 fertilizer has four times as much nitrogen as phosphate or potash. A product labeled 10-5-5 has twice as much nitrogen as phosphate or potash. And one labeled 5-5-5 has an equal amount of each nutrient.

But 5-5-5 and 10-10-10 fertilizers are not the same. Though the proportions are the same, they provide different amounts of nutrients by weight.

In the first case, 5 percent of the total weight of the bag is nitrogen (or phosphate, or potash). In the second case, the quantity of each nutrient is 10 percent of the total weight.

So, it would require a 20 pound bag of 5-5-5 fertilizer to provide the same nutrition as a 10 pound bag of 10-10-10 fertilizer.

Makes sense, doesn't it?

YOUR GRASS HAS GOOD TASTE

All water may look alike, but don't be fooled. Scientifically, H_2O may have the same basic formula, but remember that rain and snow have natural trace elements that can add to the health of your lawn.

Grandma Putt used to have barrels set out all over the place, trying to catch every last drop of precious rainwater. Why? Because the best and purest water available runs down your rain spout and out into the street every time it rains! Simple rainwater contains a mild, but high-nitrogen fertilizer; the analysis would read something like 78-21-1.

Well water is next best because it has many important trace elements, like iron, which are important to both people and plants. Well water is lower in nitrogen than rainwater, though, and it costs something to get it out of the ground! So Grandma Putt used it sparingly around her yard.

Water from your kitchen faucet has many trace elements, but it also has a lot of unwanted chemical additives. Fluoride is put in some community water to give kids strong teeth. Chlorine is used to kill germs. One bad villain coming out of your faucet is plain old sodium—salt. Too much salt isn't good for you, and it certainly doesn't do your lawn any good. In fact, many lawns are killed by this sneaky creep hiding in your water. Your plants have a definite distaste for some of these additives, so either avoid them, or get rid of them!

RISE, SHINE, AND SPRINKLE!

If you're depending upon a thundercloud to do the watering job, you'll have to be happy whenever the work gets done. But if you have a choice of times to water, Grandma Putt taught me that the best time is early in the morning, just after the sun pokes his head out from behind the trees. While the dew was still clinging to each blade of grass, we'd turn the sprinklers on, and give the lawn a good soaking.

Grandma Putt's Words of Wisdom:

"Be cool—don't cut your grass in the heat of the day."

Don't Overdo It!

Grandma Putt knew that it was more economical (and safer) to apply lawn fertilizer in small, frequent doses than in one large, massive megadose. Water-soluble nitrogen, the shot-in-the-arm ingredient which "greens up" the lawn, can cause leaf burn (or weakening of the plant by excessive growth) unless it is diluted well by watering.

The more nitrogen that is applied, the more water that will be required. But water in massive quantities would leach the nitrogen into the soil below the root level, where it is not needed. Overfertilizing also contributes to the accumulation of thatch, which interferes with the movement of air, water, and nutrients into the soil, and retards the development and growth of grass.

I know you've probably heard this before, but it's very important—*put enough water on your lawn so it penetrates deep.* If just the surface is wet, the roots will grow near the surface to drink the water where you put it. When the hot, dry days of summer arrive, the soil will quickly dry out, the roots will also dry out, and your grass will burn up. Shallow watering will one day leave you with guess what? A dead brown lawn!

Nighttime Is *Not* The Right Time

Grandma Putt's other watering rule was never to water the lawn at night! She said that if you went to bed with wet clothes, on a wet mattress, and left the window open, you too would have fungus growing between your toes! Soon, you'd get the itches and scratches. Well, your grass gets the itches and scratches too.

Folks always ask me why golf courses water all night. That's simple—people prefer to play golf in the sunshine without water being dumped in their shoes! Besides, golf courses are usually sprayed with a fungicide once a week to combat disease. So don't copy the watering habits of the local greenskeeper, unless you're collecting greens' fees!

GRANDMA'S ALL-AMERICAN LAWN

HOW TO WATER

Although watering is a simple job, it needs to be done properly. Remember, I said to water deep. Well, how deep is deep? (That's a deep subject!)

For the average lawn, the cool grasses, such as Merion and Kentucky blue, the ryes (which are both cool and warm), the red fescues, and Poa trivialis, water to depth of about 3 inches. For Dichondra, zoysia, and Bermuda, it's a good idea to water to a depth of 2 inches. Even though you have sandy soil, water deep so that the roots get used to staying down there.

How do you know when you have 2, 3, or 4 inches of water down? That's simple—make a homemade watering meter. Take a coffee can, and place it out at the farthest point that the water reaches. When the water in the can reaches whatever depth you've determined you want, stop watering.

It's a good idea to do this at least twice a week. It isn't going to do your lawn any good if you water a little every day because a little every day doesn't help at all. As a matter of fact, it does more harm than good! Shallow watering encourages shallow root growth, which weakens the grass, and makes it susceptible to all sorts of damage.

PREPARING FOR A NEW LAWN

One of the most daunting tasks a new homeowner faces is putting in a new lawn. I helped Grandma Putt do it several times at her neighbors' houses, and to me, it was always great fun—plenty of folks, digging, scraping, and leveling, with a good time had by all. If you are planning to install a new lawn where none has ever been before, here are the steps we used back in the good old days, together with a few of my more modern tips and tricks.

Step #1—Take a hand cultivator, disc and harrow, or spade and hoe, and loosen the soil. This should be done from 6 to 12 inches down, depending on the root-building qualities of the grass that will be planted.

Step #2—Pick out any rocks or debris turned up by the cultivating. *Don't miss anything!* It may be an obvious point, but grass doesn't grow real well over rocks, roots, shingles, or other debris.

Sweet 'n Low

Some grasses, particularly the bentgrasses, need extremely fertile soil along with what Grandma Putt used to call "sweet" soil which has a low acidity. If you live east of the Mississippi, you'll probably have to add lime several times a year.

I say several times for good reason. Giving your lawn a big dose of lime can give it a "stomachache." Grandma advised her neighbors to apply several small "doses" of lime over a long period of time, rather than one big application at the beginning of the growing season. She said that grass, like people, can't take such a big shock to its digestive system. In a way, it's like giving someone a whole bottle of Alka-Seltzer® to relieve a little stomachache.

Step #3—Remove any weed roots or insects that are present in the soil. Check with a reliable chemical expert—don't sterilize your soil permanently before planting grass!

Step #4—Now apply 50 lbs. of gypsum per 1,000 sq. ft. of soil. Next, if you're up North in snow country, add 100 lbs. of peat moss per 1,000 sq. ft. In the West and Southwest, add old sawdust, leaf mold, or well-rotted cow manure in the same proportion.

Topsoil Alert!

Beware of any topsoil you have to buy; don't be fooled by "good black dirt." It may be subsoil treated with sludge so that it looks like black topsoil. Color isn't what's important.

Remember all of the raking and picking over that you had to do with your own topsoil? Well, check the soil you are considering buying. If there are stones, twigs, etc., in it, then go ahead, and buy it. That means that it probably is topsoil.

If you are buying topsoil, revisit step three because you can be almost certain that any purchased topsoil will bring you lots of weeds, seeds, and insects. Good hunting!

Step #5—Next, add 50 lbs. of any good garden food with a low-nitrogen, high-phosphorus content; 4-12-4 or 5-10-5 are fine. Remember, a fat, even-growing crop of grass is happy grass!

Step #6—Work all of these ingredients into the soil. If you don't have a large lawn area, use a hoe and rake, but it's a tough, muscle-stretching job. Renting a rototiller is worth every cent you have to spend.

Step #7—Level off the cultivated soil. (Don't overwork it, and pulverize the soil completely.) Now, go over it once more, and pick up any additional stones, root twigs, and large, inert matter.

Step #8—Now, check the level of the new seedbed, making sure that it's up to the height you want for your lawn. If you're planning on laying sod, it should be approximately 3/4 of an inch below the finished lawn level. If it's not up to the height you need, bring in some additional topsoil to supplement what's already there.

Step #9—Work the soil up around the foundation of the garage, sidewalks, driveways, flower beds, and trees to force runoff and proper drainage. The idea of a completely flat lawn is a mistake, except for bentgrass, which does need a flat seedbed. Most lawns require a slight pitch or slope to assure good drainage. A lawn should slope away from a house at a grade of 10 inches for every 100 feet. That will keep heavy rainfall out of the basement, and will still allow your grass to receive the maximum water requirements to its deepest roots.

Step #10—Now smooth the remainder of the seedbed. For this purpose, use your "fertile" imagination to find some helpful tools. Grandma Putt's favorite was an old mattress spring which she kept out back. She tied a rope on the front of it, as you would on a sled, and had me pull it in big, overlapping circles, stopping only to fill in or shave off spots. Since then, I've seen a 5-foot length of chain fence, a heavy window frame, or an old section of ladder do nicely for this same purpose.

With this preparation out of the way, you're now ready to lay down some of that green in the form of seed or sod.

SIMPLE SEEDING

Despite all the modern, improved techniques of planting, old-fashioned seeding is still the safest, surest, and cheapest way to start an exceptional lawn.

Grass Seed Mixtures

Most grass seed you buy nowadays is sold in prepackaged mixtures, which I am <u>not entirely</u> against. Most of my best pets have been mongrels, and Grandma Putt taught me that different kinds of grass love to congregate together, and tell each other the news of the day. No great-looking lawn that I have ever examined contains just one kind of grass; as in Grandma Putt's lawn, different variations helped the predominant strain fight off disease and solve problems.

If Grandma Putt were alive today, I'm sure she would react to the packaged grass seed mixes like the lady in the TV commercial of a few years ago; she'd rather do it herself!

Ahh...Natural Relief

Muscles ache because of too much yard work? Whenever Grandpa Putt's did, Grandma Putt would mix up 1 cup of warm olive oil and 2 tbsp. of garlic powder, and rub it into his aching muscles. She would repeat this treatment twice a day until the aches and pains disappeared, rinsing the skin with cool water after each application.

Decisions, Decisions...

When selecting grass seed, Grandma Putt always told folks to consider the following which would affect how well selected grass seed would grow in their yard:

Soil Conditions—Some grasses will tolerate poor soil better than others.

Climate—The amount of rainfall, the average temperature, the amount of sunshine, and the wind conditions. It's very important to choose an appropriate cool- or warm-season grass.

Site—On steep slopes, grass may be difficult or dangerous to maintain. In such cases, Grandma said that a good, thick ground cover may be a better choice.

In addition to how well grass will grow, here are some other factors you should consider when making your selection:

Durability—Resistance to weeds, disease, and heavy wear and tear.

Maintenance—Requirements for fertilizing, mowing, weeding, dethatching, etc.

Appearance—Fine-textured lawns require more care than coarser ones.

Cost—Some grasses cannot be planted from seed, and cost more to install. Some require a lot of maintenance, resulting in additional time, effort, and expense.

Method of planting—You may have a preference depending upon the time of year.

That's right, there's nothing to prevent you from making your own super grass seed mixture. We did it often back in Grandma Putt's day. Here's how:

First, we decided on what variety of grass we wanted to be predominant in the lawn. You can do this today by consulting your local Agricultural Extension Service or expert at a nearby "Ag" college. If there isn't one in your area, ask your neighbors or a reputable seed supplier what type of grass thrives best in your area. In the case of a neighbor, check out his lawn before you ask his advice—it's been estimated that one in eight homeowners has planted the wrong grass for his lawn!

Once you know which grass is best, use at least 75% of that seed in your mix. For the remainder, add any one of a number of compatible varieties to it.

Selecting Seed

Remember, there are different grades of seed. Usually, the best is the most expensive. But that isn't always a safe and sure rule, so read the label! The USDA requires that packaged seed in this country clearly state on the package certain information regarding the purity, germination, other grasses, and weed or inert matter in the seed.

For instance, if the seed you're buying is Kentucky bluegrass, you'll want to know several other things. How much pure Kentucky bluegrass is in the package of seed? Make sure that the highest possible percentage is present—true to its name on the package. How long will it take the seed to germinate, and how much of it will germinate? You naturally want as large a percentage as possible to germinate. How much of the bluegrass seed is really other grasses? How much of it is made up of weeds or inert matter? All of this information should be stated on the package; if it's not, then put it back on the shelf, and pass on it.

Grandma Putt's Preferred Private Blend

For most lawns, Grandma Putt recommended one of two grass seed mixtures:

TRADITIONAL MIXTURE
40% Kentucky bluegrass
25% Delta or Windsor
    bluegrass
35% creeping red fescue

NEWER MIXTURE
50% Merion
25% Pennlawn creeping
    fescue
25% Delta, Windsor, or
    Kentucky bluegrass

If you're the antsy type who needs quick ground cover, you can add 10 percent of redtop to either mixture, subtracting from the lesser strains, and leaving the Kentucky bluegrass (Mix 1) or the Merion (Mix 2) intact.

IN THE ZONE?

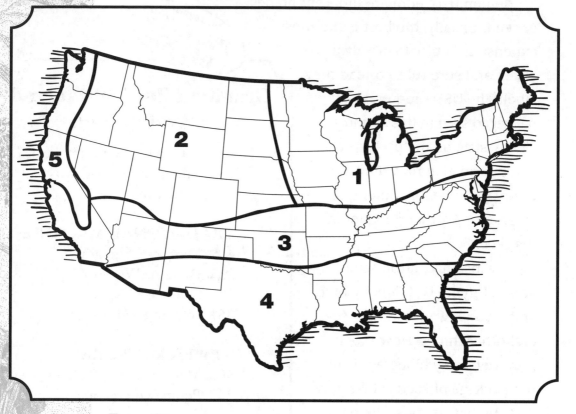

Zone 1: Kentucky bluegrass, bent grass, fescues, and improved ryegrasses.

Zone 2: Great Plains native grasses like buffalo grass, blue grama grass, wheatgrass, and in some intermountain areas, fine fescues.

Zone 3: Bermuda grass and zoysia grass. In high altitudes, bluegrass and fescues.

Zone 4: Bermuda grass, zoysia grass, Bahia grass, St. Augustine grass, and centipede grass. In the deep, deep southern wet and tropical areas, carpet grass.

Zone 5: Like Zone 1, Kentucky bluegrass, bent grass, fescues, and ryegrass.

Prepackaged Grass Seed Mixtures

If prepackaged mixtures are the only seeds available, and you don't want to contact other sources, go ahead. But be careful! *Read the labels!* Check for purity, germination, and other percentages in these packages too. Look out for anything but a minimal amount of ryegrasses. If there is any percentage of Kentucky 31, Alta fescue, or Timothy, avoid the mixture all together. These three are absolutely no good for your lawn unless it stretches for several acres. Even then, keep them away from your house.

In general, the best mixtures will be similar to the percentages in the ones I suggested you mix for yourself. These mixes are good for most lawns in the North. You can substitute other strains which will grow better in your area if you live in the South or West. Choose a mixture with one predominant strain. The theory that a mixture with many varieties in one package will do better year 'round is simply ridiculous!

Not all grasses should be planted, or grow best, from seed. The following chart shows the most commonly used sprig, stolon, or sod planted varieties.

Seed Sowing Time

Bermuda	spring
Buffalo grass	spring
Creeping bent	spring
Perennial ryes	spring-fall
Created wheatgrass	fall
Kentucky bluegrass	fall
Red fescue	fall
Redtop	fall

SELECT YOUR SEED

Common Lawn Grass Seeds	Rate per 1000 Sq. Ft.	Tone of Green	Location and Use
KENTUCKY BLUEGRASS (Poa pratensis)	2 lbs.	Medium	Sunny, will tolerate slight shade. Medium texture.
MERION BLUEGRASS (Poa pratensis)	1 lb.	Dark	Sunny, will tolerate slight shade. Medium texture.
ROUGH STALK MEADOW (Poa trivialis)	2 lbs.	Light	Wet, shade. Shiny leaf.
CHEWINGS FESCUE (Festuca rubra, var. fallas)	3 lbs.	Medium	Dry, shade and poor sandy soil. Fine texture.
CREEPING RED FESCUE (Festuca rubra)	3 lbs.	Medium	Sandy soil. Fine texture.
HIGHLAND BENT (Agrostis tenuis)	1/2-1 lb.	Dark	Sun and light shade. Fine texture.
TALL FESCUE (Festuca elatior)	6-10 lbs.	Light	Athletic fields, etc. Coarse, striated leaf.
ASTORIA BENT (Agrostis tenuis)	1/2-1 lb.	Bright	Sun and light shade. Fine texture.
SEASIDE CREEPING BENT (Agrostis maratima)	1/2-1 lb.	Medium	Sun and light shade. Fine texture.
PENNCROSS CREEPING BENT (Agrostis palustris)	1/2-1 lb.	Dark	Sun and light shade. Fine texture.
ANNUAL RYE (Lolium multiflorum)		Medium	Temporary lawns and in mixtures. Coarse texture.
PERENNIAL RYEGRASS	3-4 lbs.	Dark	Temporary lawns and in mixtures. Coarse, shiny leaf.

Common Lawn Planted Plugs	Rate per 1000 Sq. Ft.	Tone of Green	Location and Use
BERMUDA	1 sprig	Medium	Sun and dry. Course texture.
ST. AUGUSTINE	1 plug	Medium	Sun and dry. Course texture.
ZOYSIA	1 plug	Medium	Sun and dry. Course texture.

When to Seed

When to seed is just as important as how you seed. With Merion and Kentucky bluegrass, late summer and early fall are the best times to sow seed. Fall sowing gives your lawn a good head start at a time when weeds are not competing with them. The grass plants can set down their roots, make themselves at home, and get growing before going to sleep for the winter.

How to Seed

You can sow seed by either hand-broadcasting it or using a spreader. Determine the amount of seed you'll need by checking the directions on the package. If you are making your own mixture, figure the amount you will need to sow based on the requirements for the predominant strain you are using.

Fooling the Grass

Here's another shortcut Grandma Putt taught me to help grass get off to a good start, one that I still use today. Most grass grows best from August 15th to September 20th, which is the time of the harvest moon. The evenings are cool and there is more moisture in the air.

If you want your grass to germinate quickly, here's how we used to fool the seed into thinking that it's time to get up and grow! First off, Grandma Putt would brew 2 cups of tea:

Green Thumb Tip

Grandma Putt used a neat little trick that guaranteed she would never sow too much seed in any one place. She took the amount of seed she intended to use on the lawn area, and divided it into four parts. Then she'd sow one part at a time over the entire area. Although it takes four times as long, this simple trick helped her not to oversow in spots during only one or two applications.

one cup for herself, and the other for her grass seed. She used 2 tbsp. of tea and 1 tbsp. of soap per pound of seed. She mixed them in a gallon of water, placed it in a covered container, and put it in her refrigerator for 2 days.

Then she removed the seed from the refrigerator, and she had me spread it

Seed Starting Tonic

Here's a variation on Grandma Putt's method that'll energize your grass, and make it want to get up and grow! Place your seed in a mix of:

**1/2 cup of dish soap,
1 tbsp. of Epsom salts, and
1 cup of tea in 1 gallon of water.**

Put the mixture in the refrigerator for 2 days, then spread the seed out on your driveway to dry. After that, mix in a little sand, and sow it on the lawn.

out on the garage or basement floor to allow it to partially dry. Then Grandma Putt had me sweep the floor, making sure that I did a good job. I was careful not to pick up any nails, broken glass, or grease, and I tried to have some fun (ha, ha!) while doing it.

Now, you're ready to spread this combination of seed and dirt on your lawn. The grass has been tricked into going into a forced "winter" dormancy by the refrigeration, the soap softens the seed shells, and the tea provides a little boost of instant energy. Grandma Putt all the while was smiling to herself, thinking she was pretty crafty, getting me to do two jobs at the same time, and thinking I was having fun doing them!

I was taught to hand-broadcast seed, and I am still a firm believer in this method. Check the wind with that first handful of seed, or with bits of paper. Then sow away!

GRANDMA'S ALL-AMERICAN LAWN

After you're done, roll your new lawn with an empty roller. The result will be a near perfect seeded lawn!

To Mulch or Not To Mulch?

Whether or not you will want to mulch your newly seeded lawn really depends on local wind conditions, and your ability to water properly. I'm not much for mulching, especially the idea of using straw as a mulch. Straw can bring lots of weed seed into your nice, new lawn, which believe you me, will be a pretty cruel blow after all of the work you've just put in!

How-to Hint

Here's how Grandpa Putt taught me to sow seed: for your first approach, back across the area with your back to the wind, and throw the seed in the direction you are coming from. Next, go back, and rebroadcast crosswind. Then, move crosswind in the other direction. For your last approach, broadcast right into the wind. Of course, don't sow seed on a windy day. But if the wind is blowing strong, rebroadcast the seed with the wind as you did on your first pass.

EVEN SIMPLER SODDING

Sodding is one of the few home-gardening jobs that offers immediate results and immediate success. In the United States, sodding was first used for establishing new golf courses. With the building boom after World War II, sodding became a quick way for developers to establish lawns for model homes, plants, and offices. The invention of the new machinery for cutting and rolling sod encouraged growers to build up an enormous industry. While sodding is an expensive lawn planting method for most homeowners, it is still the most popular for small to mid-size lawns.

A Gardener's Best Friend

Worms are a gardener's best friend. But problems can arise if you have too many—they can leave a fine lawn in tatters covering it with their casings! So before you seed or sod, check to see what the local worm population is up to.

Grandma Putt used a couple of tricks to get rid of them. First, she'd fill a coarse canvas bag with 2 lbs. of either lime or mustard, and place it in a tub of water. After letting it soak, she'd sprinkle it over the lawn. This treatment soon brought the worms to the surface, where they could be gathered, and moved to another part of the homestead where they'd be more useful.

Another method she used was to take 10 ripe horse chestnuts, and boil them for an hour in a quart of water. She let the solution cool, then drained off the water, and sprayed it over the soil. This also brought the worms to the surface, where they could be collected and transported (for sale) elsewhere.

No Humps, Bumps, or Lumps!

Most folks couldn't afford sod back in Grandma Putt's day, so everything I know about it, I've had to pick up since then. So I'll be brief, and to the point:

If you can afford to buy sod for your lawn, have a professional lay it. It's not that much more expensive, and that way, you'll get a smooth-looking lawn without humps, bumps, or lumps. Plus, you won't have to get your hands dirty!

One problem with sodding is that nonprofessionals tend to take their new, "instant lawn," for granted. As Grandma Putt used to say… "You've got to think perpendicular." What she meant was that you have to look at more than what's above the ground. You can't afford to forget or ignore what's going on underneath it.

Plants are like people, and most times, beauty is only skin deep, and fleeting in its youth.

Underneath the grass "skin" you see, you either have a vigorous, healthy environment, or an unhealthy and poorly functioning one. Sod has to develop a strong vigorous root system in order to be able to thrive, and fight off lawn diseases and insects. So look out below!

"Top Ten" Do-It-Yourself Sodding Tips

If you insist on laying your own sod, here are my top ten sodding tips that I've gathered over the years:

Tip #1 – When selecting sod, pick a good-quality grass that grows well with this planting method. Bentgrass, Merion, or Kentucky bluegrass are the top-quality sods for the North. Zoysias, Dichondra, and some bents make good sod in the South and Southwest.

Tip #2 – Thin sod does best. Contrary to what you might think, thin sod seems to work more quickly to establish good contact with a new bed. Select sod that is no more than three-quarters of an inch thick.

Tip #3 – When you are preparing your bed for sod, make the grade an inch lower than if you would be seeding, plugging, or sprigging.

Tip #4 – To figure how much sod you will need to complete the job, multiply the length of your lawn area by the width, and then divide by nine. That will give you the number of square yards you'll need to buy.

Tip #5 – If you must keep your sod somewhere before laying it, store it grass-side-up. Keep it cool and dry.

Tip #6 – Before laying your sod, apply a layer of slow-release fertilizer to the soil surface of your bed, and make sure the bed is moist.

Tip #7 – Lay sod the way a bricklayer lays brick, with the strip ends staggered. Make sure that there are no gaps between the ends. Peg the sod down to ensure good contact with the bed.

Tip #8 – Apply a thin top-dressing of soil to the cracks between ends and joints when you're done laying it, and roll the sod with a half-filled roller.

Tip #9 – Give your new sod lawn a week to ten days to set in before you mow it for the first time. Frequent mowing will encourage the roots to begin growing.

Tip #10 – Now follow up with a good feeding and watering program. Above all else, don't overwater. It's not as necessary to keep this as soaked as the top surface of a newly seeded lawn. You want those roots to start looking for moisture and nutrients in the soil.

GRANDMA PUTT'S LAWN CARE CALENDAR

Grandma Putt always said that if God provides the sunshine, and you provide the elbow grease, then there's no reason you can't have the best-looking lawn in town. Here's a month-by-month program for you to follow based upon what we did to Grandma Putt's lawn many, many years ago.

Not much to do around the old homestead except pick up the lawn mower from the local repair shop before Ol' Joe lost it in his stockroom! Then Grandma would get out, and seed or feed right on top of the snow! There's nothing wrong with that; why, as a matter of fact, it will give your lawn a good spring start, and help it fight weeds later on.

Green Thumb Tip

Overseed your lawn in February? You bet! It's a trick I picked up from Grandma Putt that still works wonders today!

Simply fill your hand-held spreader with grass seed, and walk across your lawn, spreading the grass seed in front of you so that you are stepping on it as you go. This will keep it on the ground, and out of the birds' beaks. As you force the seed down into the snow, it picks up moisture and swells. Then when the midwinter thaw comes, the soil softens enough to swallow the seed, and then freezes over once again—holding the seed in place until it's ready to grow in spring!

If you had a problem with crabgrass last year, then this is the time to apply a preemerge weed control. Put it down during the first part of the month.

After the weather turns nice, rake the whole lawn to get rid of any remaining leaves, twigs, or other debris. It's all right to use a flexible steel or wire rake for this job if you want to; I guess Grandma didn't quite trust me because I always had to use a cheap bamboo job. The ground is usually still very damp from winter, so do it as gently as you would if someone were scratching your scalp if you just woke up (which your lawn just did).

Your lawn should be fed now to prepare it for its spring growth spurt. Apply the dry food mix at half the recommended rate if you can. There's nothing wrong with changing lawn food from time to time. Just like you folks, grass likes a varied diet.

If you didn't seed in February or March, April is still all right, as long as you do it early in the month. But you can't seed, and apply a preemergent crabgrass killer at the same time. The weed control will prevent your grass seed from germinating.

Grandma Putt's Words of Wisdom:

"Hit it hard in April, and you'll be rollin' in the green come June."

April is the time for your first dethatching and aerating of the year. After dethatching, apply a good soapy water solution. When the grass dries, mow it down to 2 inches, and don't let the April showers boost it past that height.

If April is a dry month in your neck of the woods, water every other day before 9:00 a.m., making sure to saturate the soil to a depth of at least 3 inches. Grandma Putt had me use a tin can set in the path of the sprinkler, so I could check on this before moving to another part of the yard.

Begin a regular mowing schedule in April or May, as soon as your grass seems to be growing well. Keep it cut at the optimum height to encourage good growth and discourage weed infestations. Gather the clippings, and use them on your compost pile.

This was prime dandelion month, so we'd dig out all we could for greens and wine. If you're not so inclined, apply a good broadleaf weed killer to get the lawn in shape for the summer. During the merry, merry month of May, it's time to change the lawn mower blade. Alternate every month from now on through the end of the season, keeping the one not in use well-sharpened, so it is ready to go when it is time to change it.

This was the busy lawn care month. Early in the month, give your lawn its second light dethatching of the year with a vigorous raking to get all of the dandruff out. After dethatching, aerate the soil.

In the old days, we used to use the tines of an old pitchfork. Nowadays, I wear my golf spikes whenever I work on the lawn. Of course, you can rent or buy a power rake or aerating tool which punches holes and pulls out the dirt. Any one of these tools will work. Just let your grass breathe, and it will really grow to work for you!

For any areas that have poor drainage, aerate it, and apply some gypsum at the recommended rate. Follow up with a soapy water bath.

On Grandma's wash days, I would empty the washwa-

Summer Soother Tonic

As a special treat during the summer, Grandma Putt would feed her lawn this tonic:

1 bottle of beer,
1 cup of barnyard tea,
1 cup of tea, and
1 cup of Fels-Naptha Soap Solution

in 20 to 25 gallons of water. This tonic soothed the grass while it was under stress from the hot, dry weather.

ter over different areas of the lawn. You can do the same thing much more easily and effectively. Use a mild dishwashing soap (1 cup per 20 gallons of water) applied with a hose-end sprayer. This soapy water works as a surfactant, getting rid of dirt, and warding off insects and disease. It also promotes normal feeding and fantastic photosynthesis.

Grandma's advice was to let the lawn rest in July. This is its hardest working time because it uses up lots of energy growing, fighting the hot weather, and trying to ward off diseases. So while the grass is doing all this hard work, lay off any heavy maintenance. The "light" chores included regular mowing, digging crabgrass, and weeding. And, of course, paying extra-careful attention to watering.

Spot Lawn Repair

Here's a crash course on what you should do to repair bare spots in your lawn:

Step #1—Remove all of the dead grass, weeds, clippings, and other debris.

Step #2—Loosen the soil with a rake.

Step #3—Jump-start the soil by over-spraying it with barnyard tea.

Step #4—For better seed germination, soak the seed in Grandma Putt's Seed Starting Tonic (See page 328).

Step #5—Apply a mix of seed and sand to the bare areas.

Step #6—Lightly cover the seed with soil, slightly mounding it for drainage.

Step #7—Apply a light layer of organic mulch, like straw or hay.

Step #8—Firm the surface of the soil by gently stepping on it.

Step #9—Keep the soil surface moist until the new seedlings are well established.

From August 15th on through the fall, begin to overseed the bare spots in your lawn. If you've just moved in, and the lawn is lousy, this is the time to start making friends with your soil by planting a brand new lawn.

Pay particular attention to how you water —water well as soon as the soil beneath the surface dries out. This may have to be done every day at the beginning of the month.

GRANDMA'S ALL-AMERICAN LAWN

Then watch out for insect and disease problems. August is insect month in most states and they can drive you, well...absolutely buggy! Apply the proper controls with the proper care.

Early September is still all right to seed or sod. Later in the month, give your lawn its third yearly dethatching, which needs to be gentle, too. After dethatching, we always gave the grass a good bath with soapy water.

Grandma Putt's Words of Wisdom:

"Fall is the time to give your lawn a kick-in-the-grass!"

This was also the month when it's time to really put the pedal-to-the-metal as far as whipping the lawn into shape goes. Feeding, weeding, and overseeding were top priorities because this was the prime season for grass growth and care. The warm days and cool nights made for ideal growing conditions, and you'd be *amazed* at what a little TLC will do!

As the season is winding down, apply gypsum to the lawn as a top-dressing to protect against winter damage. This is especially important for city lawns now because of salt damage from snow and ice-melting materials. Rake all leaves, and use them on your compost pile. Continue to mow, only less often.

November was the last time to fertilize for the year. Use a low-nitrogen, high-phosphate and potash fertilizer to stimulate root growth. It'll help ensure the grass's survival during the long, cold winter. Also, mow one last time, cleaning up as much debris and leaves as possible. Deposit this material on…where else? The compost pile!

Organic Blend

Here's a simple, old-time organic lawn food recipe that's perfect for a final feeding:

**2 parts alfalfa meal,
1 part bone meal, and
1 part wood ashes**

Apply it at a rate of about 25 lbs. per 1,000 sq. ft. of lawn area last thing in the fall.

This is the time of year to forget about your lawn, and dream about next year's garden. But after the dreaming, start to think about any major jobs that need to be done next year. Then bring your lawn tools into the garage, and clean them up.

We used to surprise Ol' Joe down at the hardware store by bringing our lawn mower in for a tune-up and sharpening. It may not have been any cheaper, but it sure beat the spring rush!

Late January is also the time to buy any tools you'll need for the upcoming year. Nothing is more frustrating than trying to do without the proper tools in April or May because they're already all sold out.

Believe you me, if you follow these simple steps, there is absolutely no reason why your lawn won't be the nicest, greenest grass anywhere!

EPILOGUE:
PLANT A TREE!

Some of the fondest memories of my childhood are of the days I spent beside Grandma Putt's knee, learning the ins and outs of her old-time gardening wisdom. As I wrote this book, a flood of memories came back to me, some good, some not so good, but all taking me back to those very special times.

I don't know what it is, but there just seems to be something about small boys that makes them begrudge even the happiest of tasks, and yearn to go awandering far afield. I was no different. So I'm sure that many of my fond memories of hoeing, weeding, and working in Grandma Putt's garden have grown "fonder" in retrospect than what they may have actually been at the time.

And if I seem to have gathered more "knowledge" and satisfaction in looking back toward those days with Grandma Putt than I actually gained and used on the spot… well then, for this I apologize…the knowledge and desire to absorb it was there, but perhaps I was just a little too young to completely understand it.

But more importantly, if, in reliving some of those glorious garden highlights as I have in this book, I have moved you to try, and you fail to become a successful gardener…

well then, to paraphrase old Willy Shakespeare... it is better to have gardened and lost, then never to have gardened at all!

Grandma Putt also had some wonderful words of wisdom for a friend of hers who had no apparent knack for growing things. She said, quite simply, "When all else fails, plant a tree. You can't hardly go wrong." Even today, after over 40 years of sharing my (and her) gardening gospel with millions of folks all across the country, I can't think of anything better, or wiser, to say to you.

I hope that all of you black-thumbers out there will take heart and "our" advice, and plant a sturdy young oak... or maple...or elm...and then name it after a favorite family member. Then each year, with a little help from you, it will grow in strength, and you will grow in wisdom. And perhaps, one day, as you're sitting beneath the branches of your tree, you will suddenly look up and realize it is a living testimonial to your gardening know-how. Then maybe you'll think of Grandma Putt and me, and we will, wherever we are, say...

"YOU'RE WELCOME!"

Old-Fashioned Garden Recipes Index

Fels-Naptha Soap Solution

To make this solution, Grandma Putt shaved:

a 1/4 bar of Fels Naptha or Octagon soap into 1 quart of boiling water.

When the soap was completely dissolved, she added:

1/4 cup of liquid dish soap

to emulsify the mixture and keep it from gelling. She let the mixture cool, then stored it in a suitable container until she needed it.

Chewin' Tobacco Juice

Grandma Putt made this awful smelling, but effective tonic by taking:

1/2 a handful of chewing tobacco,

and wrapping it up in a small piece of cheesecloth. She let it soak in:

1 gallon of hot water

until the mix was dark brown. She took the cheesecloth out, strained the mixture, and then stored the juice away in a suitable container until it was time to clean-up.

Super Seed Starter Tonic

pg. 13

Grandma Putt used to soak *all* of her seeds in this tonic before sowing them:

1 tbsp. of Fels-Naptha Soap Solution,*
1 tbsp. of Epsom salts, and
1 tbsp. of tea water
in 1 gallon of warm water.

Compost Starter Tonic

pg. 17

After adding grass clippings to her compost pile, Grandma Putt sprayed it with her Compost Starter Tonic, which she made by mixing up:

1/4 bottle of beer, and
1/4 cup of ammonia
in 1 gallon of warm water.

This really got her pile cookin'!

All-Purpose Organic Fertilizer

pg. 18

Grandma Putt made her fabulous All-Purpose Organic Fertilizer by mixing up:

1 part dehydrated manure,
1 part bone meal,
3 parts granite dust, and
5 parts seaweed meal

in a large, old wheelbarrow. Come chow time, she'd wheel it out into her garden, and put it into action!

Barnyard Booster Mix

pg. 40

To make a batch of Barnyard Booster Mix, Grandma Putt mixed:

50 lbs. of manure,
50 lbs. of peat moss,
50 lbs. of gypsum, and
25 lbs. of garden food

in the biggest container she could find. Then she'd set it aside until she was ready to use it.

Natural Bug Juice

pg. 50

Grandma Putt made up her Natural Bug Juice by mixing:

1/2 cup of marigolds,
1/2 cup of geraniums, and
1/2 cup of garlic

chopped, very fine, into a liquid, and mixed with 10 gallons of warm water. She then sprinkled it over and around her vegetable garden.

All Season Clean-Up Tonic

pg. 59

To keep your garden in good health, wash it down every 2 weeks with this supercharged clean-up tonic:

1 cup of liquid dish soap,
1 cup of antiseptic mouthwash, and
1 cup of chewing tobacco juice*
per 20 gallons of water.

Seed Starter Tonic

pg. 78

After planting her seeds, Grandma Putt mist sprayed them (and later, her seedlings) with this super Seed Starter Tonic:

1/4 cup of Barnyard Tea (pg. 40),
1/4 cup of soapy water, and
1/4 cup of tea
in 2 gallons of water.

Fall Garden Tonic

pg. 81

To prep the soil for the coming spring, the last thing Grandma Putt did in her garden in the fall was apply this tonic:

1 bottle of beer,
1 bottle of soda pop, and
1 cup of ammonia

per 20 gallons of water. She thoroughly applied it until the ground was saturated.

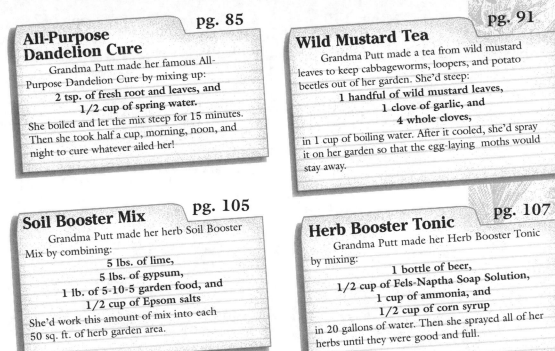

All-Purpose Dandelion Cure
pg. 85

Grandma Putt made her famous All-Purpose Dandelion Cure by mixing up:

2 tsp. of fresh root and leaves, and
1/2 cup of spring water.

She boiled and let the mix steep for 15 minutes. Then she took half a cup, morning, noon, and night to cure whatever ailed her!

Wild Mustard Tea
pg. 91

Grandma Putt made a tea from wild mustard leaves to keep cabbageworms, loopers, and potato beetles out of her garden. She'd steep:

1 handful of wild mustard leaves,
1 clove of garlic, and
4 whole cloves,

in 1 cup of boiling water. After it cooled, she'd spray it on her garden so that the egg-laying moths would stay away.

Soil Booster Mix
pg. 105

Grandma Putt made her herb Soil Booster Mix by combining:

5 lbs. of lime,
5 lbs. of gypsum,
1 lb. of 5-10-5 garden food, and
1/2 cup of Epsom salts

She'd work this amount of mix into each 50 sq. ft. of herb garden area.

Herb Booster Tonic
pg. 107

Grandma Putt made her Herb Booster Tonic by mixing:

1 bottle of beer,
1/2 cup of Fels-Naptha Soap Solution,
1 cup of ammonia, and
1/2 cup of corn syrup

in 20 gallons of water. Then she sprayed all of her herbs until they were good and full.

Perfect Soil Mix
pg. 109

Grandma Putt's perfect blend of soil for her indoor herbs was made by mixing:

1 part sand,
1 part clay loam,
1 part compost, and
1 part topsoil

Then per peck of soil mixture, she would add a pinch of Epsom salts, a handful of dried coffee grounds, and some eggshells, dried and crushed into a powder.

Healthy Herb Tonic
pg. 110

Grandma Putt kept her herbs healthy by mist spraying them with this tonic:

1 tbsp. of Fels-Naptha Soap Solution,
1 tbsp. of mouthwash,
1 tbsp. of ammonia, and
1/4 cup of tea

in 1 quart of warm water. Her Healthy Herb Tonic took care of insects and disease, while giving the plants a gentle nutrient boost.

Happy Herb Tonic
pg. 111

This tonic was made by mixing:

1/2 tbsp. of bourbon,
1/2 tbsp. of ammonia,
1/2 tbsp. of hydrogen peroxide,
1/2 tbsp. of dish soap, and
1/4 cup of tea

in 1 gallon of warm water.

Knock 'Em Dead Insect Spray
pg. 127

To make this potent brew, Grandma Putt would mix:

6 cloves garlic (chopped fine),
1 small onion (chopped fine),
1 tbsp. of cayenne pepper, and
1 tbsp. of dish soap

in 1 quart of warm water. She let it sit overnight, then she'd mist spray her plants.

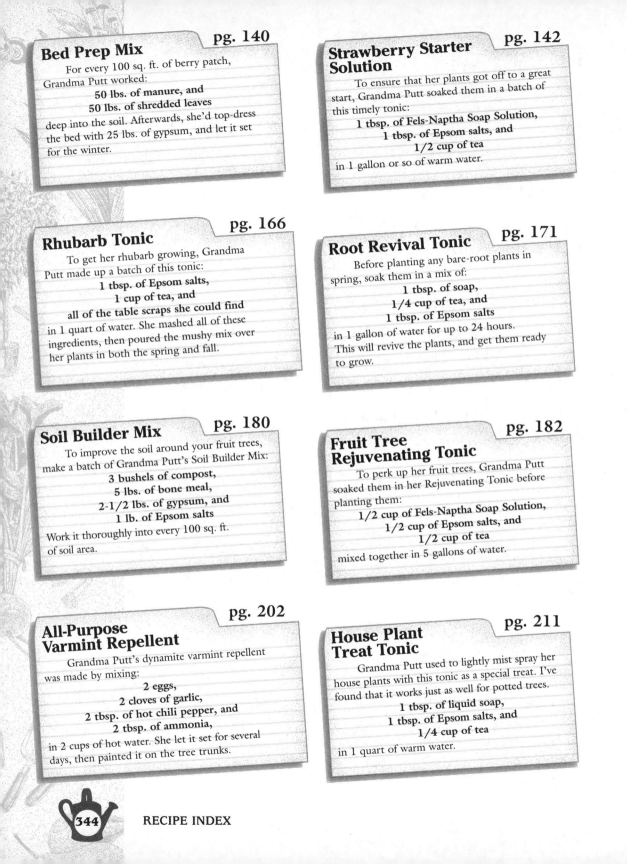

Bed Prep Mix

pg. 140

For every 100 sq. ft. of berry patch, Grandma Putt worked:

50 lbs. of manure, and
50 lbs. of shredded leaves

deep into the soil. Afterwards, she'd top-dress the bed with 25 lbs. of gypsum, and let it set for the winter.

Strawberry Starter Solution

pg. 142

To ensure that her plants got off to a great start, Grandma Putt soaked them in a batch of this timely tonic:

1 tbsp. of Fels-Naptha Soap Solution,
1 tbsp. of Epsom salts, and
1/2 cup of tea

in 1 gallon or so of warm water.

Rhubarb Tonic

pg. 166

To get her rhubarb growing, Grandma Putt made up a batch of this tonic:

1 tbsp. of Epsom salts,
1 cup of tea, and
all of the table scraps she could find

in 1 quart of water. She mashed all of these ingredients, then poured the mushy mix over her plants in both the spring and fall.

Root Revival Tonic

pg. 171

Before planting any bare-root plants in spring, soak them in a mix of:

1 tbsp. of soap,
1/4 cup of tea, and
1 tbsp. of Epsom salts

in 1 gallon of water for up to 24 hours. This will revive the plants, and get them ready to grow.

Soil Builder Mix

pg. 180

To improve the soil around your fruit trees, make a batch of Grandma Putt's Soil Builder Mix:

3 bushels of compost,
5 lbs. of bone meal,
2-1/2 lbs. of gypsum, and
1 lb. of Epsom salts

Work it thoroughly into every 100 sq. ft. of soil area.

Fruit Tree Rejuvenating Tonic

pg. 182

To perk up her fruit trees, Grandma Putt soaked them in her Rejuvenating Tonic before planting them:

1/2 cup of Fels-Naptha Soap Solution,
1/2 cup of Epsom salts, and
1/2 cup of tea

mixed together in 5 gallons of water.

All-Purpose Varmint Repellent

pg. 202

Grandma Putt's dynamite varmint repellent was made by mixing:

2 eggs,
2 cloves of garlic,
2 tbsp. of hot chili pepper, and
2 tbsp. of ammonia,

in 2 cups of hot water. She let it set for several days, then painted it on the tree trunks.

House Plant Treat Tonic

pg. 211

Grandma Putt used to lightly mist spray her house plants with this tonic as a special treat. I've found that it works just as well for potted trees.

1 tbsp. of liquid soap,
1 tbsp. of Epsom salts, and
1/4 cup of tea

in 1 quart of warm water.

All-Purpose Bug Repellent Tonic
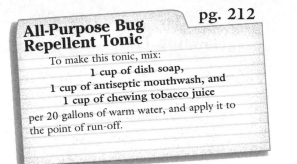
pg. 212

To make this tonic, mix:

1 cup of dish soap,
1 cup of antiseptic mouthwash, and
1 cup of chewing tobacco juice

per 20 gallons of warm water, and apply it to the point of run-off.

Nut Tree Booster Mix
pg. 217

Before planting nut trees, Grandma Putt mixed up a batch of her Nut Tree Booster Mix:

1 part Epsom salts,
2 parts gypsum, and
5 parts bone meal.

She'd work this mix into the bottom and sides of the planting hole, and sprinkle some on top of the soil after we were done planting.

Super Dry Food Mix
pg. 221

Grandma Putt's recipe for her fabulous Super Dry Food Mix was:

1 part bone meal,
1 part gypsum,
1/2 part Epsom salts,
1 part garden soil, and
2 parts All-Purpose (dry) Garden Food,

all tossed together in an old wheelbarrow, and mixed thoroughly.

Timely Tree Tonic
pg. 222

Grandma Putt sprayed her super Tree Tonic on all of her trees several times during the growing season:

1 bottle of beer,
1 cup of ammonia,
1/2 cup of tea, and
1/2 cup of Fels-Naptha Soap Solution,

mixed in 20 gallons of water in a sprayer.

Breakfast of Champions
pg. 269

This "breakfast" was made by mixing:

10 lbs. of compost,
5 lbs. of bone meal,
2 lbs. of blood meal, and
1 lb. of Epsom salts

in a wheelbarrow, and then working it into every 100 sq. ft. (10' x 10') of soil.

Perennial Planting Tonic
pg. 276

To make this power-packed perennial punch, mix:

1/2 bottle of beer,
1 tbsp. of Fels-Naptha Soap Solution,
1/2 cup of barnyard tea, and
2 tbsp. of hydrogen peroxide,

in 2 gallons of warm water, and sprinkle it over your blooming beauties.

Bed Energizing Mix
pg. 283

To get her flower beds ready to grow, Grandma Putt would make up a batch of her Bed Energizing Mix:

50 lbs. of peat moss,
25 lbs. of gypsum,
10 lbs. of garden food, and
4 bushels of compost

and work it well into the soil.

Fabulous Flower Tonic
pg. 284

Grandma Putt gave this special treat to her flowers every month or so during the growing season:

1 cup of barnyard tea,
1/2 bottle of beer,
1/4 cup of ammonia, and
1/2 cup of Fels-Naptha Soap Solution

mixed in 20 gallons of water, and sprayed over all of her beds.

Perfect Potpourri
pg. 293

To make her favorite potpourri, Grandma Putt took a pint-sized glass jar with a lid, and put these ingredients in it:

4 lightly packed cups of fresh rose petals,
3 tbsp. of mixed spices like ground cloves and allspice, and
1 tbsp. of powdered orris root

That's all there was to it!

Refreshing Rose Rejuvenating Tonic
pg. 296

Grandma Putt rejuvenated her bare-root roses by soaking them in a mixture of:

1/2 cup of soap, and
1/2 cup of tea

in 1 gallon of warm water before planting.

Black Spot Remover Tonic
pg. 298

To control black spot on her roses, Grandma Putt used to mix:

1 tbsp. of baking soda,
1 tbsp. of vegetable oil, and
1 tbsp. of Fels-Naptha Soap Solution

in 1 gallon of water. She lightly sprayed this mixture on her bushes once a week, or at the first sign of trouble.

Clipping Remover Tonic
pg. 312

To help her lawn, Grandma Putt sprayed her Clipping Remover Tonic on it twice a year:

1 bottle of beer,
1 bottle of soda pop,
1 cup of ammonia, and
1 cup of Fels-Naptha Soap Solution,

mixed in 20 to 25 gallons of water

Homemade Lawn Food
pg. 313

Grandma Putt would feed her lawn twice a year with the following mix.

3 lbs. of bone meal, and
3 lbs. of Epsom salts

mixed in with 50 lbs. of dry lawn food

She applied this mix at half of the recommended rate, 2 weeks apart.

Seed Starting Tonic
pg. 328

Here's a variation on Grandma Putt's method that'll energize your grass, and make it want to get up and grow! Place your seed in a mix of:

1/2 cup of dish soap,
1 tbsp. of Epsom salts, and
1 cup of tea in 1 gallon water.

Put the mixture in the refrigerator for 2 days, then spread the seed out on your driveway to dry. After that, mix in a little sand, and sow it on the lawn.

Summer Soother Tonic
pg. 335

As a special treat during the summer, Grandma Putt would feed her lawn this tonic:

1 bottle of beer,
1 cup of barnyard tea,
1 cup of tea, and
1 cup of Fels-Naptha Soap Solution

in 20 to 25 gallons of water. This tonic soothed the grass while it was under stress from the hot, dry weather.

Organic Blend
pg. 338

Here's a simple, old-time organic lawn food recipe that's perfect for a final feeding:

2 parts alfalfa meal,
1 part bone meal, and
1 part wood ashes

Apply it at a rate of about 25 lbs. per 1,000 sq. ft. of lawn area last thing in the fall.

INDEX

B

G

—— **H** ——

357

INDEX

——— O ———

——— P ———